THE
RIGOR
OF
ANGELS

THE
RIGOR
OF
ANGELS

Borges, Heisenberg, Kant, and
the Ultimate Nature of Reality

WILLIAM
EGGINTON

PANTHEON BOOKS · NEW YORK

Library of Congress Cataloging-in-Publication Data
Names: Egginton, William, [date] author.
Title: The rigor of angels : Borges, Heisenberg, Kant, and the ultimate nature of reality / William Egginton.
Description: First edition. New York : Pantheon Books, 2023.
Includes bibliographical references and index.
Identifiers: LCCN 2022062201 (print) | LCCN 2022062202 (ebook) |
ISBN 9780593316306 (hardcover) | ISBN 9780593316313 (ebook)
Subjects: LCSH: Reality. Borges, Jorge Luis, 1899–1986.
Heisenberg, Werner, 1901–1976. | Kant, Immanuel, 1724–1804.
Classification: LCC BD331.E423 2023 (print) | LCC BD331 (ebook) |
DDC 111—dc23/eng/20230421
LC record available at https://lccn.loc.gov/2022062201
LC ebook record available at https://lccn.loc.gov/2022062202

www.pantheonbooks.com

Jacket images: (clockwise, upper left) Jorge Luis Borges, Pictorial Press/Alamy; Immanuel Kant, Classic Image/Alamy; Werner Heisenberg, ullstein bild/Getty Images
Jacket design by Jack Smyth

Printed in the United States of America
First Edition
2 4 6 8 9 7 5 3 1

The nature of the universe, which holds
the center still and moves all else around it,
begins here as if from its turning-post.
This heaven has no other *where* than this:
the mind of God, in which are kindled both
the love that turns it and the force it rains.

—DANTE, *Paradiso* (1320)

Enchanted by its rigor, humanity has forgotten, and continues to forget, that it is the rigor of chess masters, not of angels.

—JORGE LUIS BORGES,
"Tlön, Uqbar, Orbis Tertius" (1940)

CONTENTS

PART III. DOES THE UNIVERSE HAVE AN EDGE?

PART IV. THE ABYSS OF FREEDOM

INTRODUCTION:
WHERE DID IT GO?

S HORTLY BEFORE 10:00 on the evening of May 21, 1927, a
plane dropped out of the clouds northwest of Paris. After flying over the city and twice circling the Eiffel Tower, it headed
northeast toward the normally sleepy airfield at Le Bourget. No one
could have been more surprised than the plane's single pilot, an
unknown American who looked more boyish than his twenty-five
years, to see the teeming crowds awaiting him. When he landed
his plane at 10:32 that night, the young man had been flying for
more than thirty-three hours. By the time he fell asleep early the
next morning—after fighting free from the crowds that pulled him
from his plane, talking to the crush of international press that had
gathered to cover his unprecedented feat, and taking a hot bath at
the ambassador's residence in Paris—he had been awake for more
than sixty hours.[1]

By becoming the first human being to fly alone across the Atlantic, Charles Lindbergh went from an unassuming postal pilot to the
world's most famous person—literally overnight. His accomplish-
ment was an example of extraordinary skill and courage, one that

many others had failed to achieve in the years and months before, often perishing in the process. But the crowds at Le Bourget, and later in New York, and indeed everywhere Lindbergh would go from then on, weren't just celebrating one man's exploit.

For underlying Lindbergh's undeniable skill—his flawless navigation alone and at night; his constant adjustment of altitude; his nerve-racking battle with fatigue—was a magnificent edifice of science and engineering that had just propelled a single human being in little more than a day across a distance that had previously required weeks and even months. This was an extension of the stunning human capacity for knowledge that had in recent centuries navigated the globe and built the railroads and would eventually place a man on the moon. A triumph of engineering, to be sure, but also of the laws of motion that Sir Isaac Newton had put to paper more than two hundred years earlier, and that had been powering humanity's remarkable progress ever since. For in tracing that path from Roosevelt Field in New York to Le Bourget, Charles Lindbergh had moved a greater distance in a shorter time than any human in history. Little could he know that barely a thousand kilometers from the airport where he landed that evening, the very idea of what it means for an object to move through space was being turned on its head forever.

AS LINDBERGH WAS MAKING his historic flight, another young man was being driven to distraction in a quiet dwelling in Copenhagen. That was where the Danish physicist and Nobel laureate Niels Bohr waged a daily war of attrition against his twenty-five-year-old German assistant, Werner Heisenberg, dismantling the young man's most recent paper in a relentless series of bombardments.

While not yet the full professor he would become later that year when he accepted the chair of theoretical physics at Leipzig, Heisenberg had already laid the groundwork two years prior for what would be formalized by the end of 1927 as quantum mechanics—a mathematical model of hair-curling complexity whose power is such that it continues to hold today, almost a hundred years and at least that many profound discoveries later. Heisenberg would himself win the Nobel Prize five years later for one of the two watershed papers he had written as a twenty-three-year-old. But the current battles with Bohr were about a new discovery, one that would shake the foundations of science and thought and be forever attached to Heisenberg's name.

The debate revolved around the ultimate nature of reality. Classical physics had always assumed that objects followed the same laws of motion no matter their size. However, in 1913, Bohr had demonstrated that inside the atom electrons behaved rather differently than macroscopic objects, in that they occupied distinct orbits around the nucleus and appeared to "jump" from one to the other.[2] The problem was this: If I jump from one step to another on my stairs, everyone will grant that I continue to exist along the way. Paradoxically, however, electrons show up in their new orbit without seeming to have traveled in between. Moreover, they seem not even to *exist* until they are detected, at which point they "decide" where they have been all along. It was as if Charles Lindbergh didn't exist while crossing the Atlantic, and only came back into being when he was sighted over France.

ON A SATURDAY AFTERNOON of the previous year, a deliriously happy young poet arrived at a party in Buenos Aires. Erudite, foppish, and timid, Jorge Luis Borges, known as Georgie to his friends, was attending a birthday luncheon for a fellow writer at the boating pond in Palermo Park. The source of Borges's delight was on his arm that day, a rising novelist and poet of Scandinavian descent named Norah Lange.

It had been a good year for Borges. The Buenos Aires literary scene was starting to pull back from its sycophantic adulation of the European avant-garde, whose once risqué leaders were wealthy, settled, and now far more likely to be feted and pampered by the bourgeoisie than to shock them. This shift favored Borges, whose poetry at the time tended toward the romantic and locally flavored. While thoroughly cosmopolitan, his tastes were anchored in Argentina to the point where he and his literary compatriots would shower disdain on the musicians who dared to play faddish new forms of tango at the famed Café Tortoni.

In this group of friends Norah Lange shone like a lodestar. As one of the companions would later recount, deep into a night of drinking they would slip out to the corner bar "with the goddesses of that Wagnerian paradise." Upon returning, "Norah, she of the long flaming hair, would regain her throne and scepter, extend both hands to silence the uproar, and proceed to recite . . . , her poems never failing to calm the storm and induce a sunrise of the purest emotion."[3] Indeed, in some of those poems we can sense her ardor for her lover and mentor Borges, which she likens to the "dew drawn to a freshly opened rose."[4]

Borges, for his part, felt alive like never before. And his writing reflected that. The words of a poet, of any writer, had to amount to a fusion of souls, imparting the truths of one's innermost experience; writing was to be "a full confession of the self."[5] Even under a fictional facade, the author's autobiographical substance would be "like a heart beating in the depths."[6] Indeed, it would be fair to say that the relationship with Norah had provoked some uncharacteristic writing on Borges's part. Carlos Mastronardi, a fellow writer and friend, would later recall that for one of the few times in his life Borges seemed to have little desire to be anyone other than himself. As Borges wrote at the time in an essay with the distinctly un-Borgesian title "Writing Happiness," he couldn't imagine "the negation of all consciousness, of all sensation, of all differentiation in time or space."[7] Mastronardi's surprise was justified. His friend had a well-deserved reputation for morbid obsessions and had publicly mused that a human being's sense of consciousness and identity over time was little else than a desperate illusion veiling an existential void.

Sadly, for Borges, if not for literary posterity, this reverie was not to last. On that spring afternoon at the party beside the lake, Norah shared a table with another writer, Oliverio Girondo, whose ease at conversation and charm with women contrasted starkly with Borges's own awkward demeanor. As they chatted and drank, a tipsy Norah upset a bottle of red wine. Oliverio, never at a loss for words, leaned in and quipped, "Blood will flow between us."[8] The woman who came on Georgie's arm was soon dancing with Oliverio. She would leave with him as well.

IMMANUEL KANT WAS OBSESSED with his bowels. During the summer of 1776, when elsewhere revolution was in the air, Kant couldn't take a shit. A hypochondriacal bachelor in his early fifties and an established professor at the local university, he was in most respects entirely healthy. Indeed, he would live for another twenty-eight years, far longer than most of his friends and colleagues. Still, Kant's digestive worries were a matter of great consequence. As he took his daily walks that summer, he had yet to publish a single one of the seminal works that would later earn his place as the founder of modern philosophy. His inability to get his gut in order was causing him to have confused thoughts—a considerable obstacle for someone aiming to put philosophy's house in order. Finally published five years later, those thoughts would be complicated enough for those who would endeavor to read them, but in his current state of distraction Kant could barely make sense of them himself.

Not that Kant wished his philosophy to be abstruse. Unlike some traditionalists who railed against the idea that the human mind should be planted with more ideas than those needed for each person to become adept at his or her calling, Kant believed in the democratic diffusion of knowledge. That same year the conservative thinker J. G. Schlosser wrote, "Why do you castrate oxen and colts when you prepare them for the yoke and the cart, yet wish to develop the totality of human powers in men similarly condemned to the yoke and the cart?"[9] Kant wholly and passionately opposed such prejudice. To deprive a human being, any human being, of the opportunity to cultivate his or her own mind was to undermine the free use of reason that Kant believed an essential part of being human. To achieve that universality, though, Kant's own philosophy would require both clarity and precision. Already the lecture he gave on the occasion of attaining the rank of magister years earlier had been titled "Of the Easier and More Thorough Presentation of Philosophy"—evidence of his conviction that education should be universally accessible, yes, but also a source of irritation to the generations since who have naturally found Kant's major philosophical works to be rather tough going.

It was the first of those works, published in the summer of 1781, that would lay the groundwork for all philosophy to come. The volume in question, the famed *Critique of Pure Reason,* is a doorstop of a book. As Kant's fellow philosopher and frequent correspondent Johann Georg Hamann remarked upon receiving the proofs, "Such a fat book is neither fitting for the author's stature nor for the concept of pure reason, which he opposes to such lazy-assed reason as my own."[10] But in its impressive heft Kant had distilled several decades of thinking about the very limits of human knowledge and, specifically, how a failure to recognize and take account of those limits would produce mind-boggling paradoxes, paradoxes that had been bewildering human beings for millennia.

THE MIDDLE-CLASS SON OF a classics professor, Heisenberg excelled at pretty much everything. Athletic, a committed scout and outdoorsman, and a talented pianist, he could have chosen any number of academic or artistic paths. But of all his talents, Heisenberg showed a particular aptitude for math. At sixteen he was already tutoring local university students in the subject. And it was his prowess with a pencil and an iconoclastic attitude toward long-accepted certainties that led to his first landmark: a backbreaking latticework of calculations able to account for the strange disappearances and reappearances of fundamental particles.

To Heisenberg's chagrin, in the year after he published his groundbreaking paper laying the cornerstone of quantum mechanics, an older, more established physicist published a theory he called wave mechanics. For the theorists who were wrestling with the herculean "matrix algebra" Heisenberg's approach required, the urbane Erwin Schrödinger's elegant and relatively simply calculations were a relief. Even Heisenberg had to admit Schrödinger's equation was easier to work with. To Heisenberg's great annoyance, however, Schrödinger wasn't willing to let the math stand on its own. Instead, he insisted on using the language of classical physics to try to *visualize* what was going on at the quantum level.

Brash and headstrong, Heisenberg averred that quantum mechanics constituted an entirely new physical model; if its conclusions seemed strange or even paradoxical, so be it. Schrödinger would have none of this. He believed his elegant equation described real, physical waves and that electrons, photons, and other particle-like manifestations of matter or energy appeared like frothy wave caps on a tumultuous sea. If we don't know exactly when and where such a cap will present itself, that's merely because we can't see sharply enough to make out the water beneath the surface, not because the wave isn't there.

Both Heisenberg and Niels Bohr disagreed, believing quantum discontinuity was real. But where Heisenberg was ready to jettison the continuous model of classical physics altogether, Bohr wanted to hold on to it and find a way to make the two modes communicate. This was the source of their arguments from late 1926 into the spring of 1927. In fact, the strife got so intense that in February, Bohr and his wife decided to go skiing. Without Heisenberg. It was during those weeks of relative solitude that Werner had his breakthrough.

BACK IN BUENOS AIRES, Borges nursed his broken heart. The months since Norah rejected him had been one long onslaught of recurrent humiliations. Oliverio had decamped for Europe, leaving behind a love-struck Norah and luring Borges with desperate hopes of reconciliation. But his almost daily attempts to call on Norah, which play out in a roman à clef she published less than a year later, served only to remind him how cold her heart had turned to the man for whom she had once written the most impassioned poems.

Norah dealt Borges a fatal blow on a late April day, in the form of a review she published of his latest book of poems with the icy title "Thinking of Jorge Luis Borges in Something That Does Not Quite Manage to Be a Poem."[11] The despair that ensued waxed philosophical. Where before the final rupture Borges had rhapsodized about the confessional transparency of writing, the bond it could fuse between two lovers, he now sounded his first notes of skepticism. Far from a medium of communion between two souls, language had become a "hemisphere of lies and shadows," the "fickle and contingent" meaning of words constituting "the general tragedy of all writing."[12] He now believed the promise of transcending the fundamental opacity of words was but a fantasy, a power only angels possessed, forever denied to those he termed "never-angels," the ultimate and irreducible status of mortals.[13]

The loss of his beloved changed Borges. Soon he would publish his last poem for many years, during which time he would turn almost exclusively to the short-form fiction and essays that would earn him his place in history. It would be more than thirty years before Jorge Luis Borges would be snatched from the relative obscurity of Buenos Aires by receiving, along with Samuel Beckett, the 1961 International Publishers' Prize, in an instant transforming a depressive Argentine nebbish into one of the world's most lionized and influential writers. For now, however, he snapped out of his temporary reveries and returned to a more potent suspicion that the self's experience of permanence and solidity in time and space was illusory.

In short, he started thinking about tortoises.

IN THE MONTHS PRIOR to Heisenberg's stay at Bohr's house in Copenhagen, physicists had been aware of a nagging problem. It seemed that their models could home in on the location of a particle quite well; they could also describe its momentum with impressive accuracy. Maddeningly, however, they didn't seem able to do both. As Heisenberg's friend and colleague Wolfgang Pauli put it, it was as if one of your eyes could see a particle's momentum and the other could see its position, "but if you open both eyes at the same time you will go crazy."[14]

One cold winter evening while the Bohrs were away skiing, Heisenberg took a walk in a park not far from their house. It was on this walk that he came upon his solution: the image of a discrete object moving through time and space that had been so successful for classical physics—indeed, that would manifest itself in Lindbergh's famous flight later that very spring—simply didn't apply to the behavior of reality at the quantum level. It wasn't merely that the physicist isn't able to *see* a particle's position and momentum at the same time; astoundingly, the particle doesn't *have* a momentum and a position in any meaningful sense until the physicist decides to measure one or the other.

Werner knew he was onto something. But he was sure Bohr would have objections, and he desperately wanted to get his ideas out into the world. After a rapid correspondence with Pauli, who reacted enthusiastically, Heisenberg took advantage of his mentor's absence and feverishly wrote an article he submitted on March 22 to Germany's leading journal of physics. A few weeks later he wrote a summary for nonspecialists in which he explained that quantum phenomena required us to put aside Newtonian mechanics. When it comes to quanta he wrote, "the more precisely we determine the position, the more imprecise is the determination of velocity."[15]

This fact had profound consequences for the most basic assumptions of the classical scientific worldview. Since Newton had exposited the laws of motion, scientists had accepted the notion proposed most famously by the French mathematician Pierre-Simon Laplace, that perfect knowledge of an object's position and momentum and the forces acting on it in the present will yield perfect knowledge of all its future permutations. Heisenberg's discovery put this determinism to rest. As he put it, "In the strict formulation of causal law—if we know the present, we can calculate the future—it is not the conclusion that is wrong but the premise."[16] The uncertainty principle, as it came to be known, showed with inescapable, mathematical precision that such full knowledge of the present moment wasn't just hard to pin down; it was actually impossible.

THE TORTOISES THAT POPULATED Borges's imagination were twenty-five hundred years old. One afternoon in Athens, a young philosopher named Socrates came to the Agora to meet a venerable thinker, Parmenides, who was visiting from the far-off land of Elea. Parmenides had brought with him a tall, handsome acolyte named Zeno. Zeno had become known for a brief book he had written to demolish all those who would seek to oppose Parmenides's doctrines. Motion, he argued, was an illusion. To demonstrate his point, he told a fanciful parable about the great warrior Achilles facing a tortoise in a foot race. The gist of the story was that as long as the tortoise had a head start to begin with, Achilles could never catch up. That's because to cross any distance at all, Achilles would first have to cross some fraction of it, and then a fraction of the remaining distance, and so on. A bit like making a cookie last forever by only ever eating half of what remains, even though the distances Achilles would have to cross would grow infinitely smaller, there was also no limit to how many of such distances he would have to cross. Ergo, Zeno concluded, Achilles could never catch up.

Shortly after losing Norah Lange, Borges had become fascinated with Zeno's paradox.

He reviewed the history of "solutions" to the problem, ultimately concluding that most of them were simply expositions rather than refutations. Where the great John Stuart Mill had pointed out that while Achilles may indeed run forever, that "eternity will not see the end of twelve seconds," Borges dryly countered, "That methodical dissolution, that boundless descent into more and more minute precipices, is not really hostile to the problem; imagining it is the problem."[17] It is we who create the problem, Borges realized, by the very way we imagine the race. We attribute to Achilles and to the tortoise (as we do to ourselves and indeed to all objects) a persistence in time and space. When we slice time and space into the infinitesimal chunks that Achilles and the tortoise have to cross, we simultaneously impose on them and their experience a fabricated continuity of our own design. We imagine, in other words, a continuous movement between and beneath our measurements of their progress.

The paradox of Zeno, Borges wrote, "is an attempt upon not only the reality of space but the more invulnerable and sheer reality of time . . . [E]xistence in a physical body, immobile permanence, the flow of an afternoon in life, are challenged by such an adventure."[18] Like Heisenberg working feverishly on the other side of the world, as he explored the limits of perception, Borges peered into the abyss of an apparent paradox. And like Heisenberg, instead of shying away from this paradox, he chose to reexamine his most basic assumptions about time, space, and causality.

For the rest of his long and vibrant career, Borges would remain haunted by the flow of an afternoon in life, an afternoon when his beloved's gaze turned elsewhere, and he lost faith in the persistence of his own being in space and time. Over decades, Borges would obsessively conjure characters whose special abilities and most urgent desires reveal for them a paradoxical disconnect between knowledge and the world.

The greatest wizard, Borges speculated, would be the one whose spell is so convincing that he could fool even himself into believing its appearances were real. "Would this not be our case?" he asks.[19] And then adds, "We (the undivided divinity operating within us) have dreamt the world. We have dreamt it as firm, mysterious, visible, ubiquitous in space and durable in time; but in its architecture we have allowed tenuous and eternal crevices of unreason which tell us it is false." Where do we find those crevices of unreason? Borges leaves one further clue as to the hidden protagonist of the adventure challenging our notions of time and space: "Let us admit what all idealists admit: the hallucinatory nature of the world. Let us do what no idealist has done: seek unrealities which confirm that nature. We shall find them, I believe, in the antinomies of Kant."[20]

THE STATED PURPOSE OF the colossus that Hamann received in 1781 was to put science on a sure footing. That footing had, for Kant, been shaken by the writings of a gloomy Scot by the name of David Hume, whom Kant credited with having "interrupted my dogmatic slumber."[21] (Indeed, a professor of mine once complained that the worst thing Hume ever did was awaken Kant and thus subject posterity to having to read him.) According to Hume, absolutely everything we know about the world comes from our senses. Not only does this mean we can easily be wrong about what we think we know; even worse, we have no basis to suppose that such "certainties" as Isaac Newton's laws of motion are anything other than habits we've acquired through repeated exposure to similar impressions.

This notion troubled Kant. If it were true, it would upend his faith in the universality of reason, the very basis for our claim to derive scientific laws that explain the world around us. Every attempt to say something true about the world would have no more validity than a subjective assertion. And if objective truth about the world were lost, there could be no basis for arbitrating disputes about morality or, much less, taste. Soon after reading Hume, Kant believed he had discovered a way forward. But more than a decade would pass from the first fits and starts of his thinking to the morning of July 22, 1781, when the printed and bound *Critique of Pure Reason* would land with a propitious thud on Hamann's breakfast table.

What Kant managed to work out in his *Critique* is something so profound that few people fully grasp its implications even today. Hume and pretty much everyone else had made an unwarranted assumption about what goes on when we perceive something. That assumption is that we are correct in visualizing reality in itself as being consistent with our image of it. But our perceptions, Kant realized, aren't things in the world; rather, they are versions of those things that we construct in our minds *by shaping them in space and time.* When we imagine the world as being identical to our conception of it—when we assume, specifically, that space and time are fundamentally real—our reason becomes faulty, and science responds with paradox.

Kant didn't stop there. In the second half of the book he went on to describe in detail the kinds of paradoxes that pop up when we fail to make this distinction and mistakenly assume that time and space are inherent to the world. He called one class of these errors antinomies—those crevices of unreason that Borges credited with confirming the hallucinatory nature of the world. Specifically, Kant wrote, we can picture reality as being consistent and continuous, or as being broken into discrete chunks, and we can make perfectly logical and coherent arguments supporting both conclusions *even though those conclusions explicitly contradict each other.* This happens because we assume something about reality that only comes into play when we *observe* it.

HEISENBERG WAS CONVINCED IT made no sense to think of particles having position or momentum prior to observing one or the other.

He also believed he knew *why*. A particle's trajectory, the course it runs, didn't come into being until it was realized by the act of measuring it. What we know to be the case for Lindbergh, that he continued to exist after leaving Nova Scotia and before appearing again in the skies over Paris, and that he took a specific path to get there, simply is not the case for reality at its smallest levels. Heisenberg wrote to Wolfgang Pauli of his mind-bending discovery in words that would go on to shake the foundations of modern science: the path a particle takes "only comes into existence through this, that we observe it."[22]

Like Borges's wizard, when we observe the world, we make a map or mental picture of it. And we make that map ubiquitous in space and durable in time. But there are fundamental flaws in the image we create of the world, those that Kant termed antinomies. Like an imperfection in an otherwise flawless gemstone, it would be a mistake to try to eradicate them. For the flaws are inseparable from knowledge itself.

On a walk together in 1926, a venerated older scientist pressed the younger Heisenberg on the weakness he saw disqualifying his approach—that he was jettisoning our long-held belief in the independence of reality from our observations of it. Heisenberg pushed back. Had not the renowned professor himself come up with his own epochal discovery by overturning our most basic assumptions about time and space?

"Possibly I did," Albert Einstein grudgingly conceded, "but it is nonsense all the same."[23]

ONE OF THE GREAT tools humans have developed since the rise of modernity is science. At its core science is a way of looking at the world that foregrounds intellectual humility. It refuses on principle to know more than it can know at any given time. But even the greatest scientists aren't immune to projecting their prejudices on the world. Einstein—a man so brilliant that even his self-proclaimed blunders have an irritating propensity to turn out true—also had a tendency, especially in his later years, to lecture his fellow physicists in religious terms about what they should expect to discover about the ultimate nature of reality. In fact, his now famous quips about God being subtle but not malicious, or "the Old One" not throwing dice, finally led an exasperated Niels Bohr to beg the great man to "stop telling God what to do."[24]

For all their profound differences, Jorge Luis Borges, Immanuel Kant, and Werner Heisenberg shared an uncommon immunity to the temptation to think they knew God's secret plan. Each in his own way resisted the urge to project essential aspects of how human beings experience reality onto reality itself, independent of how we know it. Indeed, Heisenberg's disruption of classical physics had its roots in an iconoclastic countercurrent to a powerful human tendency to conjure the ultimate nature of reality in our imagination, and then go out and discover it. There is indeed rigor in the world, as Borges famously wrote, but "humanity has forgotten, and continues to forget, that it is the rigor of chess masters, not of angels."[25]

Knowledge is man-made, our own way of making sense of a reality whose ultimate nature may not conform to our conceptions of it. Is the saturated red of a Vermeer part of that ultimate reality? The soft fuzz of a peach's skin? The exalted crescendo of a Beethoven symphony? If we can grasp that such powerful experiences require the active engagement of observers and listeners, is it not possible, likely even, that the other phenomena we encounter have a similar origin? When we do the opposite, we forget the role we have in creating our own reality.

In their lives, struggles, and obsessions, Borges, Heisenberg, and Kant pushed far enough against the limits of imagination, observation, and thought to unearth the antinomies engendered by that forgetting. This book is divided into four sections, each of which revolves around one of those antinomies: Are space and time infinitely divisible, or are they composed of indivisible chunks? Is there something like a supreme and unconditional being, or is everything in existence conditioned and affected by something else? Is there a spatial or temporal edge to the universe, or does it extend infinitely with no beginning or border? Are we free to choose our path in life, or is our every choice determined by the physical world we live in?[26]

The sections in turn contain three chapters, each of which focuses primarily on one of our protagonists, the influences that were decisive for him, how he grappled with that antinomy in the realm of science, literature, or philosophy, and how that struggle ultimately paved the path toward his understanding of how knowledge structures reality. Thus our story opens, however improbably, with a Russian journalist who discovers he has a gift that is also a curse: a near-perfect memory. We then join Borges as he, prodded by the desire to recover the receding moments of bliss of a shattered romance, probes the paradoxes of what memory and perception entail. Using fiction to file away at the imperfections of human knowledge, he imagines a character who can perceive and remember everything, perfectly, with no gap in space or loss in time. In so doing he reveals the very insight that ignited Kant's revolution in thought: an observation of the world can never be perfectly of the world; it always requires something else, the insertion of a minimal distance that permits it to become knowledge in the first place.

In the chapters that ensue, we delve into the realm of the impossibly small; we stretch our minds to encompass everything at once; we travel to the beginning of time and the edge of existence; and we search for an iota of freedom in the mechanistic chain of nature. As we make this journey, we will be rocked by the astonishing implications that these thinkers' collective discoveries had for our conceptions of beauty, science, and what we owe to each other in the brief time given to us in this universe.

In telling the stories of Borges, Kant, and Heisenberg, this book also tells the story of those before them who caught a glimpse of the truth, who unearthed the tenuous and eternal crevices of unreason underlying our picture of the real. It tells a cautionary tale about the danger of assuming reality must conform to the image we construct of it, and the damage that our fidelity to such a seductive ideal can wreak. Most of all, it sings an ode to the boundless potential of our knowledge, once we have worked ourselves free from the blinders imposed by imagined perfection.

Part I

STANDING ON A SLIVER OF TIME

1

UNFORGETTABLE

I T WAS ONLY MIDMORNING on April 13, 1929, but Solomon Shereshevsky was already having a bad day. The journalist had just attended the daily editorial meeting of his Moscow newspaper when his section editor called him into his office. What was Shereshevsky playing at? his agitated superior asked him. Why did he just stare at the editor while he ran over the day's stories? Was he too full of himself to take notes like all the other reporters?

Nonplussed, Shereshevsky explained that he didn't need to take notes, because he remembered everything the editor said. Then he proceeded to recite the entire meeting back to him. Verbatim.

By that afternoon Shereshevsky found himself amid a gaggle of psychiatrists at the Academy of Communist Education, among whom was a young doctor, Alexander Luria. Luria took on the task of testing Shereshevsky's memory, which he did by reading him increasingly long lists of random words and numbers and asking him to recall them. By the end of the day Luria had to admit that the capacity of Shereshevsky's memory "had no distinct limits."[1]

As Shereshevsky would later recount, until that day he had

no idea his abilities were anything other than normal. When he returned to work, he delivered to his editor the verdict of the state's psychiatric experts: his memory exceeded "the bounds of what was believed to be physically possible." His editor promptly advised him to change careers. So Shereshevsky found a circus trainer to manage him and began booking shows around the country as a mnemonist.[2]

Despite his natural talent, Shereshevsky had to work hard at his new career, and he developed techniques to push his capacity ever further. To be able to recite back the lists of numbers, random words, poems in foreign languages, and even nonsensical syllables that audience members would call out to him, he landed on the strategy of picturing them drawn on a chalkboard. When it came time to recall the lists, he would return to this mental chalkboard and simply read from it out loud. To his horror he soon discovered that the very indelibility of his memory could interfere with his performance. Closing his eyes and finding his way back to the board on which he had arranged the sounds and images, he might instead come upon the board from an earlier performance and read back that list. To counteract this danger, he found he had to mentally erase or otherwise destroy the writing on his mental board. In short, to remember better, he had to learn to forget.

This interference didn't wane with time. Luria, who continued to study Shereshevsky for decades, discovered he could flawlessly recall lists Luria had used to test him fifteen years prior. In fact, Shereshevsky waged an almost constant war against the images and associations from the past that threatened to flood his every waking moment.

It wasn't just memories that menaced his perception of the present. Shereshevsky suffered from synesthesia, sensory crossover. A sound of a certain pitch might produce a coppery taste on his tongue; numbers appeared as specific figures with rich, unchanging characteristics. For most of us, 87 is a number, say, of pages read or years lived; Shereshevsky saw it as "a fat woman and a man twirling his mustache."[3] He experienced numerals, in other words, as individuals, not instances of a general system. He once exerted intense effort to memorize a vast table of numeric sequences, failing to notice that it followed a rule of such simplicity that a child could reproduce it ad infinitum, because each line simply started with a higher integer than the previous one.

For Luria it soon became clear that Shereshevsky's remarkable ability came with an equal disability. He lived in a world of particulars, "rich in imagery, thematic elaboration, and affect," but also "peculiarly lacking in one important feature: the capacity to convert encounters with the particular into instances of the general."[4] To understand the intended meaning of a normal sentence, Shereshevsky had to overcome his sensual experience of how a word sounded here and now; he had to forget his immersion in the present and connect to a different moment in space and time, an endeavor that would at times prove impossible.

In truth, he struggled mightily with the very aspect of language that makes it function in human communication and knowledge. Even our most common expressions contain words that we use figuratively, or that have different meanings in different situations. A nightmare for Shereshevsky. The simple act of "catching a cab" would present him with a barrage of possible interpretations to contend with. As he would later explain to Luria, the word *ekipazh* means "cab," but it also means "the crew of a ship." To understand the one meaning, he had to "picture for myself not just a driver ... in the cab but an entire staff manning it. That's the only way I can make sense of it."[5] Living in a world of particulars, being constantly bathed in the immediate, makes communication a difficult affair. Language loses its ability to connect two disparate agents, to translate the experience of the one into the context of the other. But more than just a stumbling block for understanding what others were saying to him, in Shereshevsky's world, as the neuroscientist Jerome Bruner would later put it, "elements and features can be isolated, but a 'whole' or meaningful picture cannot be put together."[6] Indeed, it seems that the more perfect Shereshevsky's extraordinary memory, the less he had a coherent self who could remember.

For a brief time, Shereshevsky's feats brought him fame and a sustainable existence. But even as stories of the man who couldn't forget seeped into the outside world, life behind Stalin's iron curtain was getting harder, especially for Jews like Luria and Shereshevsky. After the war, as Stalin consolidated his power through "anti-cosmopolitan" purges, Luria lost his position for a time and took to keeping a bag packed in case the authorities came for him in the night. Shereshevsky, who had refused to lend his talents to the secret police, found himself followed and harassed, his performances interrupted, and his career eventually ruined.[7] Luria would regain his footing and become one of the preeminent neuropsychologists of the twentieth century, his analysis of Shereshevsky a profound influence for later scientists like Jerome Bruner and Oliver Sacks. Shereshevsky, for his part, learned another way of erasing or at least dampening the remembered and perceived sensorium that had become his prison house. He started drinking heavily and died in obscurity a few years later.

ON THE SPRING DAY when Solomon Shereshevsky met Alexander Luria in Moscow, Jorge Luis Borges languished in a veritable winter of discontent in Buenos Aires. Still aching for Norah Lange, Borges experienced severe despondency and responded rashly. His long evening walks through Buenos Aires took a self-destructive turn as he deliberately ventured into barrios known for their villainy. One evening as he and two writer friends made their way through the alleys of a particularly sketchy neighborhood, the tapping of the cane Borges used to aid his ever-worsening eyesight caught the attention of some local thugs, who started to bait them. To the horror of his companions, rather than join them in fleeing, Borges turned to the men and showered them with insults, such that all three friends only narrowly escaped intact.[8]

To make matters worse, while Borges slipped into an early decline, the source of his anguish had become nothing short of a literary rock star. The Buenos Aires imprint Tor had chosen ten titles from its list to release as the first ever paperbacks in Argentina. Banking on Norah Lange's growing notoriety and the titillating premise of a young woman's sexual awakening during a transatlantic crossing on a ship, its editor, Juan Carlos Torrendell, chose her most recent novel, *45 Days and 30 Sailors,* to be one of them. Never one to miss an opportunity to put on a show, Oliverio Girondo threw a party in Norah's honor that drew the crème de la crème of the literary establishment. Incidentally, the male attendees all dressed as sailors. Borges, naturally, did not attend.

Who did attend, however, were two of the world's most blazing literary lights: the Spanish poet Federico García Lorca and the Chilean Pablo Neruda, who would subsequently become, in the opinion of another writer, "the greatest poet of the twentieth century, in any language."[9] Norah became a fixture in a riotous literary scene led by Oliverio and his visiting friends Neruda and García Lorca, and often played the scandalous centerpiece of their hijinks—as when they commandeered a milk truck and drove it to one of the busiest intersections in Buenos Aires, where Norah ascended a policeman's podium and stopped the traffic for an impromptu recital of one of Neruda's most beloved poems.[10]

For his part, Borges had lost the ability to write poetry. Poetry had required a faith he no longer could muster, a faith that human language enables a connection between two souls that would amount to the creation of a unity, a single identity between them. Never mind joining souls; now Borges began to question whether even the connections we posit between two observed events—the touch of a hand, the blush of a cheek—had basis in any reality other than his own mind. And if such observations amounted to little more than ephemeral impressions, appearing for an instant, only to be lost forever in the river of time, not only could language not connect people; he questioned if it made sense to believe a person even existed on its sending or receiving end. No soul, no mind, no self at all.

In a last desperate plea, Borges dedicated his next book, *A Universal History of Infamy*, to Norah, offering her "that kernel of myself that I have saved, somehow—the central heart that deals not in words, traffics not with dreams and is untouched by time, by joy, by adversities."[11] Borges, it seems, was rapidly convincing himself that, far from a kernel untouched by time, his sense of self was a mere illusion, a sliver of nostalgia slowly drowning in a sea of evidence auguring for the "nothingness of personality." He had claimed as much in an essay he wrote with that very title as a twenty-two-year-old, in which he already began tugging at the stitching that keeps our belief in a coherent self from unraveling into ephemeral and disconnected memories. When we imagine ourselves to be a consistent self enduring in time, Borges mused, perhaps we are merely beguiled by the fact that some of our experiences seem to "occur again in an imprecise way."[12]

Memory, the twenty-two-year-old Borges had ventured, forms the core of selfhood, but memory merely concatenates a series of impressions that evoke one another. The fantasia of his obsession with Norah Lange had, for a time, banished this threat and replaced it with the idea of a self that endures over time. Now disabused of that hope, an older Borges, "a rueful and abandoned man," would again start to see the notion of a coherent self as little more than a mirage conjured when, "in a state of passion, our memory inclines to the intemporal."[13] And yet, even if that self amounted to nothing, how he longed to hold on to its fragments, memories of lost attachments that could only bring him pain.

The first essay he published after accepting the finality of his breakup with Norah dealt with the subject of hell. Tellingly, he omitted any iconic images of physical torment. Instead, he recounted a dream in which he no longer understood who or where he was: "I was filled with fear. I thought: this disconsolate wakefulness already is hell, the pointless wakefulness will be my eternity."[14] When he later read Dante's *Divine Comedy* and declared it "perhaps the highest work of literature, of all literatures,"[15] Borges felt the Italian poet had intentionally left "a splinter of Hell stuck in the heart of Paradise."[16] In what Borges would call "the most moving verses ever achieved," Dante imagines his beloved Beatrice smiling at him one last time before turning away to be absorbed into the eternally ecstatic contemplation of God that is reserved for the blessed.

In contrast to a paradise that promised the subsumption of the individual into the timeless unity of the divine mind, Borges found aspects of Dante's hell improbably attractive. For if *you* enter the inferno, at the very least *you* are there, feeling and remembering the whole time. The famously beautiful image of the illicit lovers Paolo and Francesca, whose lawless desire damned them to being buffeted about for eternity in a whirlwind together, struck Borges as rather less punitive than Beatrice's obliteration as a distinct personality.[17]

Attachment to a person or an object entails a relation sustained over time. And a relation to something sustained over time inevitably implies its possible loss. That coherence over time encapsulating the presence *and* the absence of an attachment is precisely what we call a self. As the Spanish philosopher and author Miguel de Unamuno had put it in *Tragic Sense of Life*, "I was never made to tremble by descriptions of hellfire, no matter how terrible, for I felt, always, that the idea of nothingness was much more terrifying than Hell."[18] Like Unamuno, Borges yearned for the personal attachments of love and friendship; he desired selfhood, even if selfhood could bring him only pain.

What would it entail to have an attachment and never lose it? To remember something perfectly, not as past, but as still present? Take a scene from your past, a moment that has stuck in your mind. You may see a vague picture, the flash of a recognizable face; a snippet of dialogue plays in your ear. You also probably register an emotion:

wistfulness, nostalgia. The scene may bring a smile to your face, or it may cause you to tear up. What you cannot do is re-create it perfectly, sensation by sensation.

But what if you could? What if your brain were like a powerful video recorder that stored not only every visual impulse received by your retinas at every moment but also the timbre of every sound, texture of every touch, every last whiff of aroma, and each tingle on your taste buds? What if you could access such moments at will?

Most of us would jump at the chance to revisit select moments in our past. Moments we look back on with longing now. When Odysseus and Penelope were reunited after their two-decade separation, Athena held back the long night and "likewise stayed the golden-throned Dawn,"[19] so that they could retain a little longer the ephemeral sweetness of that incomparable pleasure. But as great as that gift was, how much greater would it be to relive the moment at will. To return, in five-sense Technicolor, to a few treasured minutes of pure bliss, the flow of an afternoon in life, before everything changed.

But you can't. The more precisely you relive the past, the less it is a past you remember, and the more it becomes the present, vanishing before your eyes as the present always does. A truly perfect replay would erase its very sense of being a replay altogether because it would erase the connection between moments of time that constitute the one remembering, the self. A perfect memory is impossible because it destroys the very self who remembers. Like for Unamuno, the hell that haunted Borges's dreams was the prospect of losing that sense of self that provided the basis for all attachments, all memories. Even if the alternative was an eternity of pain.

History of Eternity, the book Borges wrote in 1935, was published the following year. While in some ways a turning point in his intellectual development, it was a low ebb in his fortunes as a writer, selling only thirty-seven copies and garnering almost no critical attention at the time. Its themes and concerns, however, would give shape to the Borges to come. Less than a decade later Borges would publish to resounding success two sets of his stories as a combined volume under the simple title *Fictions*. The second group of six stories he called *Artifices*. And the opening story is about a man who loses his ability to forget.

AS A YOUNG MAN, Kant marveled at a prediction made by one of his professors, Martin Knutzen, that a comet that had last appeared in the skies above Königsberg in 1698 would reappear at a specific date. One evening in the icy winter of 1744, Knutzen invited Kant and some fellow students to his house to gaze through the mirror telescope he had made according to Sir Isaac Newton's own design. There Kant could see with his own eyes the astonishing power of Newton's theories as the telescope revealed the stunning tale of a comet splashed across the night sky. As it turned out, Knutzen's numbers were off, and the comet of 1744 was not the same as that of 1698. But even this realization failed to dim Kant's newborn enthusiasm for the ability of reason to grasp the laws that govern the cosmos.[20]

Knutzen's faith in the power of human knowledge to derive objective laws from observations followed largely in the footsteps of the seventeenth-century German polymath Gottfried Wilhelm Leibniz, who shares credit (or blame, if you happen to be a junior in high school) with Newton for creating calculus, and even invented the first mechanical calculator, a forebear of modern computers. For Leibniz and the rationalist schools that followed him, things appeared and behaved as they did because they were programmed to do so, and the programmer who determined their behavior was, naturally, God.

For Leibniz's adherents everything that exists and moves in the world does so because God has an idea of it existing and moving. Instead of wondering if Newton's laws have objective truth and stand for all time and, if so, why they work the way they do, rationalists could have faith that those laws accurately described the interactions between all elements in space-time, because God controlled all movements for all time through what Leibniz called "preestablished harmony." Every single item in creation just needed to follow its own preset path through space-time. When a comet comes back around in agreement with calculations made with Newton's equations for gravity, we don't need to account for the planets' action on it. Indeed, the planets don't need to communicate anything to the comet; each is just flowing along the path of its preestablished harmony.

In 1770, Kant assumed the position of Full Professor of Logic and Metaphysics at the University of Königsberg. Though he had (by and large) toed the rationalist line of believing in a fundamental continuity between the way the world is in itself—the code of the world—and how it manifests itself to human senses, Kant had never been a party-line man. As he wrote about his method in a letter two years earlier to the famed poet and philosopher Johann Gottfried Herder, "With a deep indifference toward my own opinions as well as those of others, I often subvert the entire structure and consider it from several points of view in order to hit finally perhaps on the position from which I can hope to draw the system truthfully."[21] Upon assuming his professorship, Kant delivered an inaugural dissertation in Latin, as was customary. True to his word, he used the occasion to entirely subvert the structure.

For the rationalists, space and time were fundamental parts of reality. Until as late as 1768, Kant accepted this premise.[22] The inaugural dissertation hinted at Kant's shake-up of this notion right from its title, *On the Form and Principles of the Sensible and Intelligible World.* In his lecture, Kant rejected the notion that our senses directly express an underlying set of divine ideas or instructions—that we can read the code of the world, as it were. In its place he now drew an airtight border between what we experience with our senses in space and time, on the one hand, and eternal truths and principles, on the other, which exist outside space and time and remain true despite what our senses tell us.

In advancing this distinction, Kant did not, however, abandon the hope that we could derive objective truths about the causal connections between our perceptions, even as they remained subjective and variable. In other words, while we can only know what we learn through our senses, he still thought we could infer from our senses certain objective facts about the world, such as the relation between a cause and the effect that must follow that cause. But something happened in July 1771 that would decisively challenge that hope and lead Kant onto a new course of thought.

That summer a local newspaper published an anonymous essay under the title "Night Thoughts of a Skeptic." Based on its style and philosophical tone, many readers assumed that Kant's friend and frequent correspondent Johann Georg Hamann had written it. In this brief text, a skeptical soliloquist pushes his inquiries to their most devastating conclusions. Not only is every single observation we make subject to the vagaries of our subjective condition, but also any principle we attempt to draw from them, such as the existence of an objective causal relation between them, "lies merely in ourselves" and is "nothing but a determination of the mind."[23] Thus, the writer concludes, "when we say we desire to know the ultimate and operating principle," that is, when we attempt to grasp the objective reality underlying our observations, "we either contradict ourselves, or talk without a meaning."[24] There is no such thing as a law of nature; we are trapped forever in our subjective impressions, and believing otherwise is pure delusion.

According to the insomniac skeptic's provocations, both the spatial and temporal media in which all causal relations take place and the very fact of causality itself are nothing other than aspects of the subjective framework we use to make sense of the world. For Hamann, thinkers were going too far when they tried to expand knowledge with their reason alone. This philosophical hubris could only ever lead to error and despair. We need not more philosophical rigor but *faith*. Where human reason failed and had to fail, only faith could step back in and provide the grounds for our beliefs. Hamann had intended this text as a cautionary note. Moreover, he intended its message to be read by Kant.

Kant did indeed read "Night Thoughts of a Skeptic" that summer. But he did not take the conclusion from it that Hamann had hoped he would. Rather than give up on the possibility of accessing some grounds for objective knowledge of the world, rather than agree that such knowledge had to give way to faith, Kant realized that he had not been radical enough in his analysis of what happens when we observe something—even if it would take him another decade (and almost nine hundred pages) to turn that realization into the "all-crushing" *Critique of Pure Reason*.[25] At the same time, Kant realized something else. Hamann had not authored the morose essay that had awoken him from his slumber; he had translated it. "Night Thoughts of a Skeptic" was nothing other than the conclusion to David Hume's *Treatise of Human Nature*. And in that great book, Hume had gone beyond questioning our ability to learn objective truths about causality to doubt even the existence of the self trying to grasp those truths.

In his *Treatise,* Hume followed in the footsteps of René Descartes and plumbed the depths of what he could know. But instead of landing on the sure footing of "I think" as the great French thinker had, Hume encountered only baseless impressions: "When I enter most intimately into what I call *myself,* I always stumble on some particular perception or other, of heat or cold, light or shade, love or hatred, pain or pleasure. I never catch *myself* at any time without a perception, and never can observe anything but the perception."[26] Like Knutzen staring into the heavens and mistaking the comet he sees there for the one he expected to find, when we believe that our impressions belong to a self, we falsely project an expected unity on a disjointed and random series of impressions.

Hume's conviction that there was no substance connecting his disparate experiences, no *res cogitans,* or "thinking stuff," as Descartes had memorably coined the self, left him, as he wrote, "in the most deplorable condition imaginable, inviron'd with the deepest darkness."[27] Like Borges and Unamuno, Hume had found his hell, not in the threat of eternal damnation, but in the suspicion that there was no damned self in the first place. But faced with the challenge of Hume's hell, Kant discovered a profound truth about the self that Hume had overlooked—the very same truth Borges discovered when, a century and a half later, he used his newfound style of writing to push to its limits the very idea of what it means to know reality.

WHILE WE HAVE NO proof that Borges read about Shereshevsky's memory feats in the 1930s, we do know that he read ravenously and at times indiscriminately, and that stories about the mnemonist dazzling Russian audiences had circulated widely at the time. In any event, the similarities are remarkable. In Borges's story, he recounts meeting a young man in the provinces named Ireneo Funes, already well known by his fellow villagers for his quirky ability to tell the exact time of day without ever checking a watch. When Borges returns to the town two years after encountering Ireneo, he learns that a terrible accident has befallen him. Ireneo fell from his horse and injured his head and is now confined to his house. Seeking him out on the outskirts of town, Borges finds the young man lying alone on his cot, smoking a cigarette at the far end of a dark room.

The injury changed Funes in a remarkable way. Where before he evinced an unusual awareness of the passage of time, he now possesses a memory so perfect it seems to eradicate time. On his prior visit Borges had lent Funes a Latin dictionary and his copy of Pliny's *Naturalis historia*. Now, as Borges steps into the dimly lit room, he hears Funes reciting by heart "the first paragraph of the twenty-fourth chapter of the seventh book of Pliny's *Naturalis historia*," the subject of which is memory. But more than a perfect recall of past words or events, Ireneo Funes perceives everything that he has experienced or is currently experiencing, and does so in perfect, saturated, sensory plenitude. As Borges describes it,

> With one quick look, you and I perceive three wineglasses on a table; Funes perceived every grape that had been pressed into the wine and all the stalks and tendrils of its vineyard. He knew the forms of the clouds in the southern sky on the morning of April 30, 1882, and he could compare them in his memory with the veins in the marbled binding of a book he had seen only once, or with the feathers of spray lifted by an oar on the Río Negro on the eve of the Battle of Quebracho. Nor were those memories simple—every visual image was linked to muscular sensations, thermal sensations, and so on. He was able to reconstruct every dream, every daydream he had ever had. Two or three times he had reconstructed an entire day; he had never once erred or faltered, but each reconstruction had itself taken an entire day.[28]

Funes insists he has a gift beyond all reckoning, but like Luria analyzing Shereshevsky, Borges quickly realizes he also has an affliction. Like Shereshevsky, Funes bathes in the immediacy of his memories; he finds it difficult to experience the world precisely because he inhabits it so intensely. If reconstructing a daylong memory takes an entire day, that new day is consequently lost to the man who must wall himself into the sensory deprivation tank of his room so as not to be consumed by the present.

As for Shereshevsky, language for Funes doesn't seem to function properly, or at least the way it does for most human beings. Instead of understanding numbers as elements in a system of general applicability, Funes, like Shereshevsky, has an individual name and identity for every number he encounters. By the time he meets with Borges, these have surpassed twenty-four thousand. "Instead of seven thousand thirteen (7013), he would say, for instance, 'Máximo

Pérez'; instead of seven thousand fourteen (7014), 'the railroad'; other numbers were 'Luis Melián Lafinur,' 'Olimar,' 'sulfur,' 'clubs,' 'the whale,' 'gas,' 'a stewpot,' 'Napoleon,' 'Agustín de Vedia.' Instead of five hundred (500), he said 'nine.'"[29]

A language such as the one the English philosopher John Locke postulated in the seventeenth century, one with a term for every being in existence, might have satisfied Funes. But if Locke rejected the idea for being so specific as to be useless, Funes rejected it for being far too general. Funes, Borges soon realized, lacked the basic function that permits us to think in the first place—abstraction. "Not only was it difficult for him to see that the generic symbol 'dog' took in all the dissimilar individuals of all shapes and sizes," Borges recounts, "it irritated him that the 'dog' of three-fourteen in the afternoon, seen in profile, should be indicated by the same noun as the dog of three-fifteen, seen frontally. His own face in the mirror, his own hands, surprised him every time he saw them."[30]

Funes, it seems, suffers from an incapacity to make connections between even slightly distinct experiences, just as Shereshevsky did, and they both exhibit the same impatience with the generality of language. And yet a lurking paradox haunts both accounts. Shereshevsky claimed that he struggled to grasp that "the word *ekipazh*," which "definitely has to be a cab, can also mean the crew of a ship."[31] But for Shereshevsky to complain about his inability to comprehend the generality of language, he must comprehend the generality of language. *He needs to see that a word refers to two different experiences in order to find it inadequate that it does so.*

Likewise, for Funes, each and every impression is so vastly, overwhelmingly specific that he becomes "irritated" that we use the same word for a dog seen in two different moments; he is "surprised" each time he glimpses his image in a mirror. And yet, despite the power and inextricability of both his memory and his absorption into the sensory world, Funes demonstrably does span their differences. Indeed, for him to have enough self-awareness to feel irritation at our sloppy use of a word, or surprise at his own face, he must have the power, even if only in the slightest manner, to overlook the distinctions that make each unique. And this minimal forgetting, this minimum distance from a total absorption in the present, also creates the minimal condition of having a self in the first place.

Funes remembers "not only every leaf of every tree in every patch of forest, but every time he had perceived or imagined that leaf."[32] For him, each iota of the space-time continuum is utterly singular. Or so he claims. Hume also claimed this. For Hume, we could never know if there was a world of information, of necessary laws behind our sensory impressions. For him, each impression, each leaf in a garden, was condemned to be isolated, sui generis, and never an example of a general rule. But where this challenge led him to extreme skepticism, Kant drew another lesson.

Kant realized that Hume's world of pure, unique impressions couldn't exist. This is because the minimal requirement for experiencing anything is not to be so absorbed in the present that one is lost in it. What Hume had claimed—that when exploring his feeling of selfhood, he always landed "on some particular perception or other" but could never catch *himself* "at any time without a perception, and never can observe anything but the perception"—was simply not true.[33] Because for Hume to even report this feeling he had to perceive something in addition to the immediate perceptions, namely, the very flow of time that allowed them to be distinct in the first place. And to recognize time passing is necessarily to recognize that *you* are embedded in the perception.

Hence what Kant wrote in his answer to Hamann, ten years in the making. To recollect perfectly eradicates the recollection, just as to perceive perfectly eradicates the perception. For the one who recalls or perceives must recognize him- or herself along with the memory or perception for the memory or impression to exist at all. If everything we learn about the world flows directly into us from utterly distinct bits of code, as the rationalists thought, or if everything we learn remains nothing but subjective, unconnected impressions, as

Hume believed—it comes down to exactly the same thing. With no self to distinguish itself, no self to bridge two disparate moments in space-time, there is simply no one there to feel irritated at the inadequacy of "dog." No experience whatsoever is possible.

Here is how Kant put it in his *Critique of Pure Reason.* Whatever we think or perceive can register as a thought or perception only if it causes a change in us, a "modification of the mind." But these changes would not register at all if we did not connect them across *time,* "for *as contained in one moment* no representation can ever be anything other than absolute unity."[34] As contained in one moment. Think of experiencing a flow of events as a bit like watching a film. For something to be happening at all, the viewer makes a connection between each frame of the film, spanning the small differences so as to create the experience of movement. But if there is a completely new viewer for every frame, with no relation at all to the prior or subsequent frame, then all that remains is an absolute unity. But such a unity, which is exactly what Funes and Shereshevsky and Hume claimed they could experience, utterly negates perceiving anything at all, since all perception requires bridging impressions over time. In other words, it requires exactly what a truly perfect memory, a truly perfect perception, or a truly perfect observation absolutely denies: overlooking minor differences enough to be a self, a unity spanning distinct moments in time.

As Borges would show throughout his writings, the very obscurity of words that had seemed to him a betrayal of their poetic promise could, wielded the right way, procure a different salvation. The self was not nothing. It couldn't be. The very impossibility of recovering a scene from the past, of recapturing the flow of an afternoon in life, guarantees that self's persistence. But he also grasped something else. Like Kant before him, he also discovered that the conceit of slowing time down to a single frame, honing the moment of an observation to a pure present, destroys the observation itself. The closer we look, the more the present vanishes from our grasp.

Which was precisely the insight that hit Werner Heisenberg in Copenhagen as he walked in Faelled Park on that cold winter evening.

FOR ALL ITS FAMOUSLY impenetrable equations, the central debate in quantum mechanics today is not so much about mathematics as it is about language. Discoveries about the building blocks of reality can't help but invite philosophical speculation, and while there also exists a field of philosophy devoted to it, physicists are far from immune to the temptations of ontology.

Currently most particle physicists, along with the grants and positions that make their work possible, accept some version of what has come to be known as the Copenhagen interpretation of quantum mechanics. The Copenhagen interpretation takes its name from the city in which Niels Bohr and Werner Heisenberg eventually worked out their differences and arrived at a description of the relation between what Heisenberg's equations told them and the reality we live in on a daily basis. The core of the interpretation contains a compromise between Heisenberg's discovery and Bohr's interpretive framework.

Heisenberg's principle shows that the closer you home in on the location of a particle, the less you know about its momentum, that is, where it is heading and how fast it's going there. Or, conversely, you can find out a great deal about its momentum, but to do so, you lose all sense of where it is. It's like finding exactly where Lindbergh's plane is over the Atlantic, but only at the cost of knowing nothing about the path he is flying. What you can do, though, is use Heisenberg's matrix algebra—or what ultimately won the scientific community over, Erwin Schrödinger's wave equation—to enter measurements for either position or momentum and produce reliable predictions of the probable outcomes of future measurements.

Bohr's addition is a kind of philosophical explanation of why that is the case. We can think of matter and energy as either a particle or a wave. These descriptions complement each other, but neither one stands on its own. Likewise, quantum mechanics and classical mechanics apply to separate but complementary realms. Classical mechanics can translate into quantum mechanics, but the image the former gives of objects moving in space just doesn't apply to the quantum realm.

Critics of the Copenhagen interpretation reasonably ask what determines at exactly which point the laws of classical physics that work so well for baseballs, airplanes, and planets simply cease to hold for smaller entities. The same critics tend to grouse that Bohr and company made a practice of moving the border between the quantum and the classical realms whenever it seemed convenient to do so.

Most do agree, however, that within the field of quantum physics the Copenhagen interpretation has become something of an orthodoxy, with the potentially chilling effect that young researchers interested in working on the problem of "what actually is happening" at the quantum level run into an institutional inertia best characterized by the Cornell physicist David Mermin's quip "Shut up and calculate."[35] (Einstein found this attitude particularly exasperating, to the point that he would ask Copenhagen adherents if they also believed the moon ceased to exist when it wasn't being observed; Mermin, to his credit, is consistent enough to insist that "the moon is demonstrably not there when nobody looks.")[36]

Despite this general dominance of the Copenhagen interpretation, alternatives continue to sprout, each with its vocal advocates. Some of those alternatives, which can trace themselves back to Einstein and Schrödinger's realism, are collectively referred to as objective collapse models—briefly, models that don't require a human observer for probability waves to collapse into a single particle with a definite location. The Italian physicist Angelo Bassi, a leading proponent of one such model, believes that quantum mechanics can be understood to describe reality as well as predict it, if only we change our language. "You should remove the word 'particle' from your vocabulary," as he puts it. "It's all about gelatin. An electron can be here *and* there and that's it." In Bassi's view, this gelatinous substrate of reality reacts to encountering other such inchoate beings by snapping into a particle form, "like an octopus that when you touch them: *Whoop!*"[37] Crucially, this happens whether or not the inchoate blob it encounters happens to belong to a human observer.

If we can hear in proponents of the Copenhagen interpretation echoes of the philosopher Ludwig Wittgenstein, who famously wrote, "Whereof one cannot speak, thereof one must be silent," Bassi and those following in Einstein and Schrödinger's footsteps insist that a theory we can't explain in words, no matter how excellent at predicting results, ultimately isn't a theory.[38] As Bassi avers, "I strongly believe that physics *is* words."[39]

But what does it mean to put something into words? Of all the physicists responsible for developing quantum mechanics, Werner Heisenberg evinced the least concern with making the results of his and his colleagues' new discoveries conform to preexisting images of reality. His nonchalance about what reality ultimately looks like was interpreted by his colleagues as a lack of interest in "philosophical" questions. Yet Heisenberg spent decades lecturing and writing for the public on the philosophical implications of quantum physics.

In 1942, with the world engulfed in war and himself at the head of Germany's nuclear research program, Heisenberg was secretly writing a book. The "Manuscript of 1942," as it would be referred to for years, didn't appear until after Heisenberg's death in 1976, and wasn't translated until a version appeared in France in the 1980s. It turns out that during the time Heisenberg worked on creating a fission reactor for Germany, he quietly obsessed about the question of how accurately humans could come to know reality. The key to this question, he believed, lay in our understanding of language.

As Heisenberg describes the basic problem in his 1942 manuscript, science translates reality into thought, and humans need language to think. Language, however, suffers from the same fundamental limitation that Heisenberg discovered in nature. We can focus our language down to highly objective degrees, where it becomes particularly well defined and hence useful for scientists studying the natural world. But to the extent we do so, we necessarily lose another essential aspect of words, namely, their ability to have multiple meanings depending on how we use them.

The first nature of language Heisenberg calls static, and the second, dynamic. While all humans use language at varying points along these spectrums, physicists exemplify the static use, while poets exemplify the dynamic use. Where scientists very much depend on the static quality of words for their ability to pin down exact descriptions of their objects of study, they do so at a cost: "What is sacrificed in 'static' description is that infinitely complex association among words and concepts without which we would lack any sense at all that we have understood anything of the infinite abundance of reality."[40] As a result, precisely insofar as perceiving and thinking about the world depend on coordinating both aspects of language, a "complete and exact depiction of reality can never be achieved."[41]

It's hard not to hear in Heisenberg's discussion echoes of Solomon Shereshevsky's own struggles with language, or his more perfect avatar Funes's struggles with perception itself. It is as if Shereshevsky and Funes had become test cases for a sort of internal check on human knowledge, whereby the perfection of their recall and the intensity of their living in the present became a hindrance to understanding language or distinguishing perceptions from recollections. Imagine Funes as the scientist in this scenario. Funes distinguishes everything. He perceives everything as completely sui generis, not related to anything else. This utter perfection of perception allows him to distinguish "not only every leaf of every tree in every patch of forest, but every time he had perceived or imagined that leaf." Put him in a laboratory, give him a cloud chamber, and he perceives not only every line of condensation left by an errant particle but the particle itself; not only every particle, but every moment in the series of moments that defines that particle's trajectory.

But of course, he can't. Not because of some otherworldly quality of the particle—that it ceases to exist over the Atlantic and magi-cally appears when sighted over France. The scientist can't perceive the way Funes ostensibly can because the very nature of observing something as it changes over time requires that the observer gen-eralize, ever so slightly, and connect the difference between two moments in space-time. Without this slight blur, this ever so subtle distancing, this lifting up and holding steady of a standard so as to register some infinitesimal alteration, all there would be is an eter-nal present. The dog of three fifteen, seen frontally, never to be called a dog, never to be recognized, never to be *observed* in the first place.

Like Borges and Kant, what Heisenberg grasped—what he cal-culated mathematically, yes, but also what he was able to capture in language—was that to simultaneously observe an electron's posi-tion and momentum would require a perfect presence in a single moment in time, which is utterly incompatible with the mini-mum condition of observing anything at all. Not because of some spooky quality of the world of fundamental materials, but because, by its very nature, an observation must relate at least two distinct moments in space-time. In Kant's words, an observation absolutely requires distinguishing "the time in the succession of impressions on one another."[42] An observation, any observation, undermines perfect being in the present, because the observation itself brings space and time to the picture. A fundamental particle captured in a singular moment of space-time is thus, by definition, unperceivable and "absolute unity," an infinitely thin sliver of space-time, with no before or after.[43]

AS KANT WENT ON to tell Herder in his letter from 1767, his method of subverting the structure and considering it from various points of view had led him to "recognize the inherent determinations and limitations of human abilities and inclinations" and to isolate and understand such limits as they affected knowledge itself.[44] Not to condemn science to the hopelessness that drove Hume to despair, though. Kant thought recognizing and exactly describing those limits could ensure that science not run into limits of its own making. Heisenberg felt the same. As he wrote in his 1942 manuscript, each time science makes a new discovery, its "sphere of validity appears to be pushed yet one more step into an impenetrable darkness that lies behind the ideas language is able to express. This feeling determines the direction of our thinking, but part of the essence of thinking is that the complex relationship it seeks to explore cannot be contained in words." We need to guard against, to be aware of, not a barrier out there in the world, an impenetrable wall that science will eventually run up against. Rather, we should guard against creating that wall ourselves by imposing a prejudice we have about what reality must be like onto the perpetually receding future of our discoveries. In Heisenberg's words, "The ability of human beings to understand is without limit. About the ultimate things we cannot speak."[45] Or to put it inversely, by presuming we know the ultimate nature of reality, we limit our ability to understand.

In expressing this attitude, Heisenberg was paying homage to Kant, who had led the way in discovering that the key to advancing science lay in not blinding our vision with the presumption of ultimate knowledge. To get there, though, Kant first had to dive deeply into the nature of space and time; to tease apart with his intellect what the physicists of Heisenberg's day would start to discover with the benefits of cloud chambers and spectrographic analysis; to come face to face with that paradoxical moment when one sliver of space-time changes into another.

Kant didn't make this discovery on his own. An entire history of thought preceded him, and as much as he gleaned from the science and cosmology of his day, his philosophical roots pulled deeply from that history. In the next chapter we will go back to Kant's early life and education to trace those influences as his star rose among the thinkers of the eighteenth century. We will see how his most radical

insight, the one that set him on the road to revolutionizing philosophy, involved how we conceive of space and time and their relation
to reality. And we will see how he started to trace the contours of the
crevice of unreason that emerges when we imagine that the tools we
use to understand the world are of the world themselves.

2

A BRIEF HISTORY
OF THIS VERY INSTANT

ON NOVEMBER 1, 1755, THE city of Lisbon was leveled by a series of devastating earthquakes, leaving tens of thousands dead. The effect was felt far and wide—not only in the waves that emanated out through the earth's mantle, but in the questions the event raised for those trying to understand the nature of our planet and its place in the universe. Kant had been caught in the gravitational pull of such massive questions ever since his mother, full of religious fervor, had taken him by the hand and led him outside to gaze up and marvel at the beauty of God's starlit tapestry spread above them in the night sky.[1] That same night sky was later the stage for Martin Knutzen's revelation to Kant of how mathematics could decode the movements of distant objects. But Knutzen had succumbed to exhaustion in 1751, and his professorship had lain dormant ever since. Now Kant felt the need to rise to his former teacher's calling. He penned a series of widely read essays for a Königsberg weekly on the relationship between the earth's rotation and disruptions on its surface, speculating about the possibility of using science to predict disasters such as had befallen Lisbon.[2]

Clearly, at least in Königsberg's academic world, Kant was making waves of his own—curious, given how little he had published. His only book, a work on physics and cosmology called *Universal Natural History and Theory of the Heavens*—inspired by a love for astronomy that dated to his studies with Knutzen and his marvelous comet—had failed to reach the public due to the untimely bankruptcy of its publisher. Despite its lack of influence, he would attempt to use it the following year to position himself as the natural replacement for Knutzen's open professorship. In a letter to King Frederick II, he presented his book as a calling card and beseeched the king to look favorably on his application, emphasizing his "utmost submission" to his sovereign's authority and signing off as the king's "most devoted servant."[3] Unfortunately, the king ignored his letter; for financial reasons, the university decided to leave Knutzen's chair unfilled.

Despite this dearth of written work, when Kant defended the dissertation for his master's degree in June 1755, the event was attended by a large crowd of the city's most revered men of letters, who "revealed their respect by the exceptional hush and attentiveness" with which they attended to his words.[4] Later that year, Kant stepped gingerly into the spacious hall of the professor's house where he resided to give his first public lecture. In order to access the room, he had to push his way through throngs of students who had gathered for the event, milling about in the hall and overflowing into the entrance and even onto the building's front steps, which were "packed with an almost incredible crowd of students."[5] The sudden limelight clearly frayed the young teacher's nerves, for he lost his accustomed composure and stumbled through his lecture, frequently correcting himself. Despite his nervousness, the lecture was a resounding success. The audience reported "an even more lively warmth" than they had been given to expect based on the growing reputation of Kant's "most comprehensive erudition."[6]

In fact, Kant's reputation derived mostly from conversations. As friends of his would later report, Kant was a man who in the course of a normal discussion "threw off ingenious ideas by the thousands" and who, in his discourse and lectures, "was far more genial than in his books."[7]

Kant's rapid rise to prominence as a teacher and thinker at the vanguard of a philosophical movement dedicated to reason and science belied his humble origins as the fourth of nine children in a family of a harness maker. Touchingly, throughout his life Kant always esteemed and extolled his parents for their dedication to Pietism—a sect of Lutheranism that stressed prayer, humility, a personal relation to God, and biblical literalism. He praised their simple dedication to work and the fortitude with which they faced life's vicissitudes, a quality he attributed to their religious belief. "Say what you want about Pietism," he related once to his former student and eventual biographer Friedrich Theodor Rink, "the people who were serious about it were outstanding in a praiseworthy respect. They possessed the highest thing men can possess, that calm, that serenity, that inner peace, undisturbed by any passion."[8]

Kant was far less rosy-eyed, however, when discussing his education. When he was eight years old, a client of his father's named Franz Albert Schultz, who led a Bible discussion group faithfully attended by Kant's mother, noticed the child who hung on her hand at his evening Bible study group and was struck by the otherworldly intelligence that emanated from his eyes.[9] On his recommendation young Immanuel began to attend school at the Collegium Fridericianum, which Schultz would later come to direct and which taught a stark curriculum entirely in Latin, devoid of any scientific content. To be there in time, the boy would have to rise each morning before dawn, often in the winter cold—a habit he would maintain for the rest of his life even while never losing his dislike of it.

Kant hated his schooling, speaking of it as a form of "child slavery,"[10] and regarded its focus on prayer, its dissection of interior life in search of sin, and its dedication to outward shows of piety and virtue as prime examples of "the mental disorder of alleged super-natural inspirations . . . illuminatism or terrorism."[11] Indeed, much in the spirit of the Enlightenment, of which he would become one of the most influential proponents in his later life, Kant ridiculed superstitious thinking and practice in all of its forms. As he wrote to a friend at the time, he felt it unlikely that anyone ever noticed in him "any trace of a way of thinking inclined to the miraculous or a weakness that could lead to credulity."[12] All the more surprising, then, that in 1764, having finally won the attention and admiration of the literary and intellectual world with some far-ranging essays on new advances in science, rational theology, and moral philoso-phy, Kant would turn his attention to ghosts.

The spirits in question were those purported to be in com-munion with Emanuel Swedenborg, a Swedish theologian whose books detailing his visions, mystical encounters, and prophecies were becoming best sellers throughout Europe. What made Swe-denborg's approach distinct was his claim that his insights stemmed from his personal encounters with human souls after their death, encounters that served as the basis of remarkably detailed descrip-tions of the spirit world. As he wrote in his best-known book, *Heaven and Hell,* when men die, they are divided by God into groups accord-ing to their virtue; however, "though they are thus divided, still they who have been friends and acquaintances in the life of the body, all meet and converse together, when they desire it, especially wives and husbands and brothers and sisters."[13] He then warrants this remark with his personal testimony: "I have seen a father speak with six sons and recognize them and I have seen many others with their relatives and friends, who, however, because they were of diverse dispositions, from their life in the world, were soon separated."[14]

The popularity of his works was also based on reports circulat-ing of Swedenborg's miraculous ability to know and describe events occurring, for example, in the city of Stockholm when he was more than fifty miles away from the scene himself—reports that, if they were true, would violate the scientific laws that Kant had spent his career learning and teaching. Most troubling, the testimonies avowing the truth of Swedenborg's prediction were coming from sources that Kant felt to be trustworthy. But if Swedenborg was to be believed, it would mean that a mere human being had been able to experience and then communicate about a completely different world from the temporal one we inhabit, a world presumably populated by eternal, spiritual beings not confined to a local place and a limited timeline. His parents' pietistic faith had certainly made them try to instill in him a belief in eternal truths that transcended the mundane world in space and time, but such truths pertained to God, not a mere mortal like Swedenborg. Kant felt he had to investigate.

Though he put considerable time and exertion into the exercise of reading and reviewing Swedenborg's published works, Kant was clearly somewhat embarrassed by the endeavor. He published his book, *Dreams of a Spirit-Seer*, anonymously in 1766, but soon found himself apologetically acknowledging his authorship in a letter to the renowned Jewish philosopher Moses Mendelssohn shortly after learning of Mendelssohn's critical reaction. As he wrote to him, "The estrangement you express about the tone of my little work proves to me that you have formed a good opinion of the sincerity of my character, and your very reluctance to see that character ambiguously expressed is both precious and pleasing to me."[15]

It appears that the tone Mendelssohn found so unfitting was nothing other than dripping sarcasm. Reading the body of Swedenborg's work had so riled Kant that he had dropped his normally objective style and replaced it with one we might charitably describe as earthy. Indeed, Kant's conclusion starts by implying mental instability as the cause of Swedenborg's visions—"I do not blame the reader, if, instead of regarding the spirit-seers as half-dwellers in another world, he, without further ceremony, dispatches them as candidates for the hospital, and thereby spares himself further investigation"— but ultimately stoops to the scatological: "If a hypochondriacal wind should rage in the guts, what matters is the direction it takes:

if downwards, then the result is a fart; if upwards, an apparition or a heavenly inspiration."[16] Kant, it appears, had taken some offense at Swedenborg's pretension that he could directly access the spiritual world.

In the years that followed, Kant's voracious intellectual appetite would focus ever more on fundamental questions in metaphysics, but the skeptical strain he revealed in his early writing remained. One of his lecture announcements a few years later proclaimed the "true method of instruction in philosophy" to be "*zetetic,* as it was called by some of the ancients," meaning "to search for," but better known by our modern term "skepticism."[17] Doubt for Kant was "not dogmatic but a doubt of waiting," for the "method of doubting is useful because it makes the soul act not from speculation but from healthy understanding."[18]

Kant sensed a powerful strain of thought emanating from the ancient world. This strain doubted the certainties of dogma, which, like Swedenborg, would presume to speak of eternal truths beyond the reach of the human senses, and it also doubted the senses themselves, whose data wafted in the fickle currents of time and space. From its ancient sources the strain had passed through Hellenistic and Arab interpreters; it helped forge the outlines of Christian theology; and it would ultimately leave an indelible imprint on modern thought and science. Its earliest systematic formulations, though, come to us from a series of conversations conducted in the marketplaces and private houses of ancient Athens by a freethinking and at times annoyingly contrarian philosopher.

WHEN SOCRATES MET PARMENIDES and Zeno in Athens, he was still a bit of an upstart. Philosophers who had thronged the Agora for this grand occasion listened attentively to Zeno read from his book. But when he had finished, the young Socrates leaped to his feet to challenge the imposing sage and his venerable mentor, Parmenides. The visitors claimed that ultimately there exists one massive, immutable reality and that any change is an illusion. Parmenides had concocted this theory as a way of dealing with the incompatibility between the fact that things change and the apparent constancy of those things. Unlike Heraclitus and his followers, who gave up on such stability altogether and insisted that nothing existed other than change, Parmenides landed on an all-encompassing and static being as the true ultimate nature of reality, which he called simply "the one."

Now, the reader may certainly be forgiven for asking where, exactly, the problem lies with accepting that there are things and that those things change. And in fact, that's precisely what the young Socrates asked Parmenides himself: "If someone should demonstrate that I am one thing and many, what's astonishing about that? He will say, when he wants to show that I'm many, that my right side is different from my left, and my front from my back, and likewise with my upper and lower parts. . . . But when he wants to show that I'm one, he will say I'm one person among the seven of us, because I also partake of oneness. Thus he will show that both are true."[19]

In ensuing years Socrates would eventually work out the kinks in his attempt to contend with the problem of the material world's mutability, leading to the influential theory of eternal, unchanging Forms with which his student Plato would become associated. On this particular day, though, Socrates got schooled. After first exchanging knowing smiles with Zeno and expressing his profound admiration for Socrates, Parmenides drilled down into Socrates's challenge. "How neatly you make one thing be in many places at the same time!" Parmenides slyly needled the younger thinker. "It's as if you were to cover many people with one sail, and then say that one thing is also able to cover many. Or isn't that the sort of thing you mean to say?"[20]

When Socrates shakily conceded that the image could account for his position, Parmenides already had him trapped: "In that case would the sail be, as a whole, over each person, or would one part of it be over one person and another part over another?"[21] A crestfallen

Socrates soon found himself admitting that the sail in the example would indeed be divisible, and hence not one and unchanging. More to the point, he realized he'd been knocked off his perch a bit, cut down to size by a master thinker, and readily agreed to a demonstration of how to use dialectical analysis to get to deeper truths. During the dialogue that ensued, Parmenides gave a master class in what posterity would come to call the Socratic method.

But he did something else as well. He revealed a secret. The secret animated Zeno's paradoxes and reverberated through the teachings of Socrates's subsequent student Plato. It would become a keystone of Plato's student Aristotle's theories many years later, and centuries after that it would seep into the theological disputes that gave form to Christian doctrine, indelibly marking the progress of western philosophy and science. The secret Parmenides revealed to Socrates in their meeting in Athens was this: as we humans delve ever deeper in our quest to reveal the ultimate nature of reality, there is a stain in the picture that emerges, a kind of black hole that recedes ahead of us, and that we cannot seem to dispel even as the tools at our disposal evolve from thought experiments and stories to the awesome technologies that drive experimental science today. That stain is what we might call the paradox of the moment of change: the instantaneous sliver of time when something, some particle, must be both perfectly identical to itself in space and time, so as to be the thing that changes, and somehow different, so as to have changed at all.

THE YEAR HE TURNED forty, Kant's life changed. Over the prior decade his standard of living had improved considerably. His lectures became ever more popular, and the resulting increase in student fees allowed him to upgrade his housing, his wardrobe, and even his entertainment. Only some five years earlier, the coat he wore each day was so frayed that one of his friends offered to buy him a new one. Now, as he wowed his students in lecture halls, charmed noblewomen at swank dinner parties, or attended the theater with his best friend, Johann Friedrich von Funk, he was sure to stand out for the elegance of his attire. Aesthetics matter, Kant explained. Colors in particular. With a brown coat, one should wear a vest of a complementary color, such as yellow. As he strolled the streets of Königsberg, a ceremonial sword often dangled at his side.

Not that he would have used it. Kant was an attractive man, by all counts, but he was very slight of build (about five feet, two inches) and suffered from a flat chest, which constricted his breathing. Athletic prowess was not his long suit. His eyes, in contrast, had a mesmerizing effect on interlocutors. In the words of a gushing contemporary, "Kant's eye was as if it had been formed of heavenly ether from which the deep look of the mind visibly shone forth. It is impossible to describe the bewitching effect of his look on my feeling when I sat across from him and when he suddenly raised his lowered eye to look at me. I always felt as though I looked through his blue ether-like fire into the most holy [eye] of Minerva."[22]

With his style, his wit and charm, and his eyes, Kant had certainly become a man-about-town. As Hamann would later recount, Kant spent most of his afternoons and evenings in society, "not infrequently participating in a suite of playing cards, and often returning home only past midnight."[23] Kant's late evenings out, attending theater and concerts—this whirlwind of activity almost always took place in the company of Funk. And then, without warning, Kant's best friend died.

The loss of a close friend, perhaps his closest, seems to have put life on hold for Kant. While Funk lived, Kant lectured and wrote on a seemingly bewildering array of topics with a lightness to his approach, a virtuosity unencumbered by much personal commitment. Now the words he wrote to Funk's mother after her son's untimely death were understandably somber. In the letter, which he published as an open elegy to Funk, Kant characterized the variability of life as a "magic lantern" whose "play of shadows" will be cut short by a death that we overlook while in the thick of our lives. He contrasts this time, "while we are dreaming" still, with something he calls a "great destination beyond the grave." Concentrating on that eternal destination rather than on the flickering magic lantern of life, a wise man will be "rational in his plans, but without being stubborn, ... modest in his wishes, but without being censorious, trusting without insisting, and active in fulfilling his duties," all the while remaining ready for when God calls "us from this state amidst all its striving."[24] Indeed, from this point on, Kant's philosophy begins to sharpen its focus on a central goal, "something in us that we can never cease to wonder at once it has entered our sight," something that "elevates the idea of *humanity* to a dignity which one might not expect" to find among the vagaries of a given person's life.[25]

While Kant searched for this cause of wonder elevated above the flow of life in the here and now, a store of eternal values in which to anchor human dignity, he started to make social choices that reflected this search. A part-time position in one of Königsberg's libraries boosted his income enough for him to change residences, and he moved into a building owned by his publisher, Johann Jakob Kanter. The building had a bookstore and café on its ground floor, as well as a larger lecture hall where Kant's many students could come to hear him speak. Perhaps more important, Kant started to make new friends.

His new circle included an English merchant by the name of Joseph Green. Green had the peculiar passion of running his entire life according to strict maxims as opposed to whimsy or caprice. Such maxims included adhering to one's word, no matter how trivial the matter, and arriving punctually at agreed-upon meeting times no matter how inconvenient. In fact, Kant's much remarked upon regularity in his later life seems to date to the years of his association with Green, when townspeople knew it was seven o'clock in the evening because they could see Kant leaving Green's house. Of course, Green's punctiliousness had its drawbacks. Once, when Kant and Green had made a date to meet in the morning to take a trip by carriage to the countryside, Green departed at precisely eight o'clock, as planned. When he passed a slightly tardy Kant by the roadside, he ignored his friend's frantic gesticulations and continued on his way, so strictly did he adhere to his maxims.[26]

While Kant no doubt resented his abandonment by the side of the road, his friendship with Green reflected a shift in his life and thought, provoked at least in part by the pain of losing Funk. Kant was becoming increasingly convinced that humans simultaneously occupy two radically separate realms: one realm was dominated by the relative and shifting logic of time and space, while the other was guided by unchanging truths. And yet, strangely, the one realm somehow necessitated the other. Moreover, this division of human existence into two incompatible and yet mutually indispensable realms implicated all aspects of our endeavors. While he could not yet articulate his insight with the crisp, devastating logic to come, his writing and lecturing increasingly strove toward an idea that would not only clarify the nature of human knowledge but also provide a road map for the more practical question of how to determine a basis for morality.

Kant's idea in its nascent form was this: human experience is characterized by change, but for change to even be perceived as change, some fixed points must exist. Likewise, we humans are buffeted by a whirlwind of competing beliefs and desires, but the mere fact that we perceive our beliefs and desires as competing—as opposed to simply being in them and desiring and believing without reflection—indicates the existence of fixed points that underlie and anchor the choices we make, a right course of action that transcends our quotidian travails.

In a wide-ranging and influential essay he wrote during this time called *Observations on the Feeling of the Beautiful and Sublime*, Kant borrowed a famous image from the Greek thinker Heraclitus: "Everything goes past like a river and the changing taste and the various shapes of men make the whole game uncertain and delusive. Where do I find fixed points in nature, which can not be moved by man, and where I can indicate the markers by the shore to which he ought to adhere?"[27] Heraclitus's metaphor had been a description of time. For that thinker everything was flux; stability itself was nothing but delusion. Just as we believe the river to be a single thing, but in fact never enter the same river twice, the flow of time ensures that nothing we perceive as stable and persistent is in reality the same as it was. As he entered his fifth decade, Kant began to repurpose that metaphor, and to search for elusive markers on the shore of the river of life.

BACK IN THE AGORA, Parmenides pressed his advantage, and he did so by homing in on what he called a "queer creature," the instant of change.[28] What does it mean for something to change, for a movement to take place? Everything that exists, Parmenides reasoned, is either in motion or at rest. And yet, to get from the one state to another, it must pass through a moment that is somehow "neither in motion nor at rest."[29] It is precisely that moment which turns out to be the secret ingredient and primary driver of Zeno's paradoxes.

As with the paradox of Achilles failing to cross a finite space, because in so doing he would have to traverse infinite fractions of that space—or the more mundane paradox of my inability to eat a cookie, because I would have to eat infinite fractions of the cookie—all variations of Zeno's paradox result from the strangeness of the instant of change. This is because what Achilles must cross or I must eat is ultimately the same thing, infinitely many infinitesimal portions of space and time. Which is exactly what an instant of change is: an infinitely thin slice of space-time in which a thing is *both* exactly what it was before *and* what it is about to become.

All things change, and yet to change they must cease to be what they were and become what they now are, thereby negating the very permanence or stability implied by their being a thing in the first place. The thing, "in changing, it changes at an instant, and when it changes, it would be in no time at all."[30] It quickly becomes evident that even motion itself is secondary to the problem, for even an object standing completely still, when it "proceeds from the past to the future, it certainly won't jump over the now,"[31] as Parmenides put it. And if nothing "can sidestep the now, whenever a thing *is* at this point, it always stops its coming-to-be and then is whatever it may have come to be."[32] If we assume time is infinitely divisible, we can neither age nor move; and if we assume there's a minimal chunk, an atom or pixel of time something occupies, then again no *thing* moves, no *thing* changes, because continuity is broken, and its new manifestation is just that, something entirely new. Each sliver of being is imprisoned in a minuscule eternity of space-time.

Or, to put it slightly differently, we can focus on a particle, *or* we can focus on its movement, but if we want to see both simultaneously, we can't. While they may strike us as arcane, as modern physicists began to train their extraordinary instruments on those minimal pixels of space-time, they discovered that Zeno's paradoxes weren't so irrelevant after all. They weren't for Kant either.

IT WOULD TAKE KANT many years to articulate what exactly about Swedenborg's pretensions so vexed him, but when he did, the realization came like a thunderclap. The problem was this: we are so accustomed to perceiving a world extended in space and successive in time that we naturally project those qualities onto all our intellectual endeavors. Take the example of our very own personhood. Since we naturally tend to conceive of things as being extended in space and having duration in time, we implicitly apply the same structure to ourselves. We think of our self, be it our soul or our consciousness, as existing somewhere in our body. We imagine it to have come into being at a certain time, and perhaps openly believe or secretly hope it will live on past our physical demise. However, we fool ourselves when we think that this way of talking about ourselves in space and time has any validity outside space and time. As Kant put it, "One can quite well allow the proposition *The soul is substance* to be valid, if only one admits that this concept of ours leads no further, that it cannot teach us any of the usual conclusions of the rationalistic doctrine of the soul, such as, e.g., the everlasting duration of the soul through all alterations, even the human being's death, thus that it signifies a substance only in the idea not in reality."[33]

The soul or consciousness, in fact, is nothing but the unity of a sense of self over time, the bare fact that to perceive and then to articulate our perceptions something must connect from *this very instant* to another, and another after that. This connecting of disparate slices of space-time is a necessary condition of the possibility of knowing anything at all, but it is not itself a thing in space and time, a thing that survives our existence on Earth. When we believe that it is, we end up conjuring the kinds of ghost stories with which Swedenborg beguiled his readership.

The risk far exceeds simply falling for spirit-seers and treating pulp fiction as dogma. If this projection leads us as a matter of course into superstitious beliefs and underlies fanaticisms of all kinds, in the realm of science it engenders its own sorts of error and confusion. It leads us to expect nature at the smallest and largest registers to act exactly as we are accustomed to experiencing it at human registers. It leads us to impose prejudices that impede that very attribute of science that is its greatest strength: its humility; the explicit acceptance that our knowledge can always expand, will always be revised.

Kant now saw that the fact we can even experience the turbulent currents of the river of life depends on our *assuming* the existence of stable markers along the river's banks, even if we can never see them with our own eyes. Thus did he learn to distinguish what we experience in the world from *what we cannot experience in itself, but what makes it possible for us to experience anything at all.* At the same time, he realized that these projections of reason that allow us to make sense of the river's meanderings could push us too far, could inspire us to make idols out of our tools, ghosts out of the ideas we use to draw consistent conclusions about the world. And as absolutely necessary as the assumptions of permanent, ineffable truths were for producing an accurate understanding of the *physical* world, the ghosts and idols we tend to turn those assumptions into were destined to become *metaphysical* prejudices that could only hamper the success of our science. It would therefore be crucial to stay critically attuned to how we go about doing science, how we go about forming correct judgments of the world, so we can catch ourselves before our reason naturally takes us too far. Philosophy, his philosophy, if he wanted to set reason's house in order, had to embody such critique.

Finally, Kant realized that among the clues that can tell us when our reason is leading us astray are contradictions that arise when we start thinking about the necessary projections of our reason, those stable anchors along the riverbanks of change, as if they were objects in space and time. He saw that doing so leads us to draw a perfectly airtight proof for one proposition and then an equally flawless proof for its complete opposite—with no way to resolve them. We can argue with Hume, for instance, that the world consists of nothing but unconditioned impressions, and no one can dismantle our reasoning. Or we can insist the exact opposite with the rationalists, and argue that the world expresses a master code, with nothing left to chance. And again, our reasoning will appear perfect. We can drill down into this very instant and come face to face with a particle of pure, unchanging being, or we can fall unceasingly into the vanishing abyss of divisibility that gapes at our feet.

This, Kant said, is what Zeno taught us, and "to those who judged him, it appeared that he wanted entirely to deny two mutually contradictory propositions, which is absurd." Kant, however, did not find Zeno absurd.[34]

AS BORGES WOULD NOTE more than two thousand years later, Zeno proved hard to refute. Aristotle thought he was refuting the paradoxes even as he transcribed them. But generations of philosophers have agreed that his response—while certainly preferable to that of

Diogenes the Cynic, whose retort was to stand up and walk—never really dealt with the challenge head-on. For Aristotle, the reason we fall into paradox when we assume the infinite divisibility of time and space is that we are confusing potential divisibility with actual division. In theory, he argued, you could go on cutting space in half or go on homing in forever and ever on smaller and smaller units of time. But when you attempt to actualize that potential you always fall short because, as Hegel—the greatest German thinker of the nineteenth century—put it with uncharacteristic clarity, "actual motion is progression through a limited space and a limited time and not through infinite space and infinite time."[35]

What Zeno grasped, which is why merely getting up to take a walk fails to refute him, is that motion or change is self-contradictory when we mistake, as we tend to do, real things for the ideas of those things. On the one hand, we think of motion or change as something that happens to a thing itself. On the other hand, the motion of that thing is meaningless without reference to some other things, just as the change of a thing means nothing without reference to that thing at another time: "Motion is plainly relative; whether in absolute space the eye, for instance, rests, or whether it moves, is all the same."[36] But precisely for that reason, trying to bracket out the interference of other places in space or other moments in time to understand what it means for a thing to change is a little like trying to analyze color by turning off the lights: when we try to measure or define motion or change in an object *as it is in itself,* motion and change seem to dissipate before our eyes.

So more than a century later, when Heisenberg explained to Pauli that the path a thing takes through space-time "only comes into existence through this, that we observe it," this was another way of saying that things in space and time are, by definition, always in relation to other things and that someone, an observer, needs to put them in that relation.

·   ·   ·

WHILE HISTORY IS FUZZY on this point, when Elea succumbed to a tyrant, Zeno conspired to overthrow him. The tyrant then captured him and subjected him to unimaginable tortures with the aim of getting him to betray his accomplices. With his dying breath Zeno coaxed the tyrant near to him, but rather than whisper the names of his friends in his ear, as the tyrant hoped and expected, he bit it off. In other stories he bites off his own tongue and spits it in the tyrant's face before being beaten to death.[37] Thus in a strange way, Zeno's life embodies the very split his paradoxes exploit: he could be at once a thinker of frustratingly abstract ideas, arguing to anyone who would listen that change of any kind is an illusion, and yet when the time came to act, he did so with extraordinary determination. Could it not be that in some way we are all Zenos, using abstract ideas to make sense of a material world in which we ultimately must live, make decisions, act, and eventually die?

In dreaming up his paradoxes, Zeno had realized something that Kant would eventually articulate with searing precision. We never encounter our own self in this very instant as anything other than the trace of our relation to some other instant, receding before us or arising ahead.[38] But as Kant learned from being challenged by Hume, that self cannot be reduced to anything smaller or briefer than a relation between at least two slices of space-time. A truly momentary self would not be a self in the first place. Thus the very fact that we experience change means something remained unchanged. And yet, while we must presume a dimension of unchanging things, stable markers of our passage from moment to moment in the river of time, when we try to use the tools that enable us to grasp our everyday experience in space and time to *visualize* those unchanging things, we engender the very strangeness that Zeno forced the world to confront.

Still, from Zeno, from Plato, from the loss of his dearest friend, and from the quirky obsessions of a new one, Kant learned something equally profound. Just being adrift on time's river is not an option. As he delved deep into the ultimate nature of change and motion, space and time, Kant realized they not only were issues for scientists to explore but also held implications for our understanding of powerful human impulses. Yes, Swedenborg might have been a charlatan, but the thirst to believe in the extension and possible immortality of the soul is the consequence of a natural, almost unavoidable intellectual mistake. Indeed, when Kant's friend Funk died, he found himself forced to confront what is in some ways the ultimate example of the instant of change: the fact that all that we love will pass, including life itself. Even more poignantly, the very ineradicable nature of that constant, irresistible erosion of the present is what endows our life and the attachment we make in it with all of their value. We love because, and only because, we lose.[39]

Nonetheless, it is the very power of our reason, which has helped us achieve so much, that surprisingly gets in the way of recognizing this simple fact. Zeno brought Kant this clarity, because it was Zeno who revealed the paradox that undergirds these prejudices, the antinomies that erupt when we follow our very natural tendencies and desires and turn into eternal idols the tools reason gave us to make sense of the here and now. By understanding what Zeno had uncovered, Kant now began to glimpse how we need both the humility science requires and the guidance, even motivation, of our presumption of unchanging ideals. For the markers we search for on the banks of time's river motivate us in mysterious ways. Standing on the precipice of this very instant, we stare into the abyss of the eternal. Desire for that abyss fuels powerful human impulses: romantic ecstasy; religious fervor; artistic creation; compassion for others; even the courage and conviction to transcend our inclinations and do the right thing, no matter the cost to ourselves. But to believe we can exposit that abyss, that we can package it into the language and logic of space and time—to think we can visualize the impossibly small, the infinitely whole, describe the world before its beginning or after its end, know the fate written in our stars—such pretension leads us astray. It would be more than another century before technologies of observation and the mathematics of a new physics would lead us to the threshold of the kinds of observations Zeno imagined and Kant logically derived. But when they finally did, Heisenberg came to a similar realization, and brazenly, against the wishes of his elders, he designed a way of dealing with the smallest of things, the traces of this very instant, without giving in to the desire to *visualize* them.

3

VISUALIZE THIS!

B Y 1922, NIELS BOHR had become the world's leading figure in the field of atomic structure. That year the director of
the Institute for Theoretical Physics at Göttingen University
in Germany, a rigorously mathematical physicist named Max Born,
invited Bohr to give a series of lectures. The picturesque university
town would soon become one of three hot spots for the new theoretical physics along with Munich and Copenhagen. Max Born himself would become one of the field's founding fathers, before being
hounded from his post with Germany's other top Jewish scientists.
Bohr's lectures in Göttingen drew physicists from around Europe
and had all the trappings of a major cultural event. Attendees even
took to referring to the series as the "Bohr Festival."[1] It was in Göttingen that Bohr laid out his new model for the atomic structure,
with electrons confined to "shells" determined by their energy level.
And it was in Göttingen that a twenty-year-old student who was
visiting for a semester to work with Born also attended the Bohr Festival before returning to Munich to complete his doctorate. Unbeknownst to either professor, in only three more years that student

would make the first of a series of discoveries that would definitively close the door on classical physics.

TODAY WE MIGHT CALL a young man who is athletic, conscientious, and ambitious a "boy scout." In Werner Heisenberg's case, the term applied literally as well as figuratively. The younger of two brothers born into a bourgeois family in Munich, Werner was sickly as a young child, almost dying of a lung infection when he was just five. Indeed, he suffered from intermittent allergies much of his life, which makes his strong attachment to the outdoors and scouting all the stranger. When Heisenberg arrived in Göttingen from Munich to join the team of researchers there in 1922, Born said he looked "like a simple peasant boy, with short, fair hair, clear bright eyes and a charming expression."[2]

The peasant boy had qualified to work with Born for good reason. In school he had excelled in all disciplines, although early on he was drawn by the beauty of mathematics, in particular its correspondence to the real world and its seemingly magical ability to solve practical problems and predict real outcomes, a correspondence that struck him "as remarkably strange and exciting," as he later recalled.[3] His mathematical abilities quickly blossomed, and when his parents asked the sixteen-year-old boy to help a friend of the family's with her university math courses, he had taught himself calculus so he could in turn teach it to her. By the time he had to present his own skills for graduation from high school, his examiner could write with some amazement of the "playful ease" with which he solved Newton's equations of motion, "with air resistance taken into account."[4]

Despite this background, Born's initial assessment wasn't far off the mark. Heisenberg had indeed been working as something akin to a simple peasant boy—as a farmhand, in fact, trying to support himself and his family in the economic and social devastation that was Germany of the immediate postwar years.[5] His hometown of

Munich had devolved into chaos after the armistice, with armed political factions roaming the streets and claiming sections of the city as their fiefdoms. Heisenberg would recall fleeing "the sounds of shooting, without knowing where the fighting was."[6] From the dust and disruption on the streets, he found solace in the country-side and mountains, and in conversations and the world of ideas. Specifically, Platonic ideas.

One particularly violent morning, he found his way to the roof of his school building. Safe for the time being from the danger of the streets, he sat there soaking in the morning sun before fishing a volume out of his book bag and starting to read, his legs dangling from the edge of the rooftop.[7] It was Plato's dialogue *Timaeus*, which recounts the philosopher's speculations as to the fundamental makeup of the world. The son of a classics professor, Heisenberg had more occasion than most young men his age to read Greek philosophy, and he found in Plato's dialogue *Timaeus* an idealist counterpoint to the erector-set diagrams of his science classroom. In its pages the philosopher speculated that all the substances of the world were reducible to a few elements, invisible building blocks whose geometry determined their properties. Of these elemental particles Plato wrote, "The first thing the god then did was give them their distinctive shapes, using forms and numbers."[8] By way of a complex analysis, Plato decided that earth, the basis for all solids, is made of quadrangles and that each of the remaining elements—water, air, and fire—assumes its relative mobility and particular quality from its size and shape: "In all these cases the body that has the fewest faces is of necessity the most mobile, in that it, more than any other, has edges that are the sharpest and best fit for cutting in every direction."[9]

Heisenberg didn't swoon. As he later recalled, "The whole thing seemed to be wild speculation, pardonable perhaps on the ground that the Greeks lacked the necessary empirical knowledge."[10] Yet Plato had also planted a seed. When Heisenberg had learned about the structure of atoms in school, Bohr's innovations had not yet reached German schools, and as a result Heisenberg puzzled over his textbooks' deeply unsatisfying images of atoms held together in molecules by "hooks and eyes . . . , quite arbitrary structures whose shape could be altered at will to adapt them to different technical tasks"—not quite what the young thinker would expect of a physics that was supposed to be "governed by strict natural laws." As crazy as a world constructed of tiny pyramids and tetrahedrons sounded, did colored balls held together by hooks seem much saner? Wouldn't it make more sense to conceive of atoms not as concrete models taken from our everyday experience but as ideas constructed via mathematical proofs? As he would later reflect, "I was gaining the growing conviction that one could hardly make progress in modern atomic physics without a knowledge of Greek natural philosophy."[11]

The other aspect of Greek thought that infiltrated Heisenberg's early consciousness was its dialogic nature. Escape from the violence of the streets also meant leaving the city for the countryside, which Heisenberg did as often as he could. With his friends he would hike the fields and mountains around Munich, using their rich conversations as a compass to guide them out of the bedlam of their daily lives. Heisenberg would later credit these walks as being among the primary inspirations for his passion for physics, for among the topics his friends and he would discuss was the nature of the physical world and our knowledge of it.

One clear day as they walked together through the hill country to the west of Lake Starnberg, they pushed through a clearing in the trees that revealed to them the expanse of the lake as it stretched to the mountains beyond. It was on this day, Heisenberg would later recall, that his desire to understand the natural world, right down to the level of its constituent parts, was born.[12] The group had read many of the same books; works of Kant figured along with those of classical philosophy, and his influence seeped in as well. As they bantered away, free for a moment from the maelstrom in the city below, Heisenberg began to grasp a concept that would be decisive for his later work as a physicist. When we explore the natural world, we don't see things directly as they are in themselves but translate them first into mental images and then finally into concepts. It is only when we have filtered our bare impressions through concepts that we can say we have experienced them.

Concepts were words, of course, and words were what flowed back and forth in dialogues. Each dialogue could only take place within a group of at least two members. No one on his or her own owned the truth. But truth could emerge slowly from the negotiation between the participants in the conversation. What one needed to look for was something not available to any individual on his or her own. Heisenberg thought of this as "the middle ground," a place where truth emerged from the relation between elements as opposed to residing in any one of them.

One day as he walked along Leopoldstrasse in Munich, a young man from one of the other groups that roamed the city approached and told him that the youth of the city had agreed to meet at Schloss Prunn, a medieval castle several hours to the north of the city. Something needed to be done; some solution to the daily struggles needed to be found. A train trip later, Heisenberg joined a growing group of young people, mostly students but also some former soldiers who had survived the horrors of the war, in the courtyard of the castle built high into the cliffside overlooking the Altmühl river valley. There they spent many hours debating the big questions posed by their current situation: whether the fate of their own people or that of the outer world was more important; whether those who had died in the war had done so in vain; what path would bring hope to their country and their future.

As he considered the various positions, the young Heisenberg became more and more conscious of how desperately lacking the middle ground was; no solution could be found as long as each group stuck to its guns. Suddenly there appeared on the balcony overlooking the courtyard a young man with a violin. As the sound of the opening double stop of the Chaconne from Bach's Partita no. 2 in D Minor floated down into the courtyard, the assembled youth stopped arguing and listened, and Heisenberg was struck by a sense of hope and possibility: "One could speak of a middle ground, open to all sides, in Plato, or in Bach, in the language of music or of philosophy or of religion, so there must also be such a space in our future."[13]

Upon acing his final exams with customary ease in the spring of 1920, Heisenberg did what he would always do when he felt he had been working too much and needed to recharge his batteries. He went hiking with his group of friends, now officially a scout troop. His troop (called the Heisenberg group, under his leadership) had earned a reputation for pushing things a little far. He had recently fished one of his scouts out of a crevasse, and personally skied another down a mountain after the young man broke his leg. On this outing, however, Heisenberg almost did himself in. The boys stopped at a castle after a long day's hike and asked if they could sleep inside. The keepers agreed and the boys settled in—without being aware that it had served as a typhoid ward the previous year. Though none of his charges caught the illness, Heisenberg started to develop severe bellyaches and a high fever—telltale signs of typhoid. Indeed, he had contracted the deadly disease and was only nursed back to health by an uncle who happened also to be a family doctor and who managed to find him fresh eggs and milk each day despite the shortages of the postwar economy.[14]

Miraculously having managed a full recovery, the eighteen-year-old showed up for classes at the University of Munich the following fall. There he would study physics at one of the burgeoning centers of innovation on quantum theory: the institute run by the imposing and yet congenial Arnold Sommerfeld, where Heisenberg enrolled with another young superstar recently arrived from Vienna, Wolfgang Pauli. When Sommerfeld took a leave to teach in the United States less than two years later, he sent Heisenberg to work with Max Born in Göttingen, where he would become a central figure in the group responsible for what would soon be called the new Göttingen physics. But even before then, the freshman physics student in

Munich made his first in a series of advances that would set the stage for the development of quantum mechanics.

THE AGE OF QUANTUM physics began in December 1900. The man who launched the most significant scientific revolution since Galileo did not come across as much of a rebel. Indeed, he was a hardworking, somewhat conservative man of science. It would be many years before he would accept the truth of what he had discovered, and he sought for the rest of his life to avoid its implications.

Already a well-established scientist, Max Planck made his most important mark at the relatively advanced age of forty-two, when he had held the chair in theoretical physics in Berlin for the previous eight years. He spent the previous half decade working on a problem that had bedeviled physicists for some time. If a receptacle, say a metal tube, is entirely closed off at both ends save for a tiny hole and then heated up, small amounts of electromagnetic energy will escape through the hole. This so-called black-body radiation can be analyzed by a spectrograph.[15] Depending on the temperature of the tube, it will release small amounts of low-frequency waves and a much larger proportion of medium-frequency waves and then taper off again at the high end of the wavelength spectrum.

Curiously, these findings contradicted what scientists predicted should happen. If light were transmitted as a wave, as experts thought they had established, the amount of radiation should increase in proportion to the frequency of its wavelength. This makes sense. The smaller the waves spreading across a given surface, the more of them there are: think of the tiny ripples on a pond compared with the relatively scarce swells that big-wave surfers wait for off the coasts of California or Portugal. This is true of all sorts of waves. The smaller the magnitude, the higher the frequency—much as a guitar string being tightened produces a higher pitch as its vibrations stir up smaller and faster air waves—and hence the higher the number of waves. And yet, for some reason, light bucks that trend. It's a good thing it does, too. If it did not, everyday lightbulbs would bathe us in deadly high-frequency radiation every time we turned them on—a theoretical expectation that scientists call, somewhat melodramatically, the ultraviolet catastrophe. That this catastrophe didn't occur in reality was certainly comforting, but it didn't make sense. And Max Planck wanted to know why.[16]

In the summer of 1900, Planck tried something new. He turned from the theory of electrodynamics to thermodynamics, specifically to that theory's second law, which states that the entropy of a closed system increases over time. Entropy indicates a system's disorder. An egg is highly ordered. An omelet less so. An omelet you have just chewed, swallowed, and digested, even less so. While it is relatively easy to turn that egg into a meal, it is far more difficult to reverse the process. That, in a nutshell, is entropy.

Planck, ever the old-school physicist, believed strongly that laws were laws, and that when they apply, they must apply without exception. If entropy is a law, that means that eggs always become more disordered, but the reverse never happens. This conviction led him to some rigorous debates with a dour Viennese physicist by the name of Ludwig Boltzmann. Boltzmann interpreted the second law of thermodynamics to mean that the entropy of any closed system would *tend* to increase, but that didn't mean that it *couldn't* decrease in individual cases. Gas molecules will indeed tend to evenly fill a room; however, it is possible that at any given moment they could all cluster together in one part of the room. Possible, but just very unlikely. Ironically, it was by borrowing his scientific opponent's probabilistic model that Planck stumbled upon a solution to the riddle of black-body radiation.

For Boltzmann's math to work, Planck had to provisionally break smooth quantities of whatever stuff he was measuring into chunks and then subject the movements of those chunks to statistical analysis. When Planck treated light frequencies as discrete, albeit very tiny, chunks, as opposed to smoothly diminishing wave sizes, he found that the expected distribution of wavelengths reverted to what was found in the laboratory. In other words, by assuming electromagnetic waves had a kind of internal limit keeping them above a minimal size and hence below a maximal frequency, one avoided the ultraviolet catastrophe, and the number of high-frequency waves tapered off. He also managed to derive a specific value that determined the cutoff point at which the theory would conform to the experimental data. This value became known as Planck's constant. Just as the speed of light is a constant with the notation c, this constant has its own notation as well, h. As we will soon see, it would become one of the most important numbers in modern physics and a key element of the quantum revolution to follow.

Planck, who continued to believe that light was propagated exclusively as waves, accepted this limitation as a kind of mathematical heuristic, but he didn't believe it corresponded to a physical aspect of the light waves themselves. Instead, he thought this chunkiness might be a signature of the atoms emitting the light, that they could vibrate only at certain frequencies and hence admit or absorb light in specifically sized chunks, which he called "quanta." In 1918, Planck won the Nobel Prize for his discovery and is still regarded as one of the most important figures in twentieth-century science. Nonetheless, as he would later reflect, "I can characterize the whole procedure as an act of despair"; "a theoretical interpretation *had* to be found at any price, however high it might be."[17] Yet, as unpalatable as it might have been for him, Planck seems to have known he had landed on something remarkable. That very December, he told his son about his discovery while on a walk in the Grunewald forest in Berlin. He described it as "a discovery of the first rank, comparable perhaps only to the discoveries of Newton."[18]

That it certainly was. But it would take another scientist, arguably the greatest since Newton, to fully grasp what Planck had unearthed.

·   ·   ·

UNLIKE MAX PLANCK AT the time of his discovery, Albert Einstein was virtually unknown when he authored four papers that would constitute only the first volley of his immeasurable contributions to the history of science. In a year that has since gone down in scientific history as the most noteworthy since 1666, when Newton conjured up calculus, light spectrometry, and the theory of gravity in a flurry of creative genius, Einstein authored those four papers during a period of three months while working as a clerk in a patent office in Bern, Switzerland. In some ways the position he held couldn't have suited him better. His gargantuan intellect allowed him to analyze patent applications with ample time left over to keep up on developments in physics. And for the previous few years, he had turned his attention to Planck's curious discovery.

Einstein would quickly become by consensus the world's most important physicist. And yet despite his influence and incredible fame, the Nobel committee would overlook him for more than fifteen years. When he did finally get the nod (at which point, weary of being snubbed for so many years, he declined to alter his travel plans and was lecturing in Japan when the award was bestowed on him), it was not for his paper on special relativity but for his explanation of the photoelectric effect, which he advanced in a paper with the title "On a Heuristic Point of View Concerning the Production and Transformation of Light."[19] As the title conveys, Einstein intended his theory as little more than a tool to help scientists along the way toward an answer, rather than being a final answer in itself. There is little doubt that the Nobel committee and the scientists who grudgingly overcame disciplinary inertia—as well as overt anti-Semitic propaganda—to honor him went out of their way not to award the prize for relativity. Still, even Einstein himself would later say that his paper on light, among all the others that year, was truly revolutionary.[20]

As is often the case, revolutionary steps can seem obvious in hindsight. As we've seen, Planck had shown that agitated atoms emit and absorb energy only at certain frequencies but was convinced this had something to do with the atoms, not the light. Nonetheless, in his address to the Berlin Physical Society at the end of 1900, Planck unequivocally stated that his calculations showed energy emissions to be "composed of a very definite number of equal finite packages."[21] This finding astounded Einstein. As he later wrote, "All of my attempts to adapt the theoretical foundations of physics to this knowledge failed completely. It was as if the ground had been pulled out from under us, with no firm foundation to be seen anywhere."[22] In his 1905 paper, Einstein found that ground. And he did so by taking seriously the implications of Planck's discovery. If light waves were emitted and absorbed in discrete packages, this wasn't just a mathematical trick or feature of the atoms that emitted and absorbed them. Light itself had the curious ability to behave *both* as a wave and as a particle.

WHILE EINSTEIN UNSETTLED PHYSICS by showing that light could behave both as a wave and as a particle, scientists were making great strides digging deeper and deeper into the structure of those particles they already knew they had in hand, atoms. In this terrain a British physicist named Ernest Rutherford did the most important work. In his institute in Manchester, Rutherford unearthed the atomic structure we still recognize today: a nucleus orbited by a swarm of electrons. In 1912, he was joined by a young Niels Bohr, who would work with Rutherford for the next four years before returning to Copenhagen to found the institute there that would sear an indelible imprint on the physics of the twentieth century.

Perhaps Bohr's most important quality as a scientist was his pragmatic lack of devotion to any particular approach. According to Rutherford's model of the atom, electrons circled their nuclear cores like planets orbiting the sun in our solar system. The problem with this model is that it does not explain a key result of spectrographic analysis, namely, that the spectrum emitted by hydrogen atoms contains distinct dark lines between strips of color. Bohr realized that the dark lines represented energy levels that were somehow skipped as the energy emitted by the atoms' electrons increased or decreased. This told him two things. First, that electrons can change their orbits—thankfully something the earth and our neighboring planets do not do. Second, and even more strangely, when they do change, they do so instantaneously, without occupying any space between those orbits (in the atomic model these are really energy levels, not orbits). Bohr's model of the atom thus retained classical elements of Rutherford's, in that it depended on a picture of discrete particles circling a nucleus, but it also accurately predicted the experimental data that came from spectroscopy, which Rutherford's had not been able to do.

Just as with Einstein's light quanta, the electrons emitted and absorbed energy only in discrete chunks. This was consistent with their being particles. At the same time, if the electrons were indeed particles, one would assume that they would behave consistently as such and have the decency to continue existing in intermediate states. They did not. What they did do, however, was something that added to the mystery and showed scientists working on radiation and matter that their fields were inevitably converging on a common ground. When the electrons changed energy levels, the packets of energy they emitted or absorbed were calculable in precise proportion to Planck's constant.

IF PLANCK'S DISCOVERY IN 1900 unofficially ushered in the quantum revolution, Bohr's paradoxical redefinition of the electron made it clear for all that a new physics was under way.

While Bohr's centrality to the history of quantum physics is beyond dispute, many of his colleagues considered Bohr's contributions to quantum theory more philosophy than physics. And while most agreed that his theory of complementarity—according to which particles and waves are both pertinent descriptions of quantum events but neither can tell the whole story on its own—was the philosophical linchpin of the Copenhagen interpretation, even his closest allies often seemed to have different opinions about what it actually meant.

This confusion was partly due to Bohr's way of speaking and writing. He loved to parse the details of a theory in conversation, asking his interlocutor for a possible interpretation and then poking holes in it, leading to ever greater exasperation but not necessarily to greater clarity. On one occasion this method drove Erwin Schrödinger, who was visiting him at the institute in Copenhagen, to take to his room for several days, ostensibly ill, but more likely to get away from Bohr's incessant haranguing. Another Austrian physicist, Paul Ehrenfest, who, unlike Schrödinger, tended to side with Bohr in the controversies around the emerging quantum physics, would go so far as to complain of what he called Bohr's awful incantations, "impossible for anyone else to summarize."[23]

In the few years after Bohr presented his model of the atom with its strangely jumpy electrons, scientists around the world further advanced their understanding of the quantum discontinuity, including the mysterious way that Planck's constant insisted on popping up like a persistent but uninvited guest. Egged on by Einstein's claim that light also behaved as a particle, an American physicist at Caltech named Robert Millikan had spent nearly a decade working on a series of experiments intended to prove him wrong. In the process he not only firmly established that light does indeed propagate as quanta—which were now called photons—but also derived the most accurate yet value for Planck's constant. Meanwhile, Einstein, having wrapped up that little problem called general relativity, turned his attention back to quantum physics, specifically to the question of when and how the nuclei of certain atoms spontaneously "decay," emitting particles seemingly of their own accord.

This strange behavior had been recognized for almost two

decades, having been discovered by Henri Becquerel and given the name radiation by Marie and Pierre Curie. Importantly, the decay and emission of particles by these elements happened without any external influence. Einstein's epiphany this time (he had many of them) was that the sudden jumps in energy levels in Bohr's atom might work according to the same logic as the unpredictable decay seen in radioactive elements like uranium and radium. Turning again to Ludwig Boltzmann's statistical models (Boltzmann himself, long suffering from what was likely bipolar disorder, had tragically committed suicide ten years earlier), Einstein worked out a model predicting the probability that radiation of a given energy level would shift to another level. Perhaps unsurprisingly at this point, Planck's enigmatic constant again emerged as the beating heart of his equations. Bohr then adapted Einstein's findings into his own expanding atomic model by showing that distinct bands in light spectra were due to certain energy levels being more or less probable than others.[24]

Einstein's introduction of Boltzmann's probabilistic mathematics into quantum behavior was akin to opening Pandora's box into the world of classical physics. Einstein himself would resist the implications for the rest of his career, but for the time being, everyone, himself included, had to accept that, at least at the atomic level, nuclei decayed and electrons jumped up and down in energy levels—all without discrete identifiable causes. With large enough samples physicists could determine increasingly likely outcomes, but they could not know the outcome for any individual cases. Unlike in classical physics, quanta just seemed to do things without a reason.

If Einstein resisted his own findings, Bohr ran with them. His atomic model, with electron clouds forming "shells" in different numbers at different energy levels, allowed chemists to chart the similarities and differences of elements based on where they fell in the periodic table, with elements' relative stability depending on the number of electrons that "liked" being together at a given energy level. As in other cases, Bohr's gift was not to spend too much time or energy wondering why, but simply to accept and move on.

THE STRUCTURE OF THE atom laid out by Bohr had grown new layers of complexity each year, and Arnold Sommerfeld was largely responsible for its new attire. While Bohr had derived three quantum numbers from his analysis of hydrogen's spectral lines, which he assigned to the size, shape, and orientation of the presumed orbits of electrons, closer analysis of the light bands revealed that they contained even smaller hairlines within them. It had fallen to Sommerfeld to account for this further splitting by adding a new number to the mix. The new value adequately matched the experimental data, but there didn't seem to be a physical aspect of the atomic structure to pin it on, so Sommerfeld called it "hidden rotation" and moved on. Pauli—who had come to Sommerfeld's seminar already well trained in physics, having written an introduction to Einstein's two relativity theories that would go down in scientific history as a classic of the genre—didn't think much of this nonchalance. But he recognized that Sommerfeld's approach might have fertile ground in the proclivities of his new, less classically trained colleague. As he cynically told an eager Heisenberg, "It's much easier to find one's way if one isn't too familiar with the magnificent unity of classical physics . . . , but then lack of knowledge is no guarantee of success."[25]

True to Pauli's expectations, Heisenberg made full use of his detachment from prior physical certainties. When Sommerfeld handed him the task of fully accounting for the observed oddities in spectral lines, the newly minted physics student came back with a mathematical answer in a surprisingly short time. While all previous numbers had been whole integer multiples of Planck's famous constant, Heisenberg tried sequencing Sommerfeld's enigmatic fourth number in terms of half integers. Amazingly, the move mapped beautifully onto the spectral data.

This made no sense at all according to any current understanding of how quanta behave. Indeed, the one seeming consistency of the quantum discontinuities reluctantly discovered by Planck and then affirmed by Einstein was that they couldn't be further reduced. Sommerfeld initially refused Heisenberg's solution. After all, he had given the young man this task only four weeks after he had begun his studies. A brave stab, perhaps, but also rather impetuous. Soon thereafter Sommerfeld received a paper from an established theorist at Frankfurt named Alfred Landé that made precisely the same move. Sommerfeld promptly sent Landé a letter informing him that his calculation "agrees well with what has been found by one of my students (in the first semester) but which has *not* been published."[26] Even though rebuffed by his adviser and close circle, Heisenberg's first foray was not in fact a bust. It would later turn out that a whole category of quantum particles exhibits behavior that can only be accounted for using Landé's and, by extension, Heisenberg's half integers. There can be little doubt the disappointment of this stolen scoop would fuel a future resistance to second-guessing his intuitions.

WHEN HEISENBERG ENTERED THE room for the Bohr Festival in Göttingen on a balmy spring day in June 1922, he was still only twenty years old. Given the importance of the occasion and the visitor, the front of the room was entirely taken by the faculty and senior students, and he duly took his seat in the back—which did not stop him from standing up after one of Bohr's presentations to raise an objection, causing all the heads in the room to turn. Bohr for his part already knew of Heisenberg, having heard from Sommerfeld how his precocious student had come up with the half-integer curiosity. Intrigued, he went on a walk with the young man, after which they stopped for coffee and to talk physics. Heisenberg would later say his career began in earnest that day.

Over the course of the afternoon, their discussion waxed from the technical to the philosophical. Heisenberg wanted to know what Bohr really thought about the internal structure of those atoms. As the rush of mathematical discoveries in Munich, Göttingen, and Copenhagen further muddied the plausibility of an erector-set atom with planetlike electrons orbiting the nucleus, how should physicists *visualize* what is really going on inside them? Bohr's answer was typical and tapped into a propensity in Heisenberg to think in similar terms: "When it comes to atoms, language can be used only as in poetry. The poet, too, is not nearly so concerned with describing facts as with creating images and establishing mental connections."[27]

This willingness to forgo assigning distinct, classical images to mathematical values was essential to the series of extraordinary advances Heisenberg was poised to make over the next five years. As the astronomer and philosopher of science Sir Arthur Eddington would write two years after Heisenberg's greatest discovery (and ten years after definitively proving Einstein's theory of general relativity), "No familiar conceptions can be woven round the electron. . . . *Something unknown is doing we don't know what*—that is what our theory amounts to."[28] Eddington's crisp British wit also led him to draw on that of a mathematician of the prior generation whose fame would come not from science but from letters. It would make as much sense, he added, to refer to electrons and quantum numbers with words such as those penned by Charles Lutwidge Dodgson, better known to us as Lewis Carroll: "Eight slithy toves gyre and gimbal in the oxygen wabe."[29] For Eddington the words of quantum physics were no more descriptive of reality than the made-up jargon of "Jabberwocky."

In 1924, Heisenberg moved to Göttingen to take up the post of Born's assistant, which Pauli had just vacated. Progress on the atomic model had come to a standstill. As Bohr explained to a captive audience at Yale University the previous year, no one could take seriously anymore the image of electrons orbiting a nucleus like planets in a solar system. At the same time, no one quite knew what image to replace it with. Bohr's own attempt, in a paper he wrote with his then-assistant Hans Kramers and the American physicist John Slater, ended up being a dead end, although it planted a seed. In it the three scientists had tried replacing the image of a discrete electron with something they called a "virtual oscillator," in other words, some entity that behaved at the microscopic level like a rapidly vibrating pendulum or guitar string.[30] Kramers would go on to develop the idea mathematically and show that all spectrographic readings of light interference with atoms could indeed be calculated by assuming the right set of oscillators, but he resisted giving up the idea that underlying it all were particles moving in a classical way—this despite the unnerving fact that a classical description of particles simply couldn't account for the gaps that the quantum data insisted on producing.[31] Heisenberg had no such qualms.

Heisenberg reasoned that when dealing with quanta, all scientists had to go on were experimental observations. In any given experimental situation dealing with electrons, one never "saw" the particle itself. Rather, what one saw was an initial energy state and a new state, measured at two different times. Whatever image we give the electron in between those states is doomed to remain a heuristic, no more useful to us than Lewis Carroll's slithy tove. What was needed was not a different picture, a more or less slithy tove, but a dependable mathematical operation to describe the relationship between the two observable states.

Isaac Newton and Gottfried Leibniz had each developed a version of calculus to deal with measurements of curved, continuous spaces. In this sense calculus is the mathematical tool par excellence for modeling the world as conceptualized by classical physics. For the discontinuous states of quanta, though, a different math was needed. A new math for a different kind of space and time, where no baseline continuity could be assumed, but rather rupture and discontinuity. In Göttingen, Max Born was hard at work on figuring out the kinds of calculations this would require. Heisenberg, working at his side, could see that Born's endeavors were a kind of formal equivalent to Kramers and Bohr's virtual oscillators, in that both assumed gaps and differences and not points or continuities as their foundation.[32]

Heisenberg's recollection of the breakthrough rings overly modest. "The idea suggested itself," he said in a lecture at St. Andrews University in Scotland some thirty years later, "that one should write down the mechanical laws not as equations for the positions and velocities of the electrons," but rather that one should work from the other direction: namely, start with the idea of frequencies and amplitudes, and then derive positions and velocities from those values.[33]

INDEED, WHAT MERELY "PRESENTED itself" this way was an idea as revolutionary as Einstein's, twenty years earlier, that space and time are not immutable standards but are subject to change as the frame of reference relative to an observer encroaches on the speed of light. In Heisenberg's case, he decided to treat the classical notions of position and momentum in a similar way, allowing that these long-stable notions might lose their coherence at very small frames of reference. In simple terms, Heisenberg decided to invert the relationship between particles and movement: movement is not something that happens to particles; particles are something we derive from observations about movement. He now began to see particles along the lines of the "middle ground" he had dreamed of at the meeting among youth factions at the castle on the Rhine, something that emerges from relations as opposed to residing in an individual.

For his calculations Heisenberg turned to something called a Fourier series, the mathematical notation for determining the position and velocity of an oscillating point—say, a given mark on a rapidly vibrating string as it completes one cycle—as a function of its possible frequencies. For electrons, similar values could be derived from spectrographs, which are the visual equivalents of the tones we hear from vibrating strings. A brilliant idea—the problem remained, however, that the mathematics that resulted from inserting the highly complex frequencies into the existing equations were simply incomprehensible. To top it all, pollen season had arrived in full force in Göttingen, and the allergy-prone Heisenberg could barely breathe, so red and swollen was his face.

On June 7, Heisenberg left Göttingen to spend some time alone on a barren (and blessedly pollen-free) island in the North Sea called Heligoland. There he applied himself to the notoriously tricky mathematics of multiplying not individual values but the complex matrices of numbers needed to describe the before-and-after energy states of quantum measurements. Cleansed of his allergies by the sea air, Heisenberg worked feverishly day and night, performing herculean calculations. Unable to sleep one night on the island, he went to his desk and worked again, and the numbers started to click. At around three o'clock in the morning he saw the answers emerge. As he later recalled, "I had the feeling that, through the surface of atomic phenomena, I was looking at a strangely beautiful interior, and felt almost giddy at the thought that I now had to probe this wealth of mathematical structures nature had so generously spread out before me."[34] As Born quickly realized upon Heisenberg's return, in his search to model the strange behavior of the quanta, the young man had, entirely on his own, worked out a variation of linear algebra, at the time unknown to all but the most committed mathematicians.

Back in Göttingen, Born worked with Heisenberg and another physicist, Pascual Jordan, on what became known as "the three man paper," which would lay out for the first time the matrix version of quantum mechanics. In their work they saw with wonderment that the laws of movement of classical mechanics could also be derived from the new matrix mechanics they were using to describe the strange world of quanta. At the same time, another mathematically minded physicist at Cambridge with whom Heisenberg had shared his paper, Paul Dirac, was also discovering this equivalence. In both cases the key to translating the physical laws of the visible world, known since Newton, into the enigmatic numbers of quantum mechanics came down to one number: Planck's constant. Setting

Planck's constant to zero—and since it is already so ridiculously small, this is the practical consequence of any measurement of macroscopic movements—effectively removed the differences between the two. Just as Einstein had shown that the seeming consistency of space and time crumbles as one approaches one limit, the speed of light, Heisenberg had revealed that the seeming solidity of location and movement dissolved as humans approached another limit, this one hidden deeper in the crevices of space and time than anyone had ever delved. Until now.

AS HEISENBERG AND THE Göttingen team were putting the finishing touches on a new mechanics of discontinuity, another approach to understanding the movement of electrons was brewing. It began with a French aristocrat named Louis de Broglie whose fascination with physics lured him from the traditional family business of civil service. In 1925 he published a doctoral dissertation in which he proposed a mathematical equivalence between properties of matter and those of waves. Starting from Einstein's demonstration that light waves also behaved like particles, de Broglie showed that electrons, previously regarded only as particles, could also behave like waves.[35] Crucially, de Broglie's formulas applied to all matter. The larger the mass of an object, the smaller the wavelength of its frequency—which means, for all practical intents, it's not surprising that humans had never before encountered this strange aspect of things. According to his calculations, themselves emerging from Einstein's work on photons, frequencies would become a factor only when an object's mass was vanishingly small. Yet again, the standard of that size was Planck's constant.

Key to de Broglie's account was that it could also explain why electrons stayed confined to specific energy levels. By conceiving of orbits as waves of a given frequency undulating around a nucleus, de Broglie was able to show that the size of each electron shell was determined by the frequency of the wavelength associated with it.

The sharp lines in the spectrographic data made sense in that only certain wavelengths could fit into orbits of specific radii without interfering with themselves. De Broglie sent his paper to Einstein, who immediately saw its implications for Heisenberg's theory of discontinuity, commenting, "I believe that it involves more than a mere analogy."[36] Einstein, ever unhappy with the probabilistic implications of his own discoveries, thrilled to the potential evidence that continuous, physical waves could constitute the reality underlying the discontinuities that the emerging quantum theory kept running into.

His enthusiasm infected another old-school physicist who read Einstein's paper that year. Erwin Schrödinger was already an established scientist. Originally from Vienna, he had held a chair in physics at the University of Zurich for several years. A somewhat rakish bon vivant, Schrödinger was married and had several children, none of them from his wife.[37] Rather less bohemian in his physics than in life, Schrödinger had followed the advances of Bohr and his team of wunderkinder with increasing alarm. Surely no one could take seriously the notion that electrons appeared and disappeared without occupying space and time in between their appearances. So, Einstein's imprimatur on de Broglie's idea was enough to send Schrödinger searching for answers. The formula he came up with in 1926 was received by physicists with a collective sigh of relief. Here were none of Heisenberg's strange new ideas bundled into brain-racking matrix algebra. In its place Schrödinger had crafted an equation of elegant simplicity. Moreover, physicists could recognize it, because it measured things that occurred in reality, waves.

Right after publishing his new theory of "undulatory mechanics," Schrödinger showed it to be translatable into Heisenberg's matrix math, and soon thereafter Paul Dirac did the same thing.[38] Perhaps Heisenberg's mechanics weren't so strange. Perhaps they were a needlessly abstruse version of something that had been hidden all along: a wavelike reality of fields underlying our world of solid objects in space and time. One that really existed and that followed classical mechanical laws, in which substances moved and changed in space and over time, and only appeared as discrete particles to our limited senses. Before Schrödinger's equations Einstein had responded in dour terms to the direction quantum mechanics was taking, writing in a letter, "Heisenberg has laid a large quantum egg. In Göttingen they believe it (I don't)."[39] Now there seemed to be a way to avoid getting splattered by that egg.

The problem was, Schrödinger's attempts to put physics back on the solid ground of classical mechanics by visualizing what happens within atoms in terms of physical waves were not panning out. He traveled to Copenhagen to try to work out his differences with Bohr in person, but the visit turned into a nightmare as the garrulous and meandering deep thinker poked and prodded at Schrödinger's assumptions. Waves are waves in or of something, are they not? What is doing the "waving" in the case of electrons? And if waves are smooth, why do they register as particles when we measure them? As Planck had shown decades earlier, even the most recognized wave-like energy devolves into quanta when analyzed closely enough. A deeply discouraged Schrödinger would later say, "If we are going to stick to this damned quantum-jumping, then I regret that I ever had anything to do with quantum theory."[40]

Schrödinger left Copenhagen in 1926 completely fed up with his skirmishes with Bohr. On the one hand, his contention that waves were real wasn't holding water. On the other, it was by now generally accepted that his wave mechanics were equivalent to matrix mechanics and significantly wieldier. The wave equation worked, but what did it mean? Back in Göttingen, Max Born thought he had the answer. The waves in Schrödinger's equations didn't track the actual movement of real physical substance; like a data set plotted out on graph paper, they predicted the probability of where particles would be when they were eventually measured. Particles could move from point to point, and in large enough numbers their whereabouts could be accurately predicted, but any one particle at any given time could pop up pretty much anywhere.

Typically, Einstein had pointed the way when he interpreted the lines on spectrographs as corresponding to propensities of certain energy levels to radiate. But if this was the meaning of quantum mechanics, something dear to physicists would be lost for good. Scientists like Planck and Einstein had made good use of Boltzmann's statistics, but for them it was always a heuristic. Whether with collisions of cue balls or gas molecules, they assumed that we needed statistics because of technical limitations on our knowledge. If we could focus our gaze to the scale of gas molecules, we could predict their movements with the same precision we can for cue balls, and thus lower accordingly our reliance on statistical models.

At heart, physics was still deterministic. Actions led to reactions in totally law-abiding ways. With Born's move to bring in probability, something changed decisively. As he wrote in his paper in 1926, in "quantum mechanics there exists no quantity in which an individual case determines the results of a collision . . . I myself am inclined to give up determinism in the atomic world."[41] Einstein wasn't having any of it. His response to Born has been quoted, requoted, and misquoted ad infinitum (often by the great man himself), but the gist was always the same. The imposing edifice of quantum mechanics "delivers much but it hardly brings us closer to the Old One's secret. In any event, I am convinced that *He* is not playing dice."[42] The laws of physics couldn't come down to maybes; things happened for a reason.

HEISENBERG INTRODUCED THE IDEA of observation in the very first sentences of the paper that put the new physics into motion. "An attempt is made," he wrote there, "to obtain foundations for quantum theoretical mechanics based exclusively on relationships between quantities that are in principle observable."[43] At first glance uncontroversial, in fact a revolution is already at work in this statement. Just as Einstein twenty years earlier had decided to let go of something everyone "knew"—that time was the same for everyone, that my "now" is the same as your "now"—Heisenberg was letting go of the image we have of a coherent reality that exists independently of our observations of it. If it had stayed at that level, though, Heisenberg's pronouncement would have been little more than a version of the if-a-tree-falls riddle that stands in some people's minds for philosophical profundity. Heisenberg's paper, the math it contained, and the work to follow did something far more consequential. They put forth a detailed scientific interpretation of experimental evidence that demonstrated the incoherence of that commonplace understanding of reality.

What is an observation? At its very minimum, any observation entails something connecting two disparate moments in time and space. As for Kant and Borges's character Funes, a being who was truly, exclusively saturated in a present moment wouldn't be able to observe anything at all. Observation, any observation, installs a minimal distance from what it observes, for the simple reason that for any observation to take place, one here and now must be related to another here and now, and that relation needs to be registered by some trace or connector between the two. Crucially, this aspect of observing doesn't assume a conscious or otherwise human agent. It also doesn't mean, as the popular misunderstanding of Heisenberg's discovery would have it, that the tools we use to observe something always affect what we observe, although that, too, is true. Far more fundamentally, the blur of the instant of change that is a logical prerequisite for stitching together any two moments in space-time inextricably inheres in the very reality being observed. This, in a nutshell, is the uncertainty principle: you can know a particle's position or its momentum, but you can't know both.

In a deep sense, then, the laws of physics, the laws that describe how things behave, are really the laws of our observations of how things behave. Or, as Heisenberg would later say, "we have to remember that what we observe is not nature in itself but nature exposed to our method of questioning."[44] And since an observation is always an observation in time and space, the laws of physics regard operations in time and space. We may speculate about the world outside the conditions of time and space; indeed, as we will see in subsequent chapters, generations of thinkers and theologians have tried to do just that. But a nontemporal and nonspatial perspective obliterates the very idea of an observation, and hence is incompatible with any knowledge we can have of the world. In a fascinating and parallel way, the two constants that form the backbone of modern physics, Einstein's c and Planck's h, turn out to be fundamental limits built into the fabric of our observed reality: on the one hand, a speed limit at which time comes to a standstill; on the other, a size limit on how closely we can focus on the warp and weft of space-time.

It was this second limit that Heisenberg unearthed, barely a year later, with a second revolutionary paper, one that would forever bind his name to the idea of an ineradicable uncertainty at the heart of our ability to know reality.

Part II

NOT BEING GOD

4

ENTANGLEMENTS

HEISENBERG WAS BESIDE HIMSELF. He had checked and rechecked the math. He had exchanged letters with Pauli and received his support. He had sent off the paper to Germany's leading physics review, and it had been accepted. Naturally Bohr was going to object. Of course he was going to poke and prod, nitpick, split hairs. But ask him to retract? Take more time to be sure of the conclusions? The young man's obstinate streak took over. No—hadn't he allowed himself to be scooped by bowing to Sommerfeld's skepticism about his half-integer idea? It was time to follow his instincts and move ahead.

But then Bohr showed him something that let the air out of his balloon. Heisenberg had made a mistake.

It was a technical error, but Bohr was able to show that it went to the heart of what they had been arguing about all this time. As he expounded his newly derived uncertainty principle, Heisenberg called upon the method he had started to develop while hiking with his friends in the hills over Lake Starnberg: posing a problem with mental images and then turning those into concepts. He began by imagining how one might try to measure the position and momentum of an electron by illuminating it with the smallest possible wavelength of energy, gamma rays, and then examining the results of their collisions with a gamma ray microscope constructed for the experiment ("constructed" here means dreamed up). Homing in on the electron with ever smaller wavelengths of energy to better measure its position, however, would cause ever greater recoil of the particle—since smaller wavelengths equal higher energy—and thus make its momentum harder to pin down.[1] He also found that a similar uncertainty held for the variables of energy and time. Just as one could fix position but only at the expense of losing any bearing on momentum, the cost of knowing the exact time of a measurement left one utterly in the dark as to its energy level.

Even before this particular conflict, the stay in Copenhagen had started to turn south as Schrödinger's had. Heisenberg was used to collaboration and conversation. That's what the new Göttingen physics had emerged from. The last year and a half had been a dream, an extension of the Platonic Symposium of outings with good friends that Heisenberg had turned to for solace since the desperate postwar years in Munich. Heisenberg, Pauli, Pascual Jordan, Born himself—they had all come from vastly different backgrounds, but they had formed a community. Their differences were their strength. Even when they disagreed—Pauli, for example, hated the math they had come up with and stewed that "matrix must be about the dumbest mathematical word ever invented!"—their persistent back-and-forth had led to exactly the kind of middle ground that Heisenberg had dreamed of in the courtyard of Schloss Prunn.[2]

Indeed, the Göttingen physics emerged from an almost camplike life. The students spent almost all their time together—in seminars of course, but also outside, skiing, hiking, and horseback riding. In skiing Heisenberg was always the fastest. One day the friends took the institute's stopwatch, ostensibly intended for gathering experimental data, to the slopes with them to time their respective runs.

Werner tore down the slope at eighty kilometers per hour, as one of his colleagues, Wilhelm Hanle, reported, "a record for that time."[3] (One suspects that if Hanle got the velocity exactly right, he might not have known precisely where on the slope Heisenberg was.) Not that physics was ever off the table—literally. In fact, at a certain point the matronly café owner of their preferred lunch spot flat out told them they would no longer be welcome if they insisted on debating physics at the top of their voices every day, which was simply "becoming unbearable to the other guests."[4]

The time with Bohr had very much started in this spirit. They would talk physics throughout the day in the institute until after dinner, when, unsated, they would carry the conversations with them up to Werner's attic room until past midnight. As winter stretched on, though, they began to run into dead ends in their conversations. The decision to take some time with his wife in Norway was Bohr's way of getting some distance and allowing things to settle with his newly prickly assistant. Then Werner had his flash of insight, which he shared with Pauli, whose reaction was conclusive—"the rosy dawn of modernity. Daylight has come to quantum theory."[5]

Ecstatic over his discovery, Heisenberg was simply not prepared for a new round of Bohrish skepticism upon his mentor's return. Heisenberg's derivation of the uncertainty that obtained between momentum and position, on the one hand, and between energy and time, on the other, was both profound and accurate, but as an interpretation it was incomplete. The problem, Bohr insisted, was that it failed to acknowledge the wave side of what Bohr was starting to call an essential "complementarity" in quantum physics. Complementarity, he said, referred to the ineluctable fact that both wave and particle notions apply to quantum events, but that a physicist can only ever choose to measure one.[6] Heisenberg, with his gung ho embrace of discontinuity (and likely his distaste for anything that reminded him of Schrödinger and his damned waves), had failed to see that any interpretation of a quantum event would be incomplete without accounting for the fact that particles also behave like waves, and that by choosing what to focus on, the observer was in essence deciding what kind of outcome would emerge.

Heisenberg did not react well, to say the least. He not only flat out refused to withdraw the paper but also was personally offended that Bohr would pigeonhole his paper into a supporting role for his own nascent theory. The battle raged on. Like Schrödinger before him, Heisenberg felt harassed by Bohr's incessant probing and was even reduced to tears. Still, Bohr's war of attrition ultimately prevailed, and in May 1927 a crestfallen Heisenberg agreed to amend the paper by adding a postscript pointing out "essential points that I had overlooked" and crediting Bohr with bringing them to his attention.[7] Primary among these was the fact that uncertainty arises not only from the fundamental discontinuity of reality at the quantum level—that no matter how closely one looked at a particle's movement there was no way to close the gaps and find a smooth path—but from the fact that the observer always decides in advance whether to look for a wave or a particle, and that decision determines the reality one will find.

Détente shakily achieved, Heisenberg and Bohr could now ally themselves to take on the rest of the physics world. Their interpretations might have differed, but Heisenberg's principle had emerged unscathed. Whatever the tools we use, as we focus on reality at the quantum level, we must make certain choices. We can zoom in on an electron's position or on its momentum. We can further define the energy of an event or its time. But in each case, the more we focus on one factor, the greater the uncertainty of the other. And the value lodged in the pivot between one side and the other of his equation was nothing other than our old friend Planck's constant.

AFTER HEISENBERG LEFT COPENHAGEN that summer, Bohr got to work articulating as best he could the philosophical framework within which the new quantum physics could make sense to the outside world. He had several vital components to pack into one coherent picture—wave particle duality, uncertainty, and also the strange fact that quantum mechanics could explain classical physics, but not the reverse. No easy task for even the clearest thinker, but Bohr's penchant for murkiness threatened to make the situation worse.

At the end of the summer the theoretical physics world gathered at a palazzo on the idyllic shores of Lake Como in northern Italy for a conference marking the hundredth birthday of the Italian inventor of the voltage cell, Alessandro Volta. There Bohr presented his theory of complementarity publicly for the first time. Heisenberg's innovations had earned pride of place: discontinuity was, Bohr insisted, the irreducible postulate of quantum physics.[8] But he left plenty of room for Schrödinger as well. Specifically, Bohr noted that the two relations in Heisenberg's principle—on the one hand momentum and position, on the other energy and time—each contained an element traditionally associated with particles and another associated with waves. Taking a measurement therefore required choosing to focus on either a wavelike or a particle-like aspect of the quantum event, at the exclusion of the other. And yet both aspects, mutually exclusive for any act of observation, are necessarily part of the whole picture.[9] Hence complementarity: we can see different aspects of reality, depending on what we choose to observe; and those aspects complement each other; but we can never grasp the entirety of that reality.

Crucially, while Bohr acknowledged Schrödinger's waves, his theory obliterated everything Schrödinger's had sought to achieve with them. The wave equation is thoroughly classical. If you measure a given system at a given time and calculate its wave function, you will be able to calculate the same function later, with no uncertainty. The problem arises when you take a measurement prior to that later time. In classical mechanics, such a measurement doesn't alter the wave. In quantum mechanics, by taking that measurement, you have changed the future outcome of the wave function.[10]

The audience members at Como weren't knocked off their seats. Many thought Bohr might just be saying something they already understood: if you measure something, you're going to interfere with what you're measuring. But Bohr's point was far more profound. Heisenberg's principle showed that with quantum events taking a measurement decisively determined what one could know about the whole system. In some very deep sense, the measurements themselves determined the world they sought to measure.[11] This went against the very fiber of what Schrödinger, and through him Einstein, believed about the ultimate nature of reality.

As Bohr concluded his talk that day, Born and Heisenberg in turn rose from their seats and publicly endorsed his position. Because it was Bohr's lecture, and much of its grist had been worked out at his institute, their imprimatur sealed what became known as the Copenhagen interpretation of quantum mechanics—with Bohr's theory of complementarity as the philosophical framework that held Heisenberg's matrix mechanics, his uncertainty principle, and Born's probabilistic application of the wave equation together in one rather incoherent bundle. When a version of Bohr's lecture finally appeared the following year in the journal *Nature*, the editors openly hoped that it would not be physicists' "last word on the subject, and that they may yet be successful in expressing the quantum postulate in picturesque form."[12]

They weren't the only ones. Neither Einstein nor Schrödinger had come to Como. But in only a few weeks they would be ready to take a first shot at dismantling the Copenhagen juggernaut.

IN 1911 THE BELGIAN industrialist Ernest Solvay had invited the most prominent scientists in the world to a conference in Brussels to share their thinking on the state of the art in chemistry and physics. In the wake of the resounding success of the gathering, Solvay founded the International Solvay Institutes for Physics and Chemistry, which made the meetings a regular affair, holding them roughly every three years ever since with notable gaps around the world wars. In October 1927, the physics world converged for what would end up being perhaps the most remarkable gathering of physicists of all time. The last time the conference had taken place was just after the end of World War I and German scientists had been barred. Einstein, who was traveling in the United States at the time, declined the invitation in protest. But this year he was slated to come, along with pretty much every other major figure in the field. The conference's theme was "Electrons and Photons," but for all intents and purposes it was quantum mechanics.

The air in the meeting rooms at the Hotel Métropole in Brussels shimmered in anticipation of the encounter between Einstein and the young brigade of the quantum revolution. At first, however, Einstein demurred. He decided against giving the opening lecture, telling his colleagues that he had concluded, "I am not competent to give such a report in a way that would match the current state of affairs."[13] Earlier that year he had prepared a paper advancing a wave interpretation of quantum events but had withdrawn it.[14] He had been corresponding with Heisenberg, and it might have been that uncertainty was turning out to be a hard obstacle to overcome. For his part, Schrödinger did give a paper. It didn't land particularly well, and he found himself ill-equipped to respond to the sharp questioning that rained in from Heisenberg and Born.

The Copenhagen team had come prepared. Heisenberg and Born worked together as a team and delivered a joint paper, which began by throwing a gauntlet, saying, "We regard *quantum mechanics* as a complete theory for which the fundamental physical and mathematical hypotheses are no longer susceptible of modification."[15] As if this hadn't driven the point home, they further specified what they meant by complete. Quantum theory, they declared, "is distinguished essentially from classical physics by the existence of discontinuities," and "the subsequent development of the theory of radiation will change nothing in this state of affairs."[16] The gist? "Our fundamental hypothesis of essential indeterminism is in accord with experiment."[17] To use a present-day idiom, quantum mechanics was complete because the indeterminism of the behavior of individual particles was not a bug but a feature. It was baked into how reality behaves at the smallest level, and no amount of digging was going to relieve science of that apparent paradox.

With Heisenberg and Born showing little mood to compromise and the rest of the Copenhagenites, as Pauli would call them, circling the wagons, it was left to their spiritual leader to play the diplomat, a role for which the congenial Niels Bohr was particularly well suited—especially given how hard it is to strenuously disagree with someone you don't understand. While Einstein mainly listened during the presentations, a strange dance developed between the two of them at the meals that preceded and followed the scheduled lectures. Each morning a small crowd would settle in around a table where Bohr and Einstein sat speaking, and Einstein would pose Bohr a problem. Typically, this problem would take the form of a thought experiment—the genre of which Einstein was the undisputed master. Bohr would puzzle and fret and then rush off to confer with Heisenberg and Born, while Einstein would lean back with a satisfied smile on his face. By evening, though, the tables would turn, as an ebullient Bohr would point out a vital detail that Einstein had overlooked, and indeterminism would be restored.[18]

True to Einstein's style, even as he lost these skirmishes, his thought experiments lay bare the essence of the problem. Ironically, one of the problems he presented would eventually become a real experiment whose results conclusively demonstrated the reality of quantum "weirdness." Imagine, Einstein proposed, a screen with two slits at which a gun fires a stream of electrons. On the other side is a photographic plate that registers the pattern formed by the electrons as they pass through. As is well known, when waves hit such a barrier, they form an interference pattern on the plate, with lighter and darker strips representing where the new waves emerging from the two slits augment and diminish each other. Particles, if they are shot through one by one and are not able to interfere with each other as they pass through one or the other slit, should produce a pattern of two stripes on the plate.

If the Copenhagenites were correct and quantum mechanics was indeed the last word, Einstein said, as electrons pass through the slit, they pass through as elements of a probability wave, not a real wave; in other words, whatever wavelike pattern appears only accrues over time and as a result of many electrons passing through. This would be true even if the electrons passed through one after the other, since the wave of their probability would supposedly interfere with itself to create a wavelike pattern on the photographic plate. However, taken as an individual particle, each time an electron hits the plate and is registered, and hence a measurement has taken place, the probability that the same electron hits anywhere else on the plate would instantaneously collapse to zero. The electron, upon being measured in one place, would somehow, instantaneously, transmit this fact to all the other places it could have been. And this, Einstein triumphantly claimed, was impossible, because it would entail the instantaneous communication of information across an (admittedly minuscule) expanse of space and time. It would violate a well-established and proven bedrock of physics, namely, Einstein's own theory of special relativity, which put an absolute limit, the speed of light, on how fast information can be propagated. For Einstein, the interpretation of a probability wave instantaneously communicating its measurement across any expanse of space violated the theory of relativity's ban on faster-than-light communication, and this fact proved something was missing from the quantum mechanics picture.[19] For according to relativity, it is simply impossible that a decision in one place instantaneously affects the rest of reality. But that's exactly what quantum theory's most fundamental insights implied.

Einstein beamed. Measuring a particle could not be responsible for determining its pathway, as Heisenberg had famously insisted. Instead, it must be the case that the decision was already made: the particles showed up when they were measured, yes, but as they passed through the slits, they passed through the way real waves do, not as probabilities to be later resolved. And these real waves would be deterministic in a classical way. Quantum mechanics was incomplete because it hadn't yet found a way to see with precision where the particles were or the form they took before they struck the plate.

CHARACTERISTICALLY, BOHR'S ANSWER LATER that evening came in the form of an interrogation of Einstein's assumptions. Didn't his conclusion fail to account for the uncertainty principle? Einstein's claim that information about an electron's path couldn't travel faster than the speed of light took for granted how much information we could have about the situation. In fact, exact knowledge of a particle's position in space and time requires wildly inexact knowledge of its momentum and energy, rendering impossible the reduction to zero of its previous possible trajectories. In any real experiment, the equipment used for making the measurement—in this case the screen receiving the electrons—would itself register vanishingly small movements that would reinstall some uncertainty in the position and time of the electron's impact. This in turn would allow for calculating the probability of where it might have been with an exactness in proportion to that permitted by Heisenberg's equation. If one wanted to know more about the path taken by the electron, one could measure that and determine which slit it passed through, at which point, however, the experimenter would have opted to measure it as a particle and the diffraction pattern would no longer form on the screen. There was simply no way to get an electron to give you both sides of the equation in full, and therefore Einstein's complaint that quantum theory violated relativity because it assumed the instantaneous transmission of information was unwarranted.[20]

BOHR'S RESPONSE TO EINSTEIN sounds like a cop-out. Indeed, Einstein was likely quite nonplussed by it at the time. The whole point he was trying to make is that quantum mechanics can't be the whole picture, because, as he said in his address on the last day of the conference, "in my opinion it contradicts the relativity postulate."[21] Bohr's response was simply to double down on the limited nature of our knowledge of quantum events and insist that because of Heisenberg's principle quantum mechanics *was* the last word. No matter how you tweaked it, you weren't going to get more information from tiny particles than Heisenberg's math allowed.

Einstein possessed a strength that Bohr did not. Whether ultimately right or wrong, he was able to make things clear. In this case, what Einstein beautifully clarified was this: either quantum mechanics was right about the real indeterminacy of an electron's path until the moment of its measurement, or it was not. If it was not right, then physics remained deterministic, even if the knowledge of those determinations was for now, or forever, beyond our grasp. If quantum mechanics was right, however, then our fundamental understanding of reality had been misguided until now. Bohr's protests notwithstanding, an observation taken at one point in space and time would indeed appear to instantaneously affect what we know about another point in space and time, thus violating a principle decisively proven by relativity. This principle is called locality. What we can know about the world around us is limited by the velocity of light. I simply cannot know what is happening "now" at any distance from me, because information takes a certain minimum of time to cross any spatial distance, and it cannot do so faster. Period. If it does, then all bets are off. Not only can an observation affect other points in space-time simultaneously; worse yet, an observation could retroactively determine what path a particle took to get to that observation. This made no sense at all.

The two-slit experiment has now been performed over and over again. Here is what happens. A stream of electrons fired at a screen with two slits produces a wavelike interference pattern on the plate behind it. Bizarrely, the pattern remains even when you slow the rate of emission down so much that only one electron can be passing through the screen at a time. While each electron lands at a definite spot, as you run the experiment over time and allow thousands to land on the screen, they will accumulate exactly according to a wave pattern, as if the two slits had been set up in a tankful of water and the little waves emerging out the back end combined to form patterns of amplification and cancellation. In other words, while logic dictates that each electron must have passed through one or the other hole, over time they behave as if what had passed through the holes were ghosts, potential particles, amplifying or canceling each other along the way, thus producing the pattern.

Even more eerily, you can change the experiment by placing a detector at each slit to record which one the electrons pass through on their way to the screen. Now the interference pattern disappears and what you are left with is a pattern produced by a bunch of particles behaving like particles. In other words, once they have been caught in the act of passing through one or the other slit, they stop behaving like ghosts or potentialities and go on about their business as self-respecting particles.[22] This doesn't only seem to violate locality; it violates common sense.

Einstein continued to pepper Bohr and the Copenhagen contingent with questions in the years after the 1927 meeting, including three years later when they again returned to Brussels for the next iteration of the Solvay conference. On that occasion Einstein took aim at Heisenberg's principle directly, and this time he let fly a real humdinger. Imagine, he said to Bohr, a box equipped with a scale to measure its weight—something like a spring scale, but of course sensitive to absurdly small changes. The box has a trapdoor controlled by a very fast shutter, which can open and shut quickly enough to allow one photon at a time to escape. If you record the departure of a photon at an exact time and then weigh the box, comparing the mass of its contents before and after the light beam left, you will know both the time of the event and the energy, since, according to Einstein's famous equivalence, mass is convertible to energy. And this would be a violation of Heisenberg's principle, which explicitly states that one cannot know with precision both the energy and the time of a quantum event.[23]

Those at the event recall Bohr's agitation that evening as he obsessed over Einstein's problem at dinner, bringing it up to everyone who came to the table, and repeatedly going back to Einstein to ask questions and insist that he couldn't be right. Einstein, for his part, looked like the cat that had eaten the canary. When he descended for breakfast the following morning, though, Einstein would eat crow instead. For in the night Bohr had landed on what was wrong with the scenario. Einstein had forgotten to consider his own theory of relativity, which also stated that the recoil of the box when it lost the energy of the photon necessarily affected the time of the event. In minuscule ways, of course. But because the entire experiment was set up to measure such small events, even this tiny adjustment reintroduced uncertainty—at exactly the degree calculated by Heisenberg. It seemed that no matter how Einstein tried to show the flaws in quantum mechanics, Heisenberg's principle always got in the way.

After the 1930 Solvay conference Einstein seemed to accept that he wasn't going to get around the uncertainty principle by conjuring imagined physical devices. Bohr always seemed to find a way to show how measurements involving devices that had to be described with classical physics would register minute changes, and these changes would have comparatively large effects at the quantum level. The reason for this seemed to have something to do with Bohr's notion of complementarity, "the sharp formulation of which," Einstein would complain, "I have been unable to achieve despite much effort which I have expended on it."[24] This fact did not alter Einstein's conviction that something had to be missing. If Heisenberg's principle was a limit on how far down we could *see* the quantum world, that didn't mean that the quantum world didn't still work in accordance with the laws of classical physics. The Copenhagen interpretation, though, insisted that these particles had no determinate path *in reality* until they were measured, and this just could not be right.

IN THE FIRST YEARS of the 1930s Einstein's life was upended by Hitler's rise in Germany. In December 1932 he and his wife, Elsa, departed Germany for the United States, after initial difficulties securing a visa, ostensibly because of his leftist views. The incident caused some embarrassment for the U.S. government, with *The New York Times* reporting on the various states of Einstein's packing and unpacking of his bags, and led to an official apology from Secretary of State Henry Stimson, who insisted to the press that Einstein "was treated with every courtesy and consideration."[25] When Hitler took power at the end of the following month, Einstein had made it as far as California, where he stayed until March. There he did an interview with a reporter from the *New York World-Telegram* in which he stated, "As long as I have any choice in the matter, I shall live only in a country where civil liberty, tolerance and equality of all citizens before the law prevail.... These conditions do not exist in Germany at the present time."[26]

The following day, as a powerful earthquake rocked Los Angeles, Einstein left by train for the East Coast. His apartment in Berlin would soon be torn apart by brown-shirted thugs, and Einstein would never return to Germany. Instead, he would accept an invitation at the newly founded Institute for Advanced Study in Princeton, New Jersey, for what he thought would be half a year or so. He stayed until his death more than twenty years later.

Before moving to Princeton, Einstein returned to Europe long enough to officially renounce his German citizenship at the consulate in Brussels. There he attended a lecture by a physicist named Léon Rosenfeld who was working as Bohr's assistant at the time. After Rosenfeld's lecture ended, Einstein rose and, somewhat like Socrates asking one of his apparently simple questions, painted this scenario: "Suppose two particles are set in motion towards each other with the same, very large, momentum."[27] So began a thought experiment that would ultimately constitute Einstein's last best effort to dismantle the Copenhagen interpretation. While it would fail to do so, it would set in motion a series of experiments and discoveries over the next half century that would prove beyond a doubt the profound weirdness of the quantum world.

The thought experiment would take its full form two years later. Now comfortably settled in Princeton, Einstein collaborated with two colleagues there, Boris Podolsky and Nathan Rosen, to write a paper whose title effectively broadcast its thesis: "Can Quantum-Mechanical Description of Physical Reality Be Considered Complete?" The EPR paper, as it came to be known, landed in Copenhagen like a bomb. Rosenfeld later recalled, "This onslaught came down upon us as a bolt from the blue."[28] Pauli wrote frantically to Heisenberg, calling the paper "a catastrophe."[29]

In simple terms, the paper picked up on Einstein's objection from 1927, further clarifying the stakes. The two particles in question would collide and rebound in opposite directions. Assuming they were undisturbed in their flight, the particles could travel very far from each other indeed. If, however, a scientist captured and measured one of them, according to quantum mechanics and Heisenberg's principle, he or she would be able to know either its position or its momentum with great accuracy. So far so good. However, Heisenberg had also supposedly shown that the particle has no momentum or position until it is observed. And there was the rub. In observing one particle, the researcher would instantaneously know the position or momentum of the other particle, no matter how far the distance between them; even worse, by observing the one, the scientist would also instantaneously determine the outcome of any observation of the second. As Einstein had asked Rosenfeld at his lecture, "How can the final state of the second particle be influenced by a measurement performed on the first?"[30] Einstein had driven a stake through the heart of what he called spooky action at a distance in 1915 when he redefined gravity as the curvature of space-time.

Now here it was poking its head up again. Einstein just knew it couldn't be right.

The Copenhagenites again closed ranks. Heisenberg drafted a response, but finally deferred to Bohr to publish the official rejoinder. The paper—which jauntily sported the same title as the original EPR paper but this time with the presumed answer in the affirmative—turned the tables on Einstein and company by asserting that it wasn't the outcome that couldn't be right, but rather its underlying assumption of what reality must be like. The authors had imported an unjustified idea about reality into their thinking: namely, that reality existed, independent of measurements, in a visualizable form.[31] EPR thought that spooky action at a distance must mean the theory was wrong; Bohr responded rather cheekily that "the apparent contradiction in fact discloses only an essential inadequacy of the customary viewpoint of natural philosophy."[32] If reality seemed in conflict with quantum mechanics, then too bad for reality.

Einstein wasn't the only one who, in trying to show how quantum mechanics couldn't be the whole picture, ended up clarifying the stakes. Schrödinger was following the controversy quite closely as well. Later that year he published a response of his own that would win Einstein's approval and go on to become the most memorable version of the paradoxes sprouting from quantum mechanics. In his famous scenario Schrödinger describes a "hellish contraption" consisting of a box, some radioactive material, a Geiger counter, a vial of cyanide, and an unsuspecting cat.[33] According to quantum mechanics, much as an electron cannot be said to be taking a specific path until it is measured, a radioactive substance with a 50 percent chance of emitting a particle over a period of time cannot be said to have emitted or not until it is observed. As a result, the wave function of its emission will hover in a superposition of those states, emitted and non-emitted, until an observation takes place. The gist of the paper involved setting up the experiment (thought experiment of course, no cats were harmed) such that the indeterminacy of the quantum world would have real stakes in the world governed by classical physics. The Geiger counter would be set to trigger a hammer that would crack open the vial of poison when it detected an emission. If the event couldn't be said to have occurred until the box was opened and the cat observed, this would mean that the cat would have to exist in the box in an in-between state—in Schrödinger's words (for which he begged the reader's pardon), "mixed or smeared out" between life and death.[34]

Schrödinger had no problem with the idea that quantum events could be connected to one another or to classical apparatuses in determinative or causal ways. He even coined the term we use today for talking about such relations: "entanglement," the relation that develops when the two particles in Einstein's original scenario collide. As he wrote, "Entanglement of predictions arises from the fact that the two bodies at some earlier time formed in a true sense *one* system, that is they were interacting, and have left behind *traces* on each other."[35] What he contested and thought absurd was the idea that just measuring a system could cause it to take the form it has. The cat is entangled with the emission of the particle, but it is either dead or alive from the moment the vial breaks, just as the two particles are in fact in motion with specific trajectories and speeds until one of them is measured. When we measure, we learn what was already there; we don't produce it. That is reality.

It took until 1982 for a team of researchers at the University of Paris-South led by the physicist Alain Aspect (who shared the 2022 Nobel Prize for his work) to demonstrate conclusively if Schrödinger and Einstein were right, and this entanglement represents a kind of hidden state that is only revealed by measurement and not produced by it—that is, if reality at the subatomic level could be said to exist on its own, independent of observations—or if Heisenberg's theory that observations determine the underlying reality would ultimately prevail.

Unfortunately for reality, their experiment proved Heisenberg right.

EINSTEIN'S ENTANGLEMENT EXPERIMENT HAD some serious legs. Mostly pursued by physicists who wanted to confirm his position, the idea was refined by people like David Bohm in the 1950s, and his student John Bell in the decades after, and eventually carried out with greater and greater accuracy, and increasingly unambiguous results, in the 1980s and 1990s. Whether one is measuring the polarization of entangled light beams or the "spins" of entangled particles, two ineluctable facts remained: the specific attributes of the photons and particles are indeterminate until measured; and measuring one particle seems to decide the value of the other instantaneously, in apparent violation of special relativity's ban on faster-than-light communication—also demonstrating, not incidentally, that Bohr's objection in Brussels, while effective, was ultimately an obfuscation of the debate rather than a true winning shot.

Einstein's hope had always been that scientists would eventually learn that this knowledge about the distant particle or photon would turn out to be no more mysterious than, say, opening one of two boxes in which a single ball might have been placed. As he put it in a letter to Schrödinger, if we place one ball in one of two identical boxes and mix them up, "the probability is 1/2 that the ball is in the first box. Is that a complete description? no: A complete statement is: the ball *is* (or is not) in the first box."[36] To Bell's chagrin, the ingenious experiments he designed to help prove Einstein's conviction that the quantum "ball" was always there in the box, as opposed to existing in a ghostlike intermediate state until measured, ended up propping up Bohr and Heisenberg's quantum egg instead. Bell would later confess his disappointment in quite personal terms: "I feel that Einstein's intellectual superiority over Bohr, in this instance, was enormous; a vast gulf between the man who saw clearly what was needed, and the obscurantist. So for me, it is a pity that Einstein's idea doesn't work. The reasonable thing just doesn't work."[37]

Bell's experiments had involved the likelihood of measuring particles with certain spin. In very simple form, if the spins were indeed already there—balls that had always been in boxes, as it were—a certain statistical pattern should emerge in the form of an "inequality" among measured outcomes. You might think of this predicted inequality as the outcome you would expect from rolling a pair of dice many times and then tracking the number of times a certain sum shows up. The numbers two and twelve should appear with far less frequency than six or seven, for instance, because there are fewer ways to make those sums. If, on the contrary, two and twelve popped up as often as six did, you would suspect something fishy is going on. In the case of Bell's experiments, if quantum mechanics was right and the act of measurement forced the particles to assume certain states, the inequalities one would expect from uncovering preexisting but hidden spins would be violated.[38]

As it happened, experimental data in the 1970s were already accumulating that Bell's inequalities were violated and those values were not simply hidden in their quantum boxes, waiting to be discovered, but instead actively produced by the measurements. But in 1982 the Aspect experiment sealed the deal by adding an ingenious bar for quantum mechanics to clear. In this experiment, one of two entangled light beams would be randomly polarized by a switch *after* it left its source, and hence after separating from its entangled pair. The result was explosive. Bell's inequalities were violated even when light beams were randomly altered after leaving their source. Quantum entities remain indeterminate until they are measured, and measuring them seems to be able to change their entangled pairs even across distances, in apparent violation of relativity. It was like a kind of magic trick, as one commentator pointed out. It was as if twins always managed to order a different drink no matter what bar they were in and how far apart the bars were. "If one says, 'Beer,' the other instantaneously says, 'Whiskey.'"[39] And to make matters even more mysterious, you could change one twin's order in the act of ordering and, lo and behold, the other twin's order would change as well.

As magical as they sound, entangled particles are real. In a series of experiments since the early years of the twenty-first century, the Austrian physicist Anton Zeilinger (who just shared the 2022 Nobel Prize with Aspect and John Clauser for their experimental confirmations of entanglement) has managed to entangle larger and larger particles and keep them entangled for greater and greater distances. In 2004 he used entangled photons to create an unbreakable code and secure the transfer of three thousand euros from one account to another.[40] In 2007 he sent entangled particles from one of the Spanish Canary Islands across an expanse of open air to another island, some eighty-nine miles away.[41] Entangled particles called qubits provide the beating heart of the emerging industry of quantum computing, which promises to exponentially increase processing power in the near future. And yet the way measurement seems to violate not only the speed of light but the direction of time and causality can't help but strike us as deeply paradoxical. What can explain it?

Perhaps we need to think of the paradox in a different way entirely. As the Nobel laureate and creator of the field of quantum electrodynamics Richard Feynman once wrote, "The 'paradox' is only a conflict between reality and your feeling of what reality 'ought to be.'"[42] As it turns out, this is a succinct statement of something Werner Heisenberg had been saying all along.

ON THE EVENING OF January 30, 1933, Hitler had just taken control of the German government. Heisenberg was visiting the family home of his student and eventual lifelong friend, Carl Friedrich von Weizsäcker. The two of them looked out at streets from the front of Weizsäcker's home as rows of brown-shirted young men marched by in unison. As the troops' torches cast flickering shadows over the cobblestones, the scientists exchanged worried glances and wondered aloud what the changing political winds would mean for their country's future.[43]

They didn't need to wait too long. Within a month the Reichstag had burned, duly blamed on a communist interloper, leading to the appointment of Reich commissars dedicated to ensuring "order and security" in each of the German states.[44] The regime declared a boycott of Jewish-owned business on April 1 and soon thereafter began enacting laws limiting Jews in the civil service and universities.[45] Heisenberg joined other respectable non-Jewish Germans in disdaining the "excesses" of the brutal new regime, but stopped short of open criticism, and indeed as late as the following fall would express cautious optimism about the Nazis' "good intentions."[46]

Such naïveté, not to say bad faith, can't help but shock us today, but it was widespread among the non-Jewish professional classes at the time. Heisenberg, Planck, and many others in the top echelons of the German scientific establishment hoped that the political upheaval would be short-lived and that they and their Jewish colleagues would be spared due to the high social standing conferred on professors, as well as the sterling reputation German physics held in the world. They underestimated the deep-seated class antagonism of the Nazi ideology, which despised intellectualism and science in equal measure.

The short-term goal of the non-Jewish scientists was to prevent the regime from dismissing their Jewish colleagues—or, when, as was often the case, this had already occurred, to try to dissuade those colleagues from leaving the country while they worked behind the scenes to reverse those decisions. Heisenberg's own former director, Max Born, left for Italy after being placed on indefinite leave by the Göttingen administration. At first he vowed never to return, but he vacillated after Heisenberg wrote to him in June 1933 that Planck had spoken with "the head of the government and obtained the assurance that nothing will be undertaken beyond the new civil service law that will impede our science."[47] Planck had indeed had an audience with Hitler, but records are far from clear about what actually transpired in the meeting, with Planck later recalling that Hitler first denied having anything against Jews and then flew into a rage at the venerable scientist.[48]

For his part, the Austrian Schrödinger felt none of Heisenberg and Planck's loyalty to Germany. He exited his position in Berlin at the end of the summer to take up a position at Oxford. A few years later he would move back to Austria to teach at the University of Graz—which offered the dual benefit of not having Nazis, at least for the time being, while also being the abode of his current mistress, the wife of a colleague, with whom he had a daughter.[49] He would stay in Graz until Hitler annexed Austria in 1938, at which point he moved permanently to the University of Dublin. Having long considered Schrödinger a rival, Heisenberg was particularly stung by his decision, wondering aloud about the defection of a scientist who was "neither Jewish nor otherwise endangered."[50] Planck, for his part, struck a more diplomatic note, lamenting "Schrödinger's resignation as a new deep wound to our Berlin physics."[51]

Neither man seemed to grasp yet that Hitler's rise was a tragedy not just for German science but for humanity. The fact was that Heisenberg represented a branch of physics that the Nazis found especially tainted by its association with Jewish scientists like Born and Einstein, the latter of whom unsparingly used his massive public platform to publicly eviscerate the new regime. For their quiet efforts to defend quantum mechanics and Jewish scientists, Heisenberg and Planck had been labeled "white Jews" and blacklisted. Their efforts to place Heisenberg at the helm of Göttingen's institute and try to restore its former glory failed in the face of a rising torrent of public criticism from regime officials intended to deprive Heisenberg of any open academic chair. This continued even after he was notified, in November 1933, that he had been awarded the previous year's Nobel Prize. Two days later he refused to participate in a Nazi rally organized by students on his Leipzig campus, leaving the students befuddled and engaging in contradictory actions: at first marching into his classroom to disrupt his lecture in protest, and a few days later feting the newly minted laureate in typical Nazi style, with a torchlight march.[52]

The following August the regime enacted a requirement for all civil servants to sign a personal pledge of allegiance to Hitler if they wished to keep their positions. In January 1935, Heisenberg signed the pledge, although he would continue to be quietly critical and protest the regime's excesses from the inside. As he wrote to his mother in the fall of 1935, "I must be satisfied to oversee in the small field of science the values that must become important for the future. The world out there is really ugly, but the work is beautiful."[53]

For Heisenberg the beautiful work, like a violinist's mellifluous cadences floating down to calm the tumult of political strife, had become the anchor for his belief in that middle ground, a truth that exceeds any one person's or party's grasp because it can and must emerge from dialogue, relationships. Perhaps it exceeded Heisenberg's own grasp that sometimes the pull of one person's or party's version of reality is so powerful, so poisonous, it can corrupt an entire people—even a people capable of producing a beauty like that of Bach's music, like that of the science Heisenberg so wished to protect. Perhaps it escaped his grasp that there are times when the draw of a single, perverse belief is so strong that no sonata, no matter how lovely, can break its spell.

Scholars writing today often puzzle over the apparent mismatch between the courageous, boundary-breaking nature of Heisenberg's science and the cautious, passive tone of his political engagements. But perhaps the two attitudes are less divergent than they appear at first blush. In his science Heisenberg was willing to disregard the unquestioned certainty of a reality that existed beyond individual acts of observation and the interpretive efforts that link them. What this translated into in practice was a kind of preternatural patience with trying things out, a let's-wait-and-see attitude that might have expressed itself in the 1930s as a failure to recognize an actual evil in the world and react strongly against it. But if that attitude failed miserably in politics, it was vindicated in physics. For Heisenberg's

intuitions concerning the limits of our abilities to visualize the ultimate reality underlying space and time have held true to this day.

The experiments proposed in the 1950s and 1960s have conclusively demonstrated that particles do have ghostly qualities,
that entangled particles are indeed capable of something like the
"spooky action at a distance" that Einstein thought he had banished from physics.[54] Surprisingly, however, it turns out that, as the
renowned string theorist Brian Greene has put it, "special relativity
survives by the skin of its teeth." This is because, in point of fact, no
information actually travels between two entangled particles when
one is observed. What happens, rather, is that one observer now has
a knowledge of what some other observer will see if they observe the
particle somewhere else. But that same observer has no ability whatsoever to transmit that knowledge faster than light speed.[55] That
knowledge remains an interpretation from a given perspective; it
remains part of a dialogue.

Recall how Feynman suggested we needed to change our perspective to understand that the paradox of quantum mechanics is
really "only a conflict between reality and your feeling of what reality
'ought to be.'" That feeling of how it ought to be is a very strong one.
But what if it's the feeling itself that relies on outlandish impossi-
bilities? The feeling Feynman referred to is the same one that Einstein and Schrödinger hoped would be reaffirmed but never was. It's
the feeling that reality is out there independent of our observations
and measurements, yes. But more crucially it casts that feeling, that
presupposition, with a very specific image and structure, one shaped
by how our observations necessarily come to us: namely, extended
in space and successive in time.

This assumption smuggles into our thinking an implicit but
totally unacknowledged observer capable of transcending the limits of space and time. This observer takes several forms. For the
reality that makes quantum physics seem paradoxical, we implicitly adopt the perspective of, borrowing from the title of Arundhati
Roy's beautiful novel, a god of very small things. Likewise, for the

commonplace perspective from which special relativity's stretching and shrinking of space and time seem unimaginable, we import a god of very large things. In each case, the god embodies a perspective that is impossible for humans to occupy.

To know, perceive, or imagine anything at all requires us to span points in space and time, to be at some point in space-time and not at another one, and then make a bridge from one to the other. Like Funes looking in the mirror and feeling surprised at his own image (impossibly, because he supposedly can't generalize over specific impressions), it requires holding together both a sense of what's different and a sense of what's the same between two moments. It requires, as Kant reminded Hume, a synthesis of at least two discernible events. For a human or any other finite being, such a synthesis requires traversing some minimal amount of space-time. The god of very large things, in contrast, can be simultaneously at two points in space-time (indeed, is at every point in space-time) and hence can *experience* what we finite beings can only ever measure and infer: that observing a particle at one point indeed means its entangled particle will exhibit a specific value at another point. This god can do this because, unlike us beings in space and time, for this god the speed limit of light is not a factor to contend with. Simultaneity, which for us is always a projection of one observer's imagination on another place, is real only for such a god.

Likewise, for that god's partner in crime, the god of very small things, quantum changes can take place while being observed. For this god, there is no space too small, no time too short, for it to straddle both sides of a change and witness that transformation. For us, in contrast, bound by time and space, we can infer a change has occurred based on what we observe, but if prodded by Zeno or quantum data to delve down too far into the crevices of space-time, we get to a point where such change is incompatible with our observation. Indeed, a watched quantum pot, it is said, never boils.

This is exactly what another astonishing set of experiments in the 1990s showed.[56] In these experiments, carried out by scientists at the U.S. National Institute of Standards and Technology, beryllium ions were blasted with radio waves for a temporal interval that guarantees a 100 percent chance of an ion jumping up in energy levels. For any given ion and energy level, the temporal interval between when there is a 0 percent probability of an ion changing levels and a 100 percent probability of it changing levels can be subdivided, creating a time frame when there is a 50 percent chance of an ion having made the jump. True to quantum form, if a batch of beryllium ions is heated in this fashion, and measured at the half point, half of the ions will be at the higher energy level, and half at the lower. But if we now start dividing that time frame into shorter and shorter segments, looking ten times, say, over a certain period and then twenty times over the same period, peeking at the ions at each of these intervals to see whether they have changed or not, fewer and fewer end up making the jump. The experiment is limited only by how brief scientists can make the intervals between their observations, but the result is clear: "If it were possible to monitor the ions all the time then none of them would ever change."[57]

As crazy as these results sound, we should resist the impulse to shrug our shoulders and chalk one up for the paradoxical nature of the quantum world. What Feynman said in his lectures echoes what Borges showed in his own analysis of Zeno. Borges showed that Zeno's paradox arises from our having assumed the solidity and continuity of the spatial and temporal reality Achilles and the tortoise inhabit. Likewise, the very nature of what an observation requires—the bridging of two discernible points in space-time—mandates the results of these experiments. Yes, in everyday life Achilles catches up with the tortoise, and yes, in everyday life Diogenes the Cynic can banish Zeno by getting up and walking. But our everyday life is not a life of Planck scales and light speed. At the quantum level a beryllium ion can no more change its energy state while being observed than Funes can truly both be surprised at his reflection and see that reflection anew, as if for the very first time. For the ion to change while being observed, or for Funes to truly be surprised, would require space-time to be something real, something independent, the stuff in which change happens. But it's not. It's nothing more than a tool we use to relate our observations into a coherent whole. And the essential, indispensable humility that powers the scientific method depends on our resisting the temptation to think of it as real.

In the next chapter we return to Kant as he rose in the ranks of academia and began to glimpse the relation between our scientific knowledge and how we experience both beauty and the obligations entailed by our freedom. We will also see how his realization of the source of our errors had implications for his state's religious censors, and how he came upon a critical method to protect against the persistent error we make in assuming we can attain the knowledge of a god.

5

SUB SPECIE
AETERNITATIS

POOR PROFESSOR KANT. HE might have hoped that assuming the title of Full Professor of Logic and Metaphysics would lessen his workload. If so, he was soon disabused. While he would no longer depend on student fees to pay for his room and board, he continued to teach a backbreaking schedule—on top of which he now came to know the singular joys of administration.

As of the summer of 1770, a typical day for the overtaxed professor Kant began at 5:00 a.m., when his servant, a retired soldier named Martin Lampe, would roust him from bed. In this, Lampe performed one of his essential, and most difficult, tasks. For Kant's awesome dedication to his duty was matched only by his inclination to keep sleeping, especially on those dark and chilly mornings that reminded him of his days of childhood treks to the Collegium. Still, with Lampe's persistence Kant always managed to haul himself from bed. Then he would drink two cups of weak tea and smoke one pipeful of tobacco, devoting the time this took "to meditation." Though he proudly insisted on never smoking a second pipe, he ruefully confessed that the pipe's size grew substantially over the years.[1]

Now fully awake, Kant would devote the next hour and a half to thinking and writing, as well as preparing his lectures for the day. In the summer semester of 1770, on most days of the week he would lecture on logic at 7:00 a.m. He would then teach another unit of logic from 8:00 to 9:00, followed by ethics and practical philosophy from 9:00 to 10:00 and a course on the encyclopedia right after that. The demand for his teaching even extended beyond his expertise in logic and metaphysics. Two days of the week he taught classes on geography, and in the winter semester he agreed to teach (of all things) mineralogy. In all he racked up twenty-two hours of classes in a given week, not counting the regular public lectures a professor was expected to give—a truly astounding time expenditure for someone bent on bringing out a book that would change the world.[2]

To make matters worse, professors were expected to alternate taking on the position of dean. In addition to being the chief academic administrator of his faculty, Kant as dean had to serve on the academic senate that oversaw the governance of the university, deciding on disputes, complaints, and all sundry issues that sully the life of the mind. He was also supposed to administer exams to some eighty incoming students each year. This last task, apparently, was one bridge too far. He didn't even try to take it seriously, declaring himself satisfied if a student didn't exhibit "extreme neglect."[3] In typical Kantian fashion, though, he justified this lassitude with a maxim, declaring that "trees grow better when they stand and grow outside, and they bring more fruit this way than if they were grown by artifice."[4]

By the mid-1770s, Kant's writing on all manner of subjects, his inaugural dissertation and the debate it sparked among the most influential German thinkers, and his great popularity as a lecturer had made him famous in German academic circles. In 1778 the Prussian minister of education asked him if he would consider moving to Halle, one of the most prestigious universities in the realm, for a salary more than double what he earned in Königsberg. When Kant demurred, the minister raised the offer by another third and sweetened it with the honorific of royal courtier. But Kant did not want to move.[5] He had, as he wrote in a letter to one friend, "all that I wished for, namely a peaceful situation that is exactly fitted to my needs: in turn occupied with work, speculation, and society, where my easily affected, but otherwise carefree, mind and my even more capricious body . . . will be occupied without strain."[6]

In this ambience of comfort and stability, what Kant called society played a significant role. He frequented noble households for dinner, where he would usually occupy the place of honor next to the lady of the house. He had his good friends, such as the Englishman Joseph Green, with whom he kept regular company. But he also enjoyed mingling with people from different social classes. Ever a bachelor, Kant didn't keep a household in the conventional sense and always took his meals in restaurants and pubs, where he would happily engage in conversations with anyone who cared to join him. His only aversions were to pretension and to those who might make him work during his leisure time, plying the professor with questions about his writings or lectures. Indeed, he ceased to frequent one tavern when he was approached there once too often by men who joined his table "without being invited, expecting that he would lecture them at lunch and answer their objections."[7]

If the company was important to him, the food had its place as well. Kant would make deals with restaurant owners to secure the best meat and, importantly, wine. When he found a dish he particularly liked, he would compliment the chef and ask for the recipe—more out of curiosity than intent, since he would never cook himself. He would also be honest about any shortcomings he perceived. As one commentator wryly remarked, perhaps the delay of Professor Kant's long-awaited expansion of his inaugural dissertation owed to his clandestine work on a different book altogether, *The Critique of the Art of Cooking*.[8]

Indeed, Kant's great contribution to philosophy was taking longer to appear than he had expected. When he sent a colleague a copy of his dissertation in 1770, he added a note promising he would soon finish outlining "a position from which all sorts of metaphysical questions can be examined according to wholly certain and easy criteria," an endeavor he thought possible in "a rather small space" and needing only a "few letters."[9] Thus began a decade-long procrastination punctuated by intermittent declarations of an imminent publication, followed by longer periods of silence. Even his family grew restless. In July 1773 his brother Johann Heinrich wrote to him complaining of their long separation and wondering if he couldn't get a peek at Kant's ideas before they appeared on every bookstore shelf in Germany.[10] Toward the end of the same year he let it be known to correspondents that they could expect a finished version by the following Easter. When the book again failed to materialize, the German-speaking intellectual world began to grumble. As Johann Kaspar Lavater, a popular writer and author of a world-renowned guide to the science of physiognomy, wrote to the truant professor, "Say something to me even in a couple of lines. Are you dead? Why do so many write who cannot—and you, who write so exquisitely, write nothing? Why are you silent? Are you asleep?"[11]

Kant was not sleeping. In truth he was working overtime. But the problem he was working on had become much bigger. In his dissertation Kant had divided the intellectual and the sensible worlds into separate realms. The former consisted of unconditional truths; the latter consisted of judgments that were always contingent on some other state of affairs. As he worked on that problem, he realized that mixing the two realms—treating, that is, intellectual ideas as if they had extension in space and duration in time or taking mere sensory impressions for inexhaustible and incontrovertible truths—would inexorably lead thinkers to untenable contradictions. As he later reflected, "At first I saw this theory only in shadow. I tried very seriously to prove propositions and their opposites, not in order to justify a dubious theory but because I suspected I might discover an illusion of the understanding."[12]

By 1769, as he was engrossed in finishing his dissertation, the nature of that illusion had become clear to him. When we ask the most fundamental questions—what is the soul, what is the world in its totality, what is God?—our answers may be equally convincing even while utterly opposed to one another.[13] The only way this could be the case, Kant realized, was if we were mistaken about which world we were trying to describe; if, in other words, we failed to distinguish whether we were speaking about the world of the senses or the world of ideas.

If we consider space and time as an idea, any distance or moment can be further divided: Achilles will never catch up with the tortoise; I will enjoy my cookie for eternity. Taken as a sensual experience, in contrast, Achilles runs past his opponent in seconds, and I'm left wistfully eyeing my empty plate. Likewise, Kant reasoned, I can think of the entire universe as existing necessarily, programmed from the beginning of time to the end, or I can take the opposite tack and imagine that all I ever encounter are contingent, arbitrary impressions, none of which have any necessity.

These paradoxes, foreseen two thousand years earlier by Zeno, showed Kant the way. Achilles and his exasperating tortoise weren't a riddle to be solved. They were a sign that the history of philosophy had overlooked something essential about the very nature of reality itself. Achilles failed to catch the tortoise only because reason jumbled together two incompatible modes of thought and treated the *here* and *there* and the *now* and *then* of spatiotemporal existence as if they were relevant to eternal, immutable beings, and likewise treated the ineluctable mathematical fact of infinite divisibility as if it had purchase on a world in which warriors run, tortoises crawl, and cynical philosophers can just get up and walk.

Because he had grasped this truth with such clarity, it was no wonder that Kant thought he was months away from spitting out one whole coherent system. And what a system it would be. For Kant didn't just have in his sights a work that would delineate the respective worlds of sensibility and reason, and thus clarify what science can hope to know objectively. Kant now grasped that even this great advance was but the tip of an iceberg. For if such a system could be found, it would more than merely clarify the grounds of objective knowledge in the physical sciences. Astoundingly, it would also unlock a new science of art and morality, realms long thought to be either intractably subjective or beholden to God, authority, or tradition.

The problem was, something was still missing.

IN A LETTER TO the Swiss philosopher and polymath Johann Heinrich Lambert in September 1770, Kant hinted that his forthcoming book would include more than a treatise on the possibility of objective knowledge in science. Indeed, he already envisioned a practical part, a "metaphysics of morals" that he would finish that winter. In June 1771 he wrote to Markus Herz, a Jewish student from Berlin who had become a close friend and correspondent, that the book was under way and would include a "sketch of the nature of aesthetics, metaphysics and morals."[14] A few years later, still teasing out the entire structure, he confessed to Herz his interest in completing the portion on morals first.[15]

Why did Kant feel compelled to bring morality at all into his quest to understand how humans come to know the world, much less grant it such a prominent place in his endeavor? In questions concerning morality, like those concerning knowledge, Kant leaned heavily on British thinkers like David Hume, who had attributed our willingness to do good for others to a kind of moral sensibility, a feeling of pleasure that arises when we act in a way benefiting others, even if that action might lead to our own disadvantage.

True to his skeptical tendencies, in his *Enquiry Concerning the*

Principles of Morals, Hume had tried to dispense with transcendental sources for knowing the right thing to do in any given situation. Instead, he proposed a theory of morals that relied on "no arguments but those which are derived from experience."[16] Hume said his experience had taught him that selfless action is an irreducible aspect of human behavior, universally admired and esteemed, and that "a tendency to public good, and to the promoting of peace, harmony, and order in society, does always, by affecting the benevolent principles of our frame, engage us on the side of the social virtues."[17] As with his forays into the question of what we can know, Kant attended to Hume's reasoning because it provided a kind of corrective to the rationalist approach that associated the moral law with God's will and naturally presumed to know what that must be.

Nevertheless, by 1770, Kant decided that the British approach suffered from a serious flaw. As he formulated the problem around that time, "The doctrine of moral feeling is more a hypothesis to explain the phenomenon of approval that we give to some kinds of action than one which could determine maxims and first principles that hold objectively and tell us how we should approve or reject something."[18] Kant was convinced that feelings of approval or disapproval of our or others' actions must depend on something else, "a necessary internal law that makes us view and feel ourselves from an external point of view."[19] Our mere feelings, be they of sympathy or anger, pleasure or pain, could never be the basis for knowing the right thing to do, because they were always contingent, always subject to the vicissitudes of a shifting world tossed around in space and time. For Kant, the changeability of the spatiotemporal world undermined the very idea of something being right or true, which required, nay, sprang from, permanence in the face of change. The right thing to do, whatever it was, had to be unconditional. Herz wrote back to Kant that the idea made him tremble: should Kant discover such a moral law as it applied to all men, it alone would become the study worthy of a scholar.[20]

By the first years of the 1770s, Kant realized that a solution to one problem—how we know that our science yields objectively true laws and not merely a concatenation of arbitrary impressions—could lead him to the solution to other key problems: how to determine what is right and just in a world of variable norms; or how to know what is truly beautiful in a world of changing tastes and fashions. At the same time, seeing that these were all parts of one and the same question focused Kant's mind on a common difficulty underlying all of them. In a now famous letter from February 1772, Kant confessed to Herz that he "still lacked something essential, something that in my long metaphysical studies I, as well as others, had failed to pay attention to and that, in fact, constitutes the key to the whole secret."[21]

In his dissertation Kant had already determined that a crucial class of human knowledge must be independent of the sensual world. For instance, the definition of a triangle and the rules we derive about the relations among its three sides and angles are true and will remain true regardless of whether we ever encounter a triangle in our lives, and no triangular entity we do encounter will ever correspond perfectly to its ideal counterpart. The knowledge that we derive from a discipline like mathematics is a priori true; that is, it is true on its own merits and never derives a posteriori from our experiences in the world. Such intellectual representations "must have their origin in the nature of the soul [since] they are neither caused by the object nor bring the object into being." However, as Kant went on in his letter to Herz, "I silently passed over the further question of how a representation that refers to an object without being in any way affected by it can be possible. . . . [I]f such intellectual representations depend on our inner activity, whence comes the agreement that they are supposed to have with objects?"[22]

Kant had run headlong into a problem of his own making. He had tried to mend the differences between philosophers who believed that all we could know came from our senses, and would thus always remain contingent and uncertain, and those who believed that an ultimate code determined the world and the way we perceived it, eternal and unconditioned by anything else. His solution, to say that both worlds existed and that each side of this philosophical debate neglected one or the other, now posed a major problem for him. How could the two worlds ever communicate?

Kant now realized that the entire history of philosophy had been struggling with this very problem and that, in every case, philosophers had missed the point. On one side radical empiricists like Hume had given up hope that humans could find a dependable basis for deriving the laws of nature, or they had assumed that any tendency to do good was simply a fact of the world, due to the "benevolent principles of our frames," and that rigid notions of the law and justice were a superfluous overlay to instinctual behaviors.[23] On the other side, philosophers from Plato all the way to Leibniz, who did believe humans could successfully come to know the world as it is and derive laws for the Good or the Beautiful, implicitly attributed the cause for this knowledge to God: if we can know the deepest nature of reality, that's because some deity has planted a knowledge of unchanging things in our souls from the beginning or has guided the flow of our existence by way of a "preestablished harmony." But such a deus ex machina was intolerable to Kant, for whom it not only represented "the greatest absurdity one could hit upon in the determination of the origin and validity of our knowledge," but also had the additional disadvantage of encouraging "all sorts of wild notions and every pious and speculative brainstorm."[24] Indeed, Kant now knew that one of the pressing needs of his philosophy would be to cleanse humans of their destructive tendency to theorize about God and the spirit world, or use religion to say something meaningful about the world of the senses.[25]

By the time he sent his letter to Herz, Kant already knew how the components of his system needed to come together. "Without going into details here," he wrote, "now I am in a position to bring out a

'Critique of Pure Reason' that will deal with the nature of theoretical as well as practical knowledge"—which he then, with characteristic sunniness, promised to deliver in the next three months.[26] What did Kant see? And why did it take so much longer than three months to get it into print? As he would later put it, this was his Copernican Revolution. Like Copernicus removing the earth from the center of creation, Kant had decided to do away with a fundamental presupposition common to all attempts to describe how humans come to know the world: namely, that what we are trying to understand is the world itself. What we are really trying to understand, he now saw, *is our picture of the world.* And our natural tendency to think we are speaking about the world is what must be subjected to critique. Thus would be born a new "age of critique" that would initiate the downfall of humanity's submission to the age-old idols of its own creation. This would be called Enlightenment.[27]

The essence of his revolution was Kant's realization that the very coherence of the picture we make of the world depended on conditions that must hold true for a being who exists in time and space—that is, for a being for whom things are located in relation to one another and events succeed one another—to come to know anything at all. For sensory input to become knowledge of the world requires that objects be located in respect to other things, and that events be sequenced as coming before, after, or simultaneous to other events. But locating objects in respect to one another in space, or sequencing events in time, is something that pure sense perception on its own cannot accomplish. Beings who experience the world through sensory exposure need to unify and organize that exposure. In the case of our experience of the spatial relations of objects, for instance, we do this by implicitly presupposing that they exist simultaneously in a shared space. However, just like Hume diving into his impressions and not finding himself there, when we explore the space around us, we encounter things extended across it but not the space itself. Indeed, try to imagine erasing the stuff around you, item by item. First the people and furniture go. Then the architecture. Then the natural world around you. The light, the air, everything goes. What's left is space itself, and yet what's left, if we are truly deleting everything, is simply emptiness. There's no *there* there. As Kant wrote in the *Critique*, "The simultaneity of substances in space cannot be cognized in experience otherwise than under the presupposition of an interaction among them; this is therefore also the condition of the possibility of the things themselves as objects of experience."[28] Like the self, space is not an object of experience but the very condition for experiencing objects.

The problems arise, Kant realized, when we then treat those conditions, those implicit necessary presumptions, as though they were actual stuff in the world. Consciousness, for instance, isn't for Kant some mysterious entity that needs to be explained; rather, it is nothing other than the necessary presumed unity that allows there to be a timeline against which I order and distinguish my perceptions. Likewise, the whole of space, the cosmos, is nothing other than a necessary projection that allows me to distinguish and order objects in relation to one another. As Borges would quip a century and a half later, we must suspect "that there is no universe in the organic, unifying sense of that ambitious word."[29]

The mental faculty responsible for these necessary projections of unity is, for Kant, the Reason in the title of his famous *Critique*. The ultimate purpose of the book, why he calls it a critique of reason, is that while reason's drive for unity is necessary for any experience of the world in space and time, that same faculty doesn't know its own strength. Reason's amazing ability to unify the disparate exposures of inherently limited beings into a coherent narrative tends to run roughshod over those same limitations. In the case of the self that can blur the differences in moments of space-time enough to allow objects to appear to us at all, reason turns a necessary condition of the possibility of experience into an independent substance, even endowing it with superpowers like the immortality of the soul.[30] In the case of the presumption of a shared space that unifies the manifold of our perceptions into objects, reason turns it into a "collective unity of a whole of experience."[31]

Such a collective unity, "an individual thing containing in itself all empirical reality,"[32] this all-encompassing whole—"*Deus sive natura*," Spinoza would call it, God or nature—only such a being could be truly unconditional, self-contained, and not contingent on anything else. A being containing everything, all at once, determining each of its parts from beginning to end. In his influential treatise *The Problems of Philosophy*, the English philosopher and mathematician Bertrand Russell declared that the goal of philosophy was to free itself from the biases of individual perspectives and to see the world "as God might see, without a *here* and *now*, without hopes and fears, . . . in the sole and exclusive desire of knowledge . . . as impersonal, as purely contemplative, as it is possible for man to attain."[33] But in practical terms, what would such a knowledge look like? The ideal of "seeing" the universe *sub specie aeternitatis* has existed for millennia, but those who have grappled deeply with this ideal have all tended to founder on the same shoal. As beings who must know the world in time and space, the notion of a knowledge unconstrained by time and space is quite simply inconceivable.

Take one metaphor for knowledge, that of sight. Sight grants us an image of the world, yes, but an exceedingly partial one. Not only do we see very few images in any given moment, but even when we envision an object, we can only ever do so one aspect at a time. Now try to generalize or expand on that ability. Even to stretch the visualization of a single object beyond a single facet quickly runs aground. What is a cube when simultaneously viewed from all six sides? We quickly see that freeing the constraints of our perspective in such a way doesn't sharpen our understanding of the cube; instead, it obliterates it. Indeed, the very "cubeness" or "cubity" of the cube depends on our *not* being able to see more than three sides at a time. When we start to push the boundaries of this thought ever wider, this limitation becomes all the more apparent. Not only all visual discernment but every possible form of knowledge we can obtain about the world depends, radically and entirely, on its limitations in time and space. Seeing everything simultaneously or knowing all time in the blink of an eye would obliterate the very connection between objects and instances that constitutes knowing. Thus, although god-like knowledge in its ostensible freedom from bias may seem like a desirable goal, its realization even in theory leads to an absolute contradiction in terms.

While individual cognition always presupposes an uncondi-tioned whole, this whole is itself never an object of perception or cognition, nor can it ever be. What I can know is always conditioned on an unconditioned whole that I must presume to exist but that remains unknowable. Put another way, the minimum condition of any experience whatsoever is not being a god, whether a god of very small things or of very large ones. And, as it happens, this pat-tern of projecting the existence of the cosmos as an unconditioned whole, and then receding to the limited sphere of human action, was the trick Kant fell upon to link the question of knowledge with the question of morality, and that opened the door onto his critical system.

By turning his gaze to the question of what is necessary for an object to appear in the first place, or what is necessary for a moral question to emerge in the first place, Kant realized that there were basic principles that would apply in all cases—at least for any being like us, whose basic form of existence was to be located in space and time and limited in what it can see and know. For while what we say about the world may never be universal, necessary, and true, we nonetheless *can* derive universal, necessary, and true statements from the very faculties that allow us to experience the world. For this to happen we must presume a unified subject, even though we cannot grasp it as an object, operating in a unified space-time whole, even if we cannot grasp that as an object either. We presuppose those unified substances as if they were objects of cognition for an eter-nal being, but then accept that they are not ours to know, that we are fundamentally limited to representations of that whole in space and time. And it is those representations we study when we do science, not the fundamental nature of the world itself. To put it in the words Heisenberg would use so many years later, in physics "we have to remember that what we observe is not nature in itself but nature exposed to our method of questioning."[34]

Likewise, while we can't derive universal, necessary, and true laws governing our duty by observing a bunch of customs and presuming they approximate the moral law, we can derive unconditional duties from what would be the condition of the possibility of our asking in the first place what the right thing to do is. For this to happen, we must generalize from our inclinations, then survey different practices and compare them with those inclinations, and finally ask ourselves whether there is something we *ought* to be doing differently. We thus presume an independent, unconditional standard for our actions, the way a perfect being would behave and a way we should behave that would be other than simply doing what we feel like doing. And yet an actually omniscient and omnipotent being for whom all time and space were immediately present would suffer no ignorance, no blindness, and for that reason have no possibility of making any decision, ethical, unethical, or otherwise. The freedom to choose, and choose poorly, is thus intrinsic to not being God.

When Kant realized that our knowledge must presume an unconditioned whole and then pull back from it and see itself as conditioned or limited by that whole, when he saw that in a similar way our morality must presume an unconditioned duty as a standard against which to judge its own conditional behaviors, he accomplished two things. On the one hand, he realized that accepting those intrinsic limitations would enable science to know more exactly what it measures and would enable morals to determine more exactly how we should behave. On the other, he showed how our natural tendency to extend our epistemological and moral certainty beyond those limitations will produce untenable paradoxes, unless we account for and limit that tendency.

In a word, Kant came to terms with not being God.

IN THE LAST YEARS of the 1770s, Kant had settled into a comfortable rhythm. After a good meal with one of his friends, he would take a long walk down to the river, maintaining that nothing freed the mind for important thoughts like a good walk in the fresh air. One of his early biographers would claim that this pathway, which would later be dubbed "the philosophical footpath," was as responsible as anything else for giving birth to *The Critique of Pure Reason.*[35] But pleasant strolls on their own might not have been enough to get Kant across the finish line if it hadn't been for a novel. The novel was a satire of professorial lassitude written by Theodor Gottlieb von Hippel. The main character, lampooned as "Professor Grand-father," has settled into the comforts of his position and ceased work entirely, becoming like "stagnant water." Kant laughed with other readers at first—until he realized, with the publication of the book's second volume the following year, that he was the butt of the joke. A decade of silence from Germany's most famous thinker had taken its toll.[36]

Message loud and clear. Kant stopped dawdling and started writing. The months leading up to publication were a whirlwind of productivity. But when the *Critique* finally hit the bookstores, the initial response was perplexity. Here was the book his public had been awaiting for years, and now that it had arrived, hardly anyone could understand it. As the grenade-lobbing Hippel would put it in a letter to another reader, "Have you read Kant's Critique? There's a darkness in it that is trying to picture itself. Too highfalutin for me. What can help me rid myself of it?" For his part, Hamann would write to Herder in October 1781, "I'm in my third reading of Kant's book and am stuck. I think I'm going to need a fourth."[37] Still, the multiple reads would eventually pay off. People soon began to grasp what Kant had accomplished. The age of critique Kant had foreseen was born.

If Kant went through a period of silence in the decade leading up to the publication of *The Critique of Pure Reason*, in the years that followed he didn't seem to shut up. Indeed, Kant's production for the ensuing decade was nothing short of monumental. Not only did he write a major popular introduction to moral philosophy, the *Groundwork for the Metaphysics of Morals*—perhaps still his most widely read book—but he followed that with the full exposition of his moral philosophy, *The Critique of Practical Reason*; an important second edition of *The Critique of Pure Reason*; a book on the foundations of the natural sciences; and finally, at the end of the decade, his extraordinary third *Critique*, focusing on questions of aesthetic judgment, all punctuated by several widely read essays that set the tone of national philosophical debate about politics and history. Amid this flurry of activity Kant, who was by now getting on in years, also lectured extensively and, of course, continued to answer the call of his institutional duties, serving as dean several times during this period.

He also bought a house. While no longer subject to the uncertainties of renting his quarters, as he had his entire professional life to that point, Kant now began to learn the headaches of being a homeowner. As he prepared to move in, he hired a general contractor, to whom he initially expressed his gratitude, writing to him that in taking over the supervision of his building, "you have thus taken a great worry from me because I am entirely ignorant in such things. I have no doubt that the master craftsmen, whom I have told to follow your instructions, will follow them without objections."[38]

Unfortunately, the craftsmen in question didn't quite live up to Kant's expectation. They proposed renovations that ended up being impossible; they purchased too many bricks; and, naturally, they pushed back the agreed-upon completion date, causing Kant considerable worry as to whether he would have a home to live in by the time he vacated his rental. In short, Kant finally found an anchor of certainty in a world of change—the unreliability of contractors.

Kant had also made the unfortunate choice of purchasing property that abutted the city's prison. If he had reason to criticize false piety before, the theatrically loud prayers of the inmates, with which they intended to publicize their good intentions in a desperate appeal for clemency, were driving him batty. Within days of having moved into his new house, Kant wrote a letter of complaint in which he not-too-subtly suggested that the prisoners might have less reason "to complain about the presumed danger to the salvation of their souls" if they were to sing with the windows closed, and perhaps even "without screaming with all their might."[39]

While his perception of false piety served as the trigger for this complaint, it also lay in the background of Kant's thinking on morality in general. As he had already shown in his *Critique of Pure Reason,* while positing something like God, an unconditioned and absolute creator, was a logical necessity for thinking through the conditions of possibility of knowledge in time and space, such a being could only be presupposed as an idea, a kind of ultimate guarantor of coherence, about whom we can know and say nothing of substance. Claims to know anything more could only ever devolve into fanaticism in one's own interest or, worse, in the interests of some authority intent on depriving a subject of her freedom. As might be expected, raising such points threatened to trespass on the domain of those who had reason to think that they, and not Professor Kant, were the appropriate arbiters in matters of faith.

In early 1792, Kant submitted an essay to a widely circulated monthly in Berlin with the title "On Radical Evil in Human Nature." After it appeared in April of that year, Kant immediately submitted another essay, this one called "Of the Struggle of the Good Principle with the Evil Principle for Sovereignty over Man." But when his Berlin editor presented this paper to the royal censors this time, they rejected it, explaining that while Kant's first essay was philosophical in nature, the second trod into the realm of theology. In the end Kant got around the censors by including both articles as chapters in a book titled *Religion Within the Limits of Reason Alone,* which was eventually approved for publication by the philosophical faculty of the University of Jena and appeared in print in 1793.

In this book Kant threw down the gauntlet, declaring that existing religions should be understood as historically specific vehicles for what he called the religion of pure reason. Any given religion, its practices, and local beliefs were like an outer, changeable garment enveloping an inner, universal truth of morality. Kant now proposed to translate Christian doctrine into these universal moral truths. Whereas the battle in his two most important books on ethics had been between personal inclinations and universal duty, he now shifted this to a struggle between two kinds of maxims: good ones, which abide by the moral law and take as their lodestar only universal aims; and evil ones, which are corrupted by our inclinations. The problem lay in distinguishing the two kinds of maxims. How can we know for sure that we are following a selfless maxim rather than one that hides within it a kernel of personal gratification?

Kant recognized in this problem something he had seen in his work on pure reason: an antinomy.[40] Either one's maxims are pure of personal gratification, or they are not. If they are pure, then one is born with only good in one's heart and cannot be personally credited for having chosen a righteous path. If, on the other hand, one's maxims are corrupt from the start, how would it be possible for a human to make the choice to extirpate those evil maxims, "since extirpation could occur only through good maxims, and cannot take place when the ultimate subjective ground of all maxims is postulated as corrupt."[41] The only way out of this dilemma, he saw, was to posit as an axiom that people must be responsible for what they become, even if one can never point to an actual moment when one can know that one is free from any and all determinations. If we didn't posit this freedom, Kant went on to clarify, a person "could not be held responsible . . . and could therefore be *morally* neither good nor evil."[42]

And this act—presupposing our ultimate freedom and responsibility as if we were a free and unconditioned agent, despite being immersed in a world of contingencies that we cannot control—translates into the language of moral philosophy the core idea of Christianity, namely, the incarnation of God's eternal perfection in the temporal world. Like a finite human embodying the infinite ideal of God, the person who presupposes freedom in this way is only then willing to sacrifice selfish inclinations through hard work, discipline, remorse, all in the service of a universal ideal. Indeed, in his own land's reigning religious doctrine Kant had found a historical example of the very method he had derived for determining what we can know for certain about scientific or moral laws. One presupposes a self-contained cosmos that one can never fully know, one presupposes a perfect moral law that one can never fully embody, precisely to derive the standards of what one can know and ought to do.

Kant's translation of Christianity into his own system of moral philosophy earned him the opprobrium of the censors in Berlin. But it also revealed something profound about the origins of some of his deepest philosophical insights. Kant had inherited his belief in the moral law through Martin Luther, who in turn had learned it from Saint Augustine. Luther believed God's commands were given to humans despite their inability to infallibly follow them, just as parents urge their children to walk before it is physically possible for them to do so.[43] Augustine, for his part, had understood this conflict to be essentially between humanity's temporal nature and God's eternal truth.[44]

This idea, so powerfully expounded by Augustine in his narrative of conversion to Christianity, had its roots in a tradition of thought that circulated around the Mediterranean basin in the first centuries CE, when the cult of Christianity was emerging in fits and starts. Its proponents were many and varied, but one stands out. He was an Egyptian by the name of Plotinus, and in his book *The Enneads* he expounds the doctrine of time as the moving image of eternity that was so influential to Augustine and that seeped into the ground-waters of Kant's intellectual upbringing.

Curiously, it was this very book that Borges was reading as he searched for respite from his overwhelming despair and that inspired him to create the fiction that would turn him into one of the most influential writers of the twentieth century. In the next chapter we will see how Borges used these ideas to recover from his depression even as he explored the antinomy of a total and unconditioned knowledge.

6

IN THE BLINK
OF AN EYE

I N THE YEAR 325 the Roman emperor Constantine called for an
assembly of Christian bishops to gather in the town of Nicaea,
now Iznik in modern-day Turkey. While it may seem arcane to
many of us today, the theological question at hand was of burning
importance to those in attendance. On one side of the room were
ranged those who were convinced by the teachings of Arius, a presby-
ter from Egypt who held that God the Father should be understood
as separate and hence superior to Jesus the Son, whom God had
created and who in turn must have had an origin in time. Aligned
against the Arians were the adherents of Eustathius, the bishop of
Antioch, who countered that Jesus could not be secondary to God
but must be understood as an equal and hence also eternal manifestation of God's substance in human form. Such was the force of
Eustathius's arguments that the assembly of bishops voted almost
unanimously to adopt this view and declare Arianism a heresy.[1]

Born some thirty years after the bishops met in Nicaea, Saint
Augustine of Hippo adopted and codified the idea of Jesus's full

and equal participation in God's divinity despite having been born, lived, and died as a man.[2] Indeed it was his nuanced interpretation that provided Augustine with the defense he needed against Arianism, since it allowed Jesus to be both human and divine, an incarnation in the temporal world of God's unalterable eternity, the "mediator between you the One and us the many, who live in a multiplicity of distractions by many things."[3]

What Saint Augustine was expounding was the mystery of the Incarnation, the theological centerpiece to Christianity, repeated each week since the early centuries of the church by its millions of adherents when they intone in unison that Christ is "true God from true God, begotten not made, consubstantial with the Father."[4] This Nicene Creed emerged from the conference called by Constantine in 325, but Augustine was drawn to it primarily because it solved (or at least encapsulated) for him the fundamental mystery of human existence. How do limited, temporal beings like us participate in the universal, eternal All that is God? We can do so only partially, he decided, because there is one who does so fully, one who is both man, and hence was born, lived, suffered, and died, and also divine, and hence embodies without any loss or difference the entirety of God's universal being. Augustine had learned of this mystery by reading Plotinus.

Plotinus was born in the early years of the third century CE in Egypt, then an outpost of the Roman Empire. As a young man he studied the revitalized Greek philosophy flourishing at the time, but he had heard rumors of a great fount of wisdom in the East. Curious to learn more, he enlisted in the army of the emperor Gordian III and joined his doomed campaign to conquer Persia. Afterward he settled in Rome and quickly ascended the ranks of the capital's most respected teachers. He followed a strict Pythagorean practice in his dress and eating habits, abjuring all meat, and his teachings took on a mystical, personalized flair.[5]

Of particular interest to Plotinus was the concept of eternity, which would prove so inspiring to Augustine. Plotinus didn't conceive of eternity as an endless, boring extension of the present. Instead, he imagined eternity as everything, all existence, all space, and all time, captured at once, in the blink of an eye. Eternity wasn't the endless expansion of time; it was the absolute negation of time. We humans experience things in time because we are limited and cannot fully grasp the absolute unity of all things. The time we inhabit, he taught, is nothing but the moving image of eternity, an insignificant second hand sweeping over the face of a vast, immobile clock, never grasping more than a fraction of its surface. However, we could be certain that this eternity existed. For, as Kant would also see a millennium and a half later, our very ability to experience any given moment in time logically necessitates the existence of a reality that transcends those moments, a greater unity that "upholds things, that they not fall asunder."[6]

Augustine turned Plotinus's vision into a personal, existential quest. He called his life a "distension in several directions" and saw himself "scattered in times whose order" he didn't understand.[7] Christ's incarnation of God's total, all-encompassing being promised him the only path to salvation, a path that leads from the "storms of incoherent events" tearing to pieces the entrails of his soul, to "that day when, purified and molten by the fire of your love, I flow together to merge into you."[8] But for all its personal urgency, Augustine's quest would become a universal touchstone, his idea of eternity the ultimate template for the desire that animates our fallen, temporal lives.

BY EARLY 1934, BORGES had sunk into the black bile of despair. His stories and poems from that time reek of death and are pockmarked with razor-sharp references to suicide. In one story, an actor receives a passionate onstage kiss from his beloved, only to be rebuffed in her dressing room—after which he offs himself. In another, a medical student suffering from feelings of inadequacy enters a pawnshop to purchase a revolver but deviates from his intent at the last moment, buying instead a phonograph with the money he would have spent on ending his life.[9]

If the second story vaguely suggests art as a path to redemption, for Borges that path would stretch on for several more excruciating years, during which the solace of death never ceased to beckon. Yet thankfully, for posterity and the world of letters, he managed to resist temptation. And what kept him afloat, even if only barely, was a small, nagging problem. The problem of eternity.

Granted this problem wasn't new. (How could it be?) Borges had obsessed about infinite time already in the 1920s in essays like the one on Achilles and the tortoise, or the one titled "The Duration of Hell." In these cases and others, he grappled with the idea of eternity as the endlessness of time, be it internally, as one chops it into ever smaller pieces, or externally, in the hell of quite literally one damned thing after another. Each of these visions tormented him with the afterimage of a lost love, ever receding in the drift of time. With his new thoughts on eternity, however, Borges added another dimension to his approach. He started rereading Plotinus.

His daily life shrouded in the misery of depression, Borges fell hard for the gravitational pull of Plotinus's vision of eternity. This was not the bad infinity of one day of suffering after another (after another . . .) that plagued his contemplation of the duration of hell; nor was it the obliteration of the self that he saw as somehow worse. Here beckoned a vision of utter plenitude, simultaneously grasped, with no toll paid to the ravages of time. Here was Perfection. Here was Bliss. And yet Borges could still not find a satisfactory explanation for how we participate in the eternal if, as Plotinus had put it, humans are always in time.[10] There could be only one answer. Something in us escapes the temporal, even as we inhabit that realm.

It was this something that Borges glimpsed as he paged through his worn copy of Plotinus. To be human, Borges saw, is to straddle the impossible border between ephemerality and eternity, loss and permanence. From the vantage of a sifting, vanishing time we project an eternity hopelessly out of reach. Like the exile who, "with a melting heart," recalls "expectations of happiness," we "gather up all the delights of a given past in a single image."[11] Eternity is nostalgia, the inextinguishable desire for what we've lost.[12]

Not everything was doom and gloom, though. In 1932, Borges had met a writer some fifteen years his junior by the name of Adolfo Bioy Casares. They were introduced to each other at a luncheon hosted by the writer and socialite Victoria Ocampo, to whose great exasperation the two men promptly withdrew from the other guests and fell into deep private conversation about, naturally, books. When she urged them not to be "such shits" and to come back and talk to her guests, they opted to leave instead so they could continue their conversation un-harangued.[13]

Unlike Borges, who couldn't have been more of a city slicker, Bioy was a scion of the landed gentry. He was studying law in Buenos Aires when they met but soon ditched his studies—ostensibly to dedicate himself to his family's lands, but really to free himself for a pursuit much closer to his heart: reading and writing. A few years after bailing on Ocampo's luncheon, Bioy invited Borges to stay with him at his estancia not far from the city. Borges did his best to adapt to the environs, going so far as to claim he knew how to ride—a fiction soon debunked by his propensity to slide off the far side of every horse he tried to mount.[14]

Shortly after Borges's strange little book *A History of Eternity* appeared to bewildered reviews in 1936, Bioy became one of the few people to purchase it. In addition to the essay on Plotinus, another on Nietzsche's concept of the eternal return, and a discussion of competing translations of the *One Thousand and One Nights*, Borges had included a brief review of two versions of an obscure Indian novel. Bioy was so captivated by Borges's review that he ordered the novel from a bookseller in London, only to learn that it didn't exist. Bioy had become one of the first to fall for what would become a standard Borgesian trick—inserting fictions into the real world in the form of obscure footnotes, invented references, or seemingly scholarly studies of concocted writers.

The little review that so confused Bioy dealt with a novel called *The Approach to Al-Mu'tasim,* ostensibly authored by a Bombay-based attorney named Mir Bahadur Ali. The novel first appeared in 1932 in an edition so cheap "its paper was virtually newsprint," with promotional copy touting it as the first detective novel written by a Bombay native. Accolades in the local press spurred Bahadur Ali to release an updated, illustrated edition in 1934. This is the one that was then purportedly reprinted in London "with a foreword by Dorothy L. Sayers, but with the (perhaps merciful) omission of the illustrations"[15]—the version, of course, that Bioy unsuccessfully attempted to track down.

The (nonexistent) novel tells the story of a law student who falls in with the worst kind of people, men who seem not to possess the slightest spark of decency. Amid such ethical squalor, the student one day witnesses a single act of kindness, a "moment of tenderness . . . in one of the most abominable men." Thunderstruck, the student hypothesizes that he must be seeing in this roughneck a trace of goodness left by another person—a friend the man once had, one who perhaps had been likewise imprinted by another friend before him—and he comes to the conclusion that *somewhere in the world there is a man from whom this clarity, this brightness, emanates.*[16] The student follows the traces from person to person until he at last arrives at the store of a modest bookseller in Persia, at the back of which a glowing light emanates from behind a tawdry curtain. The student calls out the name he has since learned, Al-Mu'tasim; a voice bids him enter and the novel ends.

The idea of being thunderstruck by an unexpected act of decency recalls something Kant once wrote about the call of duty. What astonished Kant about the moral law was how it ensured that humans would always be more than mere servants to their base desires, more than cogs in the giant machine of nature, blown every which way by the fluctuations of time and place. We see evidence for the existence of this moral law everywhere, he said; in the least impressive of our fellows, in the most abominable of men, we can at times glimpse an act of righteousness, a spark of goodness. And when we do, Kant wrote, we can feel our spirit bow down in respect, even if we wish to resist that feeling and remain aloof.[17]

Like Kant, the student in Bahadur Ali's book witnesses an unexpected act of goodness and feels his spirit bow down. But then he does more. Instead of recognizing there the influence of a universal moral law, he decides the goodness must have a specific source, an embodiment. One person who incarnates all that goodness, all that selflessness. One person who has left his trace on others, a trace the student must follow. An incarnation of goodness in a fallen world.

In this fragmentary, cryptic story the first bloom emerged of a radical new style nourished by the loam of ancient thought: a work of fiction disguised as a review or scholarly article, replete with footnotes mixing real and imagined sources, all in the service of excavating some mysterious source. The mystery ignites a quest, a search for some being, place, book, or poem that incarnates a unity we yearn for but can never achieve—eternity, as Borges put it, in the style of desire.

Astonishingly, inevitably, what we see emerge here is the same insight Kant fell upon as he sought to unify his system in the years leading up to his *Critique:* that the very idea of temporal and spatial diversity requires us to posit an ultimate unity that can never itself be the subject of our experience, but one we nonetheless endow with reality and incarnate as the object of our deepest desire. For Kant that object of desire was both the motor of science and what reason needs to guard against, lest we ever believe we've found it. For Borges that object is the motor of literature, indeed of life, and yet, in story after story, he always sounds a note of caution. For as Borges would learn, to find that object, to enter that ultimate reality, is something no temporal being could ever survive.

.   .   .

WHEN BORGES WAS THIRTEEN years old, his father, Jorge Guillermo Borges, published a trio of poems under the common title "Momentos." In them, the disillusioned lawyer whose mother had emigrated from England lamented the passing of time, the loss of those moments of love and ecstasy that we yearn for but that then pass in the blink of an eye, only to be looked back on in regret and longing.[18] Perhaps under the influence of a midlife crisis, perhaps wishing to rekindle his romance with his wife, Leonor Acevedo, Jorge Guillermo decided to move his family to Europe, eventually to live in the country of his mother's family. The first stop, however, would be Geneva, Switzerland. There the couple's two children, Jorge Luis and his sister (who happened to be named Norah), could stay safely under the care of Leonor's mother, while the grown-ups toured the capitals of Europe in search of lost time.

World history upset these best-laid plans. War broke out while the lovebirds toured Germany, so they rushed back to neutral Switzerland and enrolled Jorge Luis in the school founded by John Calvin. They apparently didn't think this a necessary step for Norah, who took painting lessons at home and would eventually enter the École des Beaux-Arts.[19] Unlike Norah, who learned to love Geneva and whose French became so fluent she would start inserting French words into their conversations at home, Georgie didn't thrive. Even back in Argentina, speaking his own language, he had been mercilessly bullied and usually kept to himself. Now with the additional barrier of a language he didn't know and didn't show much aptitude for, he became even more isolated.

While not much better at German, he did develop more of a taste for it and fell under the spell of Arthur Schopenhauer, of whom he would write, "If the riddle of the universe can be stated in words, I think these words would be in his writing."[20] Desiring to learn to read in this new language, he chose as one of the texts Kant's *Cri-*

tique of Pure Reason. Another was the Viennese writer Gustav Meyrink's novel *Der Golem,* about a Czech rabbi who tries to create life
and produces a monster instead. Understanding the mystical creation of life itself proved an easier lift than reading Kant. *The Golem*
ended up being the first book in German that Borges managed to
read in its entirety, and it landed on fertile ground.

Around this time, he made his first friends, two Jewish boys,
Maurice Abramowicz and Simon Jichlinski, both of whom shared
Borges's love of literature and ideas. Now seventeen, he began to
liberate himself from the confines of his family life, staying out late
with his friends, caught up in rapt conversations.[21] It's possible that
his great affinity for Jewish culture dates to these early friendships.
Indeed, Borges would later develop a passing familiarity with Jewish
mysticism, specifically with the writings of the Jewish philosopher
Gershom Scholem, whom he knew personally and named twice in
a poem inspired by Meyrink's novel (although he impishly claimed
to have used the philosopher's name only because he couldn't come
up with any other word that rhymed with "golem").[22]

According to Hassidic lore, the method for animating a golem
involved inscribing the Hebrew word for truth, *emet,* into the creature's forehead. Because the creature should be destroyed immediately upon creation, this would be done by erasing the first letter,
leaving behind *met,* or death. The letter to be erased, and hence the
very breath of life, was the first letter of the alphabet, aleph.[23] In
Borges's poem the rabbi eyes his monstrous creation with a mixture
of tenderness and horror, and asks himself, "Why did I decide to
add to the infinite series yet another symbol? Why to the vain skein
that unravels in the eternal did I add another cause, another effect,
another care?"[24] This tension between the eternal and the temporal
world of causes and effect is the same one that emerged in Borges's
review of Bahadur's apocryphal novel. And in that story's last line,
Borges pointed to another tradition as a precursor to this idea, the
same tradition he discussed in a short piece he wrote around the
same time called "A Defense of the Kabbalah."

Kabbalah refers to the practice of rabbinical interpretations that posited the Torah scrolls as shadows or copies of an eternal Torah written in fire. Kabbalists reasoned that, unlike the letters we human must contend with, scattered in times whose order we don't understand, those of the original and eternal Torah are not subject to the contingencies of space and time. Attempting to reconstruct that original timeless text, the kabbalists parsed the Torah through allegorical readings, numerology, and anagrams.[25] The *Sefer Yetzirah*, or *Book of Creation*, taught that the twenty-two letters of the Hebrew alphabet were God's building blocks, which God combined to come up with the complexity and variety of existence, starting with the first letter: "Aleph with all and all with Aleph; Beth with all and all with Beth; and so each in turn . . . [A]ll creation and all language come from one name."[26] Our languages, fallen far from their divine source, still carry those traces of divine inspiration; the older and more sacred a language, the closer it comes to that source. Thus, in the first phoneme of the first Hebrew letter, aleph, the kabbalists found the very power of naming, of creating, of engendering life itself.[27]

While the time in Geneva lasted longer than Jorge Guillermo had intended, it would eventually come to an end. Typically, this happened only once Georgie had finally grown a taste for it. Along with friends, he had also found love. Emilie, of green eyes and flowing red hair, a first and chaste romance that would cast the mold for a future, more devastating infatuation. His domineering mother, Leonor, foreshadowing future impediments, did not approve. The girl was working class. Borges's father, who once thought sending his bookish son to school with a dagger would solve his severe bullying problem, this time decided the boy should take someone to bed. He gave Georgie an address in the red-light district and pushed him out the door. The young man dutifully followed his father's instructions, but his anxiety mounted as he neared his goal. Not terribly confident even under normal circumstances, Georgie failed to perform. Traumatized, mortified, he went for a medical consultation and was diagnosed with a weak liver. His father decided it was time to leave Geneva, and Emilie, for climes that could warm up his son's tepid blood. Thus did Borges experience his first great heartbreak.[28]

Time is loss. Time is heartbreak. Time is desire for timelessness. Almost thirty years later, in the wake of a more momentous affair, Borges would bring this concatenation of influences and ideas together in a story that would become the eponymous tale in one of his most successful books and a story that for many readers around the world would come to exemplify his unique literary vision. In that story he imagined a villa in Buenos Aires where a mysterious object lay hidden under the cellar stairs. A disk only a few centimeters in diameter, containing within it all the space of the cosmos "with no diminution of size."[29]

Fittingly, he called that object an Aleph.

IN "THE ALEPH," BORGES's alter ego comes across (perhaps all too accurately in some respects) as a snobbish wet blanket of a man, haunting the villa and family of his departed beloved, Beatriz Viterbo. The villa, now inhabited by her poet cousin Carlos Argentino Daneri, has become Beatriz's de facto mausoleum. But the price he pays for the license reluctantly given to him to visit is having to read, and worse react to, Carlos Argentino's atrocious poetry. It turns out the man has nothing less in his sights than a poetic compendium, in almost no discernible order, of everything in existence. At the time of Borges's telling, he has put into verse such sundry climes as a stretch of the Ob River, a gas refinery in Veracruz, several hectares of land in Queensland, "and a Turkish bath not far from the famed Brighton Aquarium."[30]

Carlos Argentino's production of peripatetic poetry comes to a screeching halt when he calls the character Borges in a panic to tell him that his house is slated to be demolished by the property owners. While Borges begins to protest in horror at the loss of this shrine to Beatriz, Carlos Argentino praters on, bemoaning that the destruction of the house will make it impossible to write his poem. This is because, he clarifies to Borges, in one corner of the cellar there is an Aleph, "one of the points in space that contain all points."[31]

Borges's confusion quickly morphs into the suspicion that Carlos Argentino must be mad, which doesn't stop him from heading over to the villa to witness his psychotic breakdown in person. It is only after making his way down the darkened stairs and lying on the cellar floor at Carlos Argentino's bidding that he realizes his folly, that he has allowed himself to be "locked underground by a madman, after first drinking down a snifter of poison."[32] He closes his eyes for a moment, and the thought swiftly departs when he opens them and sees the Aleph.

At this point, he says, his telling of the tale runs into an irresolvable roadblock, "the enumeration, even partial enumeration, of infinity."[33] The Aleph, he writes, "was probably two or three centimeters in diameter, but universal space was contained inside it, with no diminution in size. Each thing (the glass surface of a mirror, let us say) was infinite things, because I could clearly see it from every point in the cosmos."[34]

Here follows one of the most captivating poetic lists in literary history, as Borges attempts what he has already declared impossible, namely, to enumerate the infinite. He details an extraordinary panoply of random moments and experiences, memories and perspectives, writing,

> I . . . saw a silvery spiderweb at the center of a black pyramid, . . . saw convex equatorial deserts and their every grain of sand, . . . saw a copy of the first English translation of Pliny (Philemon Holland's), saw every letter of every page at once . . . , saw tigers, pistons, bisons, tides, and armies, saw all the ants on earth, . . . saw the horrendous remains of what had once, deliciously, been Beatriz Viterbo, saw the circulation of my dark blood, . . . saw the Aleph from everywhere at once, saw the earth in the Aleph, and the Aleph once more in the earth and the earth in the Aleph, saw

my face and my viscera, saw your face, and I felt dizzy, and I wept, because my eyes had seen that secret, hypothetical object whose name has been usurped by men but which no man has ever truly looked upon: the inconceivable universe.[35]

This existence of everything, in the blink of an eye. The inconceivable universe, out there, at this very instant. Here, in one extraordinary run-on sentence, Borges managed to encapsulate a philosophical insight that catapulted him from the intimacy of love and loss to the edges of the knowable universe. This insight had coursed through the hidden veins of culture and science from Plato through Jewish mysticism to Christian revelation, from the *Critique* of Kant that he had read as a child to learn German to the very principle that Werner Heisenberg had unleashed contemporaneously with Borges's own brief moment of happiness, the flow of an afternoon in life that he had hoped to capture and transmute into eternity.

This is the insight that the Aleph expressed. To have a self, to experience anything at all, required the existence of the vast totality of space around him, of a past preceding him and a future yet to come. And yet that secret, hypothetical object, the inconceivable universe, was destined to remain hypothetical, secret, forever.

AT A PARTY HOSTED by Bioy in the winter of 1944, Borges met Estela Canto.[36] A journalist who was enjoying a rising reputation as a writer, Estela appreciated Borges's work but was unimpressed by his frumpy appearance, not to mention his apparent lack of interest in her. This changed when they met by chance on their way to another evening gathering at Bioy's house, and Borges suggested they walk together for a few blocks. The walk ended up taking several hours and led to a drink at a local bar. At one point in their conversation Estela quoted Bernard Shaw in English. This clearly caught Borges's attention, for she later recalled he mentioned specifically that it was the first time he had "come across a woman who likes Bernard Shaw."[37]

The two began to meet occasionally to stroll the city's streets. It was on one of these walks that Borges confided to Estela that he was at work on a story about "a place that contained all other places in the world."[38] On another occasion he showed up unannounced at her apartment with a gift. It was, he told her, an Aleph, and it would show her "all the objects in the world." When she undid the wrapping, all she found was a kaleidoscope. Her confusion did nothing to dampen his enthusiasm, however, and he babbled on about how he planned to make the story he was working on the first of many he would dedicate to her.[39]

Borges soon became fixated on the idea of Estela as his version of Dante's Beatrice, the girl the poet fell in love with, who died young and would reappear in his *Divine Comedy* to lead the poet from the depths of the inferno to the apotheosis of God's paradise. In that association he was certainly helped along by her name. Estela is a name derived from Latin and old French meaning "star." Each volume of the *Divine Comedy* ends with the same words, *le stelle,* the stars. The theme reached its climax in March 1945, when Borges invited Estela on an outing to a town just to the south of the capital where he had summered with his family as a child and spent a few, rare happy moments. Specifically, he wanted to take her to an inn, the Hotel Las Delicias. The inn had seen better days. As Estela would later recall, "The dining room, vast and badly lit, was almost empty. The food on the fixed-price menu was as bad as might be expected in a boardinghouse." Still, she noted, none of this seemed to bother him, and "he was happy and excited in this old dining room, which had been robbed of its former splendor."[40]

As they ate the mediocre fare and then later made their way across the equally shabby grounds, Borges cited passages from Dante's *Paradiso* in which Beatrice guides the poet to the mystic rose at the heart of God's eternal heaven, "which holds / the center still and moves all else around it."[41] In that vision, Dante described looking up at the center of all creation, where he "saw a point that sent forth so acute / a light, that anyone who faced the force / with which it blazed would have to shut his eyes, / and any star that, seen from earth, would seem / to be the smallest, set beside that point, as star conjoined with star, would seem a moon."[42] Reveling in the ecstasy of Dante's ethereal lines, Borges dropped to his knees and popped the question.

"I'd be very happy to, Georgie," Estela replied, "but don't forget that I'm a disciple of Bernard Shaw. We cannot get married without first going to bed with each other."[43]

While Borges at first took Estela's answer to be an affirmation, he apparently found it difficult to deliver the goods. His mode of courtship soon devolved into inviting Estela to tea at the home he shared with his mother, whose snobbery irritated Estela mercilessly. In the end, she would blame the old dame's behavior and Borges's cloying attachment to her for having "destroyed any possibility" of their relationship developing further.[44] In the meantime, though, Estela's presence in his life had given enough wings to his imagination for him to finally produce a successful story collection titled *The Aleph*.

AT THE OUTSET OF his essay on eternity, Borges made a passing, almost unnoticeable mention of something that had occurred some two decades earlier in a patent office in Bern, Switzerland. From that office burst a "relativist scare" that brought to light the problem of "synchronizing each person's individual time with the general time of mathematicians."[45] Indeed, one of the most profound of Einstein's discoveries in 1905 had been that our common notion of universal time had no basis in reality. This notion, codified by Newton in the image of God's clock ticking away behind all human perceptions and actions, seems, at first glance, an obvious assumption to make about reality: namely, that it exists, "out there," as a vast, simultaneous *now*. For each of us, this vast now consists of the form of the mental images we make of whatever else is happening in the world right now, at this very moment. My children asleep upstairs as I write these words; my friend in Boston making his morning coffee; my wife in Austria already up and about in the city; the *Perseverance* rover making its way across the surface of Mars; the James Webb Space Telescope training its mirrors on the origins of space and time. The problem is that vast now can only ever be a mental construction. That's because information, all information, takes time to travel. So, if I could look up through the ceiling to my kids, the information that they are sleeping would take some (admittedly, absurdly short) time to reach me. If my friend in Boston were to FaceTime with me while making his coffee, my experience would be imperceptibly delayed; slightly more for my wife in Austria. At 1.5 million kilometers away, the JWST would send emissions subjected to a noticeable lag. For its part the poor rover's rovings could take more than twenty minutes to arrive at my computer screen, depending on where Earth and Mars were in their orbits.

So, this vast present moment extends around us like an almost infinitely wide and infinitely thin disk of space-time and we just can't see it, right? Not exactly. While in the classical Newtonian view of the cosmos it makes sense to talk about a stable reality being shared right now throughout space, Einstein showed that this idea really depended on our ability to measure time and compare those measurements with one another. And this, of course, requires sending messages back and forth. Thus, it makes no sense to ask whether events are indeed happening at the same time or if they in fact happened at successive times until we measure them and communicate those measurements. But since measuring and comparing take time, not only can deciding if events were simultaneous only occur at a later time, whether they were in fact simultaneous will also change if one or both of the parties doing the measuring are in motion with respect to the other.[46] In other words, it turns out that there is no stable reality coinciding with what we imagine the present moment, out there in space, to be. Like Heisenberg's electron, it doesn't exist until we observe it.

And still, we imagine it. Like the Aleph below the stairs, we project the vast, inconceivable universe outward in space with every thought and every observation we make, just as we require a past from which we stem and a future toward which we hope. Such projections aren't arbitrary; they are implied by the most minimal experience. Yet to treat them as though they existed in that form on their own, outside our experience, is to treat our image of the universe, which contains all space and time, as if it were something in space and time. To treat it, in other words, as if it were real.

It isn't. And yet the dream of its reality has captivated the world from time immemorial and continues to hold us in its spell today.

From the darkened streets of his memories of loss, as he gazed hopefully onto vistas of new promise, Borges made out the contours of a poetic, scientific, and philosophical vision that had the power to shatter that spell. It was a vision that would unite physics and ethics in a strange, new architecture of the cosmos and an ultimate vindication of human freedom. But before reaching that point, Borges would follow that vision into a new antinomy, to the very paradoxical edge of a boundless universe, a universe he could start to glimpse from the twilight of his advancing blindness and the intricate passageways of a seemingly infinite library.

Part III

DOES THE UNIVERSE HAVE AN EDGE?

7

THE UNIVERSE
(WHICH OTHERS CALL
THE LIBRARY)

L ONG BEFORE HE GAINED fame as one of the world's most beloved writers of children's fiction, C. S. Lewis earned his reputation as a scholar of medieval literature. He taught this subject first at Oxford University before moving to Cambridge in 1954 to assume the newly created Chair of Medieval and Renaissance Literature, a position he would hold for the rest of his career. One of the subjects Lewis lectured on at both storied schools was how people in the Middle Ages imagined the cosmos.

Like Kant, Lewis was filled with awe by the starry skies above. On occasion he would invite his students to walk with him at night and look up at those skies, and challenge them to cast aside their accustomed, modern way of viewing the heavens. "Whatever else a modern feels when he looks at the night sky," he would tell them, "he certainly feels that he is looking *out*—like one looking out from the saloon entrance on to the dark Atlantic or from the lighted porch upon dark and lonely moors." But the cosmos didn't appear that way to the poets and natural philosophers of the Middle Ages, Lewis went on to explain. If you succeeded in seeing with medieval eyes, he told them, "you would feel like one looking *in*."[1]

What could it mean to look out at the night sky, or any sky for that matter, and feel that we are looking in? To do this, we might begin by imagining that the surface of the earth on which we stand is not curved convexly, bending away from the soles of our feet, but rather concavely, like the inside of a bowl, such that, way out there, beyond any visible horizon, the earth's surface slopes gently *up* to eventually encompass everything we see. In this inverted cosmos, no matter where we stood on the surface of the earth, we could stare straight up and point toward the exact same point. But even if we could manage to twist our minds around this way, we would surely be tempted to wonder *why* anyone would concoct such a bizarre cosmic architecture. The reason medievals did so stemmed from a long-standing debate about what it meant for the cosmos to be *somewhere* at all.

University life in thirteenth-century Europe was dominated by a movement now known as Scholasticism. The Scholastics' primary aim was to reconcile the teachings of Aristotle—whose works had arrived in Europe via the translations and commentaries of Arab philosophers—with their own culture's dominant Christian theology. One of the ideas they adopted from Aristotle was his physical model of the heavens: imagine our earth as a giant marble encased in multiple, nesting, perfectly smooth layers of glass, each moving independently of the one below it and carrying the orbs we see above us in the sky—the sun, the moon, the planets, the blanket of stars. The outermost of these spheres imparted its motion to the others without itself needing another sphere to contain it and give it motion. This primum mobile, or first mover, appealed mightily to Christians, just as it had to its Muslim importers—not least because it seemed to offer a physical embodiment of a popular and intuitive proof for the existence of God (who was, after all, a pretty good candidate for the ultimate cause for which no other cause is needed).

While God as the first mover made for a nifty trick, reconciling all of Aristotle's teachings with Christian ideas was more of a stretch. A particularly thorny problem arose from Aristotle's definition of what constitutes where something is. The place something occupies, he believed, is "the innermost, motionless surface of the containing body in direct contact with the contained body."[2] This was important because it helped explain the concept of motion: namely, an object's change in relation to its place. But if the outermost container of the cosmos itself had no container, how could it be said to move? Even more nerve-racking, if the cosmos as a whole had nothing surrounding it, might one not infer that it is impossible for anyone, even God, to move it?

In 1277 the bishop of Paris, one Stephen Tempier, had an answer for the Scholastics. He issued a proclamation ordering the university professors to stop instructing God what He couldn't do. The list of 219 Condemnations in the bishop's decree covered an enormous array of topics and censored specific books, but a good chunk of them dealt with the irksome (for the ecclesiastical authorities) hubris of philosophers who thought they had the standing to decide on God's limitations.

So God could, it seemed, make the cosmos move, even if there were nothing outside the cosmos *in which* to make it move. This then raised the head-scratching question of relative to what, exactly, the cosmos was moving. Luckily, the Scholastics had a number of thinkers to whom they could turn for help—specifically the Arab commentators and translators who had brought Aristotle's teachings to Europe. The most influential of these was named Ibn Rushd, a twelfth-century polymath from the south of Spain whose interpretations of Aristotle were so widely read and respected that he became known as the Arab Aristotle.

As a young man Ibn Rushd had been called into the presence of the sultan, himself a learned man, who had shown great interest in discussing deep theological questions. After some pleasantries and general inquiries about his family and provenance, the sultan jumped right into the deep end and, to the young philosopher's considerable alarm, asked him what people were saying about the heavens, specifically, "Are they eternal or created?"[3] Not surprisingly, Ibn Rushd had given this some thought. Indeed, his answer would ultimately leave its enduring imprint on Christian as well as Islamic theology. Aristotle had believed that the earth and the system of crystalline spheres encapsulating it had existed for all time. Monotheists like Ibn Rushd and his sultan, however, believed that God had created the cosmos, which seemed to suggest that it had a beginning in time. Ibn Rushd's response to this apparent contradiction was, in essence, to have his cake and eat it, too. The cosmos was both eternal *and* created by God.

Crucially, this solution had consequences for the place of the cosmos as well. Aristotle's giant system of nested crystalline spheres had *nothing* around it. But nothing couldn't really exist—nature, as the philosopher had taught, abhors a vacuum. So, what would you find if you managed to work your way to that outermost layer and tried to stick your hand out beyond it? Ibn Rushd's approach solved this tricky question, too. For just as the cosmos could be eternal—and hence have no beginning or *edge* in time—and yet still have been created by God, the cosmos could exist in space with nothing outside it—and hence have no edge in space—and yet still be something objectively movable for God. The cosmos could be said to be moving because its place was not determined by an external physical container; rather, it was determined by the very center it revolved around.[4] The cosmos was contained by its own central point.

Ibn Rushd's model, while not fully adopted by the theologians, had remarkable staying power. It was the model C. S. Lewis had in mind when he tried to reorient his students to medieval ways of viewing the heavens, although Lewis had his version not from Ibn Rushd but from its adaptation by Dante. As he wrote in *The Discarded Image*, "A few astonishing lines from the *Paradiso* ... stamp this [image] on the mind forever. ... The universe is thus, when our minds are sufficiently freed from the senses, turned inside out."[5]

The Italian poet's *Divine Comedy* recounts in first person the mystical journey of his alter ego through the gates of hell down through its nine circles to the lowest point of creation, literally the nether parts of Lucifer, buried upside down in ice. From the nadir of creation that is Satan's scrotum, the poet describes ascending to the surface of the earth, up the mountain of purgatory, and from there begins, in the third book, his ascent to the pinnacle of paradise. Improbably, bewilderingly, Dante managed to inscribe in his journey the model of a cosmos whose center is its own container.

To pass from the earth to the center point of the heavens, one must come to a point where one's orientation flips, where what was up becomes down. More essentially, if even harder to put into words, one's outward movement must also flip and become an inward movement—such that no matter what direction one chooses to gaze, one is looking at the same central point. In a key passage in *Paradiso*, Dante manages to do both. Arriving at the upper reaches of the sky, he describes a point where "our atmosphere . . . sprinkles snowflakes downward with its frozen mists," and yet now, instead of the snow falling downward, he sees "the upper air adorned, snow-flaking upward with triumphant mists that for a while had stayed with us there."[6] There in the heights, among the snowflakes suspended in indecision about which way to fall, the pilgrim looks down as the sun races by below his feet. He turns helplessly to his beloved, who urges him to step "onto the swiftest heaven . . . whose nearest and most exalted parts are all so uniform, I cannot tell which Beatrice selected as my place."[7]

Indeed, it does not and cannot matter where Dante steps onto the primum mobile, the swiftest heaven, for in the architecture he has created for this journey, all paths outward converge on the same point:

> The nature of the universe, which holds
> the center still and moves all else around it,
> begins here as if from its turning-post.
> And this heaven has no other *where* than this:

the mind of God, in which are kindled both
the love that turns it and the force it rains.
Only one circle's light and love enclose it,
as it encloses the rest . . . and that precinct
only He who girds it understands.
No other heaven measures this sphere's motion
but it serves as the measure for the rest.[8]

Gazing up and outward, Dante sees the enclosing circles of heaven around him become progressively smaller and more intense in light and joy until, ultimately, his eyes find that one central point, infinitely small and infinitely bright, that, paradoxically, encloses all of existence in its embrace.

It was to this eternal solace—this "amazing and angelic temple that has as boundaries only love and light," this self-contained cosmos that knows no outside in space or before or after in time—that Borges's mind fled as he contemplated the bad infinity of words on pages, pages in books, and books on shelf after dusty shelf lining the municipal library whose outdated catalogs it was now his job to maintain.[9]

ON JANUARY 8, 1938, BORGES began to work at the Miguel Cané municipal library. With no university degree and no prior experience other than poorly paid, part-time writing work for literary journals, he was in no position to be choosy. And so he found himself walking ten blocks to take a tram across town to one of Buenos Aires's less desirable neighborhoods, where he would spend his days cataloging the sparse collection. Had he the space to himself, he might have appreciated it more, but he was far from alone. There were, he would later recount, "some fifty of us doing what fifteen could easily have done."[10] To make matters worse, his co-workers weren't exactly bookworms. They spent their days chatting about soccer and betting on horses, when they weren't busy harassing the female patrons.

One day one of them happened to spy the name Jorge Luis Borges in a biographical note. Rather than be amazed to find out their colleague was a writer, the men laughed about the coincidence of the shared name. Borges also drew his co-workers' ire when at first he logged too many books. He would need to slow down, they told him, unless he wanted them all to be out a paycheck.[11]

There was one bright side to his new job. What it lacked in challenge, interest, or pay it more than made up for in free time. Exhausting his limited quota of books shortly after arriving each day, Borges was free to fill his remaining time reading the few titles he could find of any literary value or jotting down his own ideas. Indeed, some of the foment leading to his literary explosion in the early 1940s came from these days lost among the unread books of an underused library on the south side of Buenos Aires. For the time being he also had one other position that at least provided some connection to the literary world: editing a biweekly section on books for the magazine *El Hogar.* But in December of that year, something happened that would deprive him of even those small blessings.

Borges shared an apartment with his mother, Leonor, as he would continue to do until her death years later. On Christmas Eve she sent him to fetch a young woman who was to have dinner with them. Running late, Borges ascended the darkened stairs of the girl's apartment building in a rush, only to smash his head on a window frame that had swung out into the stairwell. At first he tried to recover at home, but soon he became feverish and even lost his power of speech. At the hospital the doctors diagnosed him with septicemia; for a while it was far from clear that he would survive. Even after he recovered, Borges feared he would suffer some permanent damage to his mental abilities, and he became even more focused on writing something new, something that would make a name for himself.[12]

The story he wrote during his convalescence wore the guise of a scholarly article about some recently unearthed pages by an obscure French writer named Pierre Menard. Absurdly, the work in question included the Frenchman's reproduction, verbatim, of two chapters plus another fragment of Cervantes's great novel, *Don Quixote*. These were not simply a modern version of the Spanish master's work, the story's author insisted. Nor were they, perish the thought, mere copies. No, Pierre Menard had labored for years, writing countless drafts, all toward the end of producing "a number of pages which coincided—word for word and line for line—with those of Miguel de Cervantes."[13]

Menard, Borges writes, contemplated a number of ways for accomplishing his goal. He could, for example, endeavor to forget his nationality, his language, and three hundred years of history so as to *become* Miguel de Cervantes. No, he decides, that would be too easy. Or rather, of the many ways in which the task was impossible, that would be the least interesting. It challenged Menard far more to arrive at Cervantes's exact words while remaining a Frenchman of the twentieth century, thus overcoming the cultural differences, the history that had passed, and all the literary events in between—including, most vexingly, the publication of *Don Quixote* itself. In an ironic coup de grâce, Borges transcribes a passage from Cervantes's original novel and juxtaposes it with the identical passage from Pierre Menard's version, ignoring the perfect repetition of the texts to extol the improvements of the latter. He professes to be impressed, for example, by Menard's use of an archaic style in a foreign language, in contrast to the relative banality of Cervantes's reliance on "the Spanish of his time."[14]

With "Pierre Menard," Borges delved into the nature of creativity, of originality, a topic that concerned him greatly. Early in the story, the narrator quotes the French author's own notes, in which he put his creation on a par with the greatest of the ages and with the most far-reaching philosophical or theological proofs. The final term of such a proof, he wrote, whatever that term may be—"the world around us, or God, or chance, or universal Forms—is no more final, no more uncommon, than my revealed novel."[15] The sole difference, Menard went on to explain, is that while "philosophers publish pleasant volumes containing the intermediate stages of their work," he had erased the work he had done, the multiple, even countless drafts of his production.[16] Menard, in other words, had realized the famous parable of monkeys with typewriters and simply condensed infinite time in order to produce the desired outcome. "The task I have undertaken is not *in essence* difficult," he noted. "If I could just be immortal, I could do it."[17] Individuality, style, creativity—none of this mattered, it seemed, for given sufficient time, all books that could be written would be, simply by random chance. Nothing in the universe could truly be original, for everything can be generated by chance.

Borges published his story in May 1939, after some months of convalescing from his injury. That summer he lost his editorial job at *El Hogar,* leaving him nothing but his pitiful position and even more pitiful salary as assistant librarian. Following on the heels of "Pierre Menard," Borges wrote an essay that made explicit the same anxiety about artistic originality that had imbued the former story. In this case, the setting was a library.

In that essay Borges picked up a theme he had learned from his earlier readings on the Kabbalah, according to which God had made the universe out of a combination of letters. He noted that from Aristotle on thinkers had been fascinated with the idea that given a set of homogeneous elements differing only in position, order, and form, with enough time one could construct an entire world. While the Greek philosopher Leucippus would famously call these homogeneous elements atoms, and claim that all of existence originates from the random collision of such basic beings, his ideas would later be ridiculed by other thinkers, among them the Roman orator Cicero, who countered that "if . . . the twenty-one letters of the alphabet . . . were thrown together onto the ground . . . I doubt whether chance could possibly create even a single verse to read."[18]

Cicero's challenge was pounced on by generations to follow, leading to the most famous version of the thought experiment, in which a "half-dozen monkeys provided with typewriters would, in a few eternities, produce all the books in the British Museum."[19]

It was Lewis Carroll who pointed out that because the number of combinations, while enormous, is finite, there must be an upper limit to the number of possible books that can be written. Given enough time, the question would ultimately become not *what* book shall I write, but *which* of the infinite books already written shall I repeat. (As the comic George Carlin once asked, Why do people keep telling me to put it in my own words when they're the same damn words everyone else uses?)

Lost in his municipal library, lost in life, Borges was beginning to question if he could ever put anything in his own words, if he would ever write anything of consequence. Perhaps no creation could ever be of consequence. Perhaps nothing new whatsoever could be fashioned in a world whose limited materials combined over an apparently infinite time. In fact, he had encountered this very harrowing idea while reading the German philosopher Friedrich Nietzsche. Nietzsche, who had lost his mind before dying of pneumonia the year after Borges's birth, proposed this notion in his prophetic book *Thus Spoke Zarathustra*. The number of atoms in the world being finite, he said, "*in an infinite stretch of time, the number of possible permutations must be run through, and the universe has to repeat itself.*"[20] Indeed, it must repeat itself, and in fact has been repeating itself, eternally.

Nietzsche's point in devising this logical fairy tale (or nightmare, depending on your outlook) was to create the backdrop for his existentialist prototype, the famous *Übermensch* who would brave the cosmic absurdity of the eternal recurrence of the same and accept or, better yet, affirm his destiny, forever willing himself to live the same life, repeatedly, throughout eternity. But Borges, being Borges, had nothing quite so heroic in mind.

After acknowledging the inconceivable astronomical lengths of time one would need to attain before even one perfect repetition of the universe's arrangement of finite particles would take place, Borges adds a slight yet decisive disturbance into the mix. Partisans of the eternal recurrence forget, he reminds us, "that memory would import a novelty that negates the hypothesis."[21] Just as the perception of a moment is impossible without a self who connects that moment with another and who, hence, by definition is never wholly in that moment—just as a memory can never be a perfect repetition of a moment of the past without ceasing to become a memory and simply *becoming* that moment in the past—the perfect repetition of all things is utterly meaningless without someone present at both moments who can register that repetition. And yet that same presence destroys the perfection of the repetition. The very element that allows for the fantasy of infinite repetition of the same is, by necessity, something new, and hence not a repetition.

Borges then presses his advantage even further. The very presumption of infinite time and, for that matter, infinite space that permits Nietzsche's speculations is but a mere fantasy born of that observer who inevitably imports something new and different into every repetition, every recollection. For no one has ever observed infinity. Infinity is nothing other than the incapacity of beings who inhabit time and space to imagine an edge, a border, an end point to that time and space. Talking about the infinite time in which things must eventually recur has no more meaning than referring to the "Infinity to My Right." In other words, Borges adds, "if time is infinite to our intuition, so is space."[22]

With this twist Borges invoked none other than Immanuel Kant. Space and time, as Kant wrote, are the necessary forms taken by our *intuition* of an otherwise chaotic influx of sensory data. This explains why Borges's next step was to unpack Kant's first antinomy, the problem of whether the universe has a beginning in time or an edge in space. For, as Kant showed, if we conceive of the universe as if it were an object in time and space, we run headfirst into an impossible contradiction. When we imagine it being finite, we come to its edge in time or in space. But that edge must be somewhere, and hence we are forced to imagine something beyond it. However, when we try to imagine the universe without a limit, encompassing all time and all space, our imagination fails, and we are still forced to ask *where* it is, or *what* came before. But the universe is not a thing in time and space that can be either finite or infinite; the antinomy is provoked by thinking of it as if it were. The questioner, the observer, brings something unique, namely, a finite self, to each and every perception in time and space; this very observer produces bad infinities the moment he or she tries to step into the shoes of the god of very large things by transforming the limited connecting of moments and places necessary for any perception into the unlimited realm of everything at all times.

And this move, this unwarranted expansion, Borges realized, is exactly analogous to the one Nietzsche performed when he conceived of the eternal recurrence of the same. For, "without a special archangel to keep track, what does it mean that we are going through the thirteen thousand five hundred and fourteenth cycle and not the first in the series or number three hundred twenty-two to the two thousandth power?"[23] There is no such special archangel, of course, no external and independent standard against which to measure our observations. But like Kant's anchors along the river of change that is our life, our desire to assume the perspective of such a bedrock standard becomes the driving force of our science. At the same time, the fact that we never can occupy that ultimate vantage is also the guarantee that our drive for knowledge will never end.

How do we avoid falling into the trap of thinking that the god of very large things is out there, in space, in time? How do we avoid turning our incapacity to conceive of a beginning to time into a monstrous paradoxical recurrence digesting every individual effort into the uniformity of random cosmic excrement, the moronic product of a galactic orchestra of monkey fingers blindly bashing away on meaningless keys?

Borges pondered this mystery on endless commutes, these doldrums ostensibly brightened by the working man's holiday bonus of a two-pound package of maté, the strong herbal tea Argentines sip obsessively from the gourds they carry with them almost everywhere they go. As he hauled his satchel of herbs the ten blocks from the tram station toward his lonely bed, Borges's eyes would well with tears as he realized how these paltry tokens served only to underscore his menial existence. Overwhelming, ponderous tedium, hammered home by his employer's attempted kindness. His literary friends wondered what had happened. Was this some ironic ploy, a great writer's witticism written onto the pages of his life? Unfortunately not. For Borges, at this time, such toil was all he could hold down.[24]

And still, in the hours of freedom found in the library's basement or on its rooftop, away from the banter about soccer and women, or on the evening tram, clattering along darkening streets back to the apartment he shared with his mother, reading was what saved him. Specifically Dante's *Divine Comedy*, whose poetic depiction of the journey from the midpoint of one man's particular time and place to God's universal, central, all-encompassing presence outside the warp and weft of time granted him "one of the most vivid literary experiences" of his life.[25] Indeed, not only the story but the very structure of Dante's solution to the problem of the place of the universe opened a door for Borges.

There is only one way to close off the regression into the infinite that occurs when we assume the vantage of the god of very large things, he thought. It is to understand, with Dante, with Saint Augustine, with Plotinus before them, that *non in tempore sed cum tempore incepit creatio*—the creation begins not in time but with time. As Borges wrote in the essay inspired by the monotony of stacking the shelves at the Miguel Cané, our world has but one chance to escape that subaltern horror, that "vast, contradictory Library, whose vertical wildernesses of books run the incessant risk of changing into others that affirm, deny, and confuse everything like a delirious god."[26] That way is this: we must describe for it an alternate architecture, a paradoxical geometry whose notation was only worked out in the late nineteenth century but whose concepts have permeated the mystic and theological musings of poets and philosophers alike since time immemorial. That world, our library, was finite, yes, but boundless as well, its architecture inverted such that its center was everywhere, and its circumference, nowhere.

IN 1941, BORGES PUBLISHED a collection of eight of the stories he had been working on over the last few years. The book, the first he had released since *A History of Eternity* five years earlier, immediately cut a rift into the Argentine literary world. The journal *Sur,* for which he was a frequent contributor and whose board was stacked with admirers, treated the publication as a major cultural event. Bioy quickly published a review in which he touted Borges's new style of writing as having discovered "the literary possibilities of metaphysics."[27] His hopes high, Borges entered it into the National Awards for Literature competition.[28]

More conservative than the *Sur* writers, the selection committee wasn't sure what to make of the strange collection of stories. Were they even stories? An essay about a French writer who copied some chapters of *Don Quixote;* an investigation into a secret society that had created a fictional world. At least the story Borges had chosen for the collection's title, "The Garden of Forking Paths," a spy story set in a prior conflict between Germany and England, had some recognizable trappings of fiction. Still, one identifiable genre out of the entire set didn't pass muster, and so the committee passed on Borges, again. The judges preferred more familiar subjects.[29]

The circle around *Sur,* many of whom were members of a group called the Argentine Society of Writers, rallied around Borges and responded by publishing a special issue of the magazine dedicated to his work and hosting a dinner in his honor. In fact, the battle lines were being drawn over the thinly hidden contours of a political and cultural divide that had started to emerge in Argentina in the shadow of World War II. The literary establishment's snubbing of Borges came in the barely disguised language of anti-Semitism: "exotic and decadent work" exhibiting "certain deviant tendencies of contemporary English literature."[30] The selection committee was packed with writers who tended toward the nationalist side of politics and who found Borges's international, intellectual style elitist and overly "cosmopolitan."[31] Borges, for his part, ever willing to engage in tit-for-tat battles, built on public statements he had already made against Hitler and in favor of the Allies and denounced the nationalists as Germanophiles and a potential fifth column in Argentina.[32]

The conflict festered until the onset of the following year, when Borges's admonitions became true. In June 1943 a pro-Axis group of military officers staged a coup and were quickly supported by nationalist factions, who stormed the streets and trashed British-owned businesses and homes. The junta that formed a few days later made establishing nationalist themes in literature and culture a top priority, publicly condemning those, like Borges, who exhibited too little interest in properly Argentine themes.[33]

In this political maelstrom Borges decided to double down on his artistic choices and his fervent opposition to what he saw as literature written in support of fascism. In 1944 he created a new grouping of stories he had written since the publication of *The Garden of Forking Paths*, calling this collection *Artifices*. Rather than publish them alone, he reissued the former collection and put both out in a single, two-part book under the simple title *Fictions*.

Fictions would go on to become one of Borges's most noted, republished, and translated collections. It would play a large role in earning him the first International Publishers' Prize almost two decades later, awarded to an author "whose existing body of work will, in the view of the jury, have a lasting influence on the development of modern literature."[34] Among its pages was one of the tales from the first group of stories that Borges had put out in 1941, a story that picked up on the themes he outlined in the little essay that he had written years earlier in the Miguel Cané library. This tale would go on to be debated and imitated, illustrated by renowned artists and pondered by philosophers and mathematicians alike.

Almost entirely lacking in plot or character development, it became a classic of existentialist and absurdist literature from its first indelible words: "The universe (which others call the Library)."[35]

IN "THE LIBRARY OF Babel," Borges sketches a vision of hell in exquisite architectural detail. A narrator's voice is revealed to be that of "a librarian," one of many who have existed and will exist in the future, who spend their lives roaming the hexagonal rooms of the Library.[36] Four of each hexagon's walls are lined with books, the other two opening onto vestibules that in turn lead into the next set of hexagons. Running up and down each hexagonal room and each vestibule is a spiral staircase leading to identical rooms above and below. On each of the rooms' four walls are arranged five bookshelves; each shelf contains thirty-two books; each book "contains four hundred ten pages; each page forty lines; each line, approximately eighty black letters."[37]

The books, we soon learn, contain combinations of twenty-five orthographic symbols. These include twenty-two letters along with spaces, commas, and periods. Like the kabbalists in their *Book of Creation*, the librarians who wander the Library's chambers learn that all the diversity in the universe is the result of combinations of these symbols. Somewhere in the Library is one book that contains nothing but *a*'s; elsewhere, no one knows where, another lies whose pages contain nothing but *a*'s with the sole exception of one solitary *b*. And on and on it goes.

Over the centuries the librarians have studied countless volumes and have converged upon a set of theories about the nature of the Library. According to the consensus, two basic principles govern the collection: the Library contains every book of the set length that can possibly be constructed out of the given orthographic symbols; and no two of those books are identical.[38]

That's it. It seems so simple. And yet do we have any idea how large such a collection would be? The great semiotician and novelist

Umberto Eco disregarded the question, calling it irrelevant to the story's meaning.[39] Still, let's go there. The mathematician William Goldbloom Bloch did, and what he found out was nothing short of astonishing.

Using combinatorics and scientific notation, Bloch calculated the number of distinct books in Borges's library as being $25^{1,312,000}$, a number somewhat larger than a one followed by 1,834,097 zeros.[40] Since numbers in the abstract can fail to reach readers who aren't trained mathematicians, Bloch goes on to compare the size the Library would need to be to contain that number of books with the size cosmologists estimate for our universe. Suffice it to say, our cosmos doesn't fare well. Slightly overstating the current projections of its size, we can estimate that our universe has enough space in it to accommodate a mere 10^{84} books—if, that is, the universe consisted of nothing but books stacked as tightly as possible. But if that were the case, our known universe could fit into Borges's Library $10^{1,834,013}$ times (that is not even counting the fact that the Library consists of large amounts of space in addition to books, which in fact would make it immeasurably larger). If we packed protons tightly into our known universe, we might cram in about 10^{124} of the subatomic particles; in other words, in comparison to the Library, our entire universe is much, much, much smaller than a proton.[41]

Despite the awe-inspiring, truly unimaginable size of the Library, the next most salient fact is that it is not infinite. Since (echoing our facile proclamations on the unicity of snowflakes) there are no two identical books in the Library, this means that as vast as it is, there is an upper limit on the Library's size. And this fact in turn means that somewhere, light-years upon light-years away, above or below, to the left or the right, the Library should come to an end. It should have an upper floor, with no hexagons above; it should have a last cell, with no opening in the wall.

But such borders are, according to the basic architecture that Borges has outlined, impossible. Each and every cell is identical in shape, size, and number of books. The Library is uniform, which means that you can't, even in theory, find a cell whose upper or side limits are closed, making them different from all the others. Like the medievals, like the ancients, Borges is forced to grapple with the edge of a universe that is presumed to encompass all. Like the medievals, like the ancients, he solves it by curving space:

> Idealists argue that the hexagonal rooms are the necessary shape of absolute space, or at least our *perception* of space. They argue that a triangular or pentagonal chamber is inconceivable. (Mystics claim that their ecstasies reveal to them a circular chamber containing an enormous circular book with a continuous spine that goes completely around the walls. But their testimony is suspect, their words obscure. That cyclical book is God.) Let it suffice for the moment that I repeat the classic dictum: *The Library is a sphere whose exact center is any hexagon and whose circumference is unattainable.*[42]

The "classic dictum" is one that has often been cited by mystics and philosophers as a definition of God as a sphere whose center is everywhere and circumference is nowhere. It is also an exact analogue of the architecture Dante invented for his cosmos, building on theological and cosmological answers to the conundrums of the location of the universe and God's ability or inability to move it. But modern mathematics has another name for it. A hypersphere.

Like the vastness of Borges's mathematics in the Library, a hypersphere, which is a four-dimensional object, isn't really imaginable for beings like us who inhabit three spatial dimensions. But we can extrapolate from lower-dimensional objects to get a sense of it. To begin with, imagine any sphere, say the surface of a basketball. Now imagine being a microorganism whose life is confined to that surface. Directions in your world would include left and right, forward and backward, but up and down—in this case, inside and outside the rubber surface of the ball—simply wouldn't exist for you.[43]

Now imagine that you have studied cosmology and trained

your telescopes on the far reaches of your space. As light reaches you from farther and farther away, the sources of that light, while at first diverging from each other, at a certain point begin to converge. When you aim your telescope far enough into the distance, it turns out that you are looking toward the very same point in space (namely, the other side of the basketball) *no matter what direction you turn your gaze.*

What we have imagined is still a two-dimensional object and hence perfectly graspable in three dimensions. The only step that remains is to extrapolate from this model by imagining that the two-dimensional creature whose perspective you occupied is now three-dimensional, while maintaining the strange fact that if you get your information from far enough away, it doesn't matter which direction you look when looking out, you are still looking at the same point. In other words, exactly as the medievals did when they looked up at the sky, you are now looking inward toward some central point, a point that, paradoxically, encompasses all of existence.

The Library Borges constructed is hyper-spherical in shape; when the librarian dies, he tells us, "compassionate hands will throw me over the railing; my tomb will be the unfathomable air, my body will sink for ages, and will decay and dissolve in the wind engendered by my fall, which shall be infinite."[44] An enormous but finite collection of books; an infinite fall. The only solution is a hypersphere, finite in size but boundless in shape. And yet an important difference remains between Borges's vision and that of Dante. Crucially, the certainty that anchors Dante's cosmos is that all-encompassing center, this heaven that "has no other *where* than this: the mind of God, in which are kindled both the love that turns it and the force it rains."[45] For Borges, lost in the seemingly endless aisles of an absurdist library of despair, the center is wherever one is, and that circumference, that impossible, all-encompassing point and origin, nowhere. Or, at least, unattainable.

Unattainable, perhaps, but still a consummation devoutly to be wished. And this was Borges's brilliant riposte to Dante's cosmos, the rebellious response of a man denied love, denied redemption at every turn, a "rueful and abandoned man" who, like Kant before him, faced the challenge of a meaningless and lawless world, a universe of fleeting impressions tossed together by happenstance, and refused, against tradition and temptation, both the path of utter despair and that of blind devotion.[46]

For just as the minimum coherence that permits a chaotic jumble of impressions to congeal into the flow of an afternoon in life requires a being whose existence transcends total absorption in that sensory manifold, our awareness of the vast and apparently infinite span of existence in space and time imposes on that wild expanse an order, a rigor, a necessary structure.

We create that order, but we imagine it preceded us. Treading water in the bad infinity of space and time, we can see no end. We are like the librarians who, searching for a final vindication of their existence, "squabbled in the narrow corridors, muttered dark imprecations, strangled one another on the divine staircases, threw deceiving volumes down ventilation shafts, were themselves hurled to their deaths by men of distant regions."[47] Superstitions rise and fall, like that of the Book-Man: that somewhere in the Library's uncharted expanse there must be a book that explains it all, "the cipher and perfect compendium *of all other books,* and some librarian must have examined that book; this librarian is analogous to a god."[48] Desperate for this redemption, desperate that life be more than the random purging of a vast combinator, Borges's librarian prays, "Let heaven exist, though my own place be in hell. Let me be tortured and battered and annihilated, but let there be one instant, one creature, wherein thy enormous Library may find its justification."[49]

Without such justification, no individual exists, nothing is created, nothing new. "To speak is to commit tautologies," Borges writes, for absolutely nothing that one can say has not been said countless times in countless volumes.[50] And yet, and yet . . . Borges recognized that even feeling lost requires an organizing principle, a scintilla of freedom, a modicum of salvation. Since those "who picture the world as unlimited forget that the number of possible books is *not*," Borges ends by proposing a hope, one gestured to by Nietzsche's eternal return: an eternal traveler would, because there is a limited number of ways to organize a limited number of volumes, eventually find the same volumes repeated in the same order, "which, repeated, becomes order."[51] But Borges knew that such an order, on its own, is not enough.

Like Kant sparked to hope by Hume's despair, Borges saw that the very memory needed to see a recurrence as a recurrence would of necessity be an alien element. The order thus discovered, that underlying rigor, is one of chess masters, not angels. But it is a rigor nonetheless. Like Dante's cosmos, the universe that others call the Library is contained by its center; unlike Dante's, that center isn't God. It is, instead, the very observer whose absorption into the whirling, buffeting, random chance generator of temporal and spatial existence requires a minimum of abstraction, an iota of order, an atom of rigor just to feel lost and absorbed in the first place. It is, indeed, that very observer for whom the conditions of possibility of knowing anything at all also require that universe turn itself inside out, become a hypersphere whose central point envelops all existence.

IN 1964, A SCANT twenty years after Borges published his *Fictions* and more than half a millennium after Dante wrote his *Divine Comedy*, two astronomers working out of a research facility in Holmdel, New Jersey, noticed an annoying residue of static in the highly sensitive readings their radio telescopes were making of distant space. They assumed it must be due to the pigeons that insisted on roosting up there and crapping all over the dish. So they climbed onto the apparatus and carefully scoured it. To no avail. It turns out they were listening not to pigeon droppings but to the microwave radiation left over from the origin of time. But these traces of the big bang had no specific origin. No matter what direction they trained their instruments, the cosmic background radiation was identical. Their discovery confirmed that Dante was right. No matter where we train our gaze on the starry skies above, we look inward toward the very origin of space and time. Thus freeing our minds from our senses, we find that the universe is, indeed, turned inside out.

8

GRAVITAS

IN THE SUMMER OF 1922, a young physics student took a train from Munich to Leipzig to hear a great man speak. The speaker, Albert Einstein, had by then ascended to the pinnacle of scientific achievement and renown. He had overturned generations of thinking about the nature of light; he had redefined humanity's basic understanding of time and space; and he had explained how gravity works, replacing equations that had withstood the test of two centuries with an even more accurate theory. It thus came as a shock to a starstruck Werner Heisenberg when, upon entering the lecture hall, he spied pamphlets being passed around denouncing Einstein as a "Jew" whose perverse theories had undermined the simplicity and elegance of classical physics.

Heisenberg had come to Leipzig brimming with excitement and committed to a notion of science as the perfect embodiment of the pursuit of truth. The pamphlets he found there came from the pen of one of Germany's top scientists, the Nobel laureate Philipp Lenard, whose anti-Semitic persecution helped ensure that Einstein's own Nobel would come years late and for reasons other than his relativity theory. Heisenberg was so distraught by this attack on the dean of modern science that he left the hall without even noticing that the man lecturing that day was not Einstein, who had canceled his trip out of anger at Lenard's abuse. Returning to the cheap quarters he had rented, Heisenberg saw they had been broken into and his few meager possessions stolen. Eviscerated, the young man returned to Munich that same night. The next day he sought out temporary work as a woodcutter to earn the money he would need to replace the items he had lost.[1]

It would be another four years before Heisenberg would meet Einstein. By then he had graduated from a neophyte to a core member of the scientific avant-garde, revolutionizing physics with his bizarre new quantum mechanics. Einstein and his older colleague Max Planck still ruled the physics world from their perch at their institute in Berlin, which Heisenberg called the chief "citadel of physics in Germany."[2] Keen to learn more about the uprisings in Copenhagen and Göttingen, the luminaries invited Heisenberg to give a lecture on his work. After the presentation, Einstein invited Heisenberg to his house, where he peppered him with friendly but critical questions. The older man seemed particularly exercised by Heisenberg's nonchalance concerning what was actually going on inside the atom in the time spans separating the experimenter's observations.

It didn't really matter what was going on beyond the reach of our instruments, Heisenberg blithely insisted; it only mattered what one could measure, because "a good theory must be based on directly observable magnitudes."[3] Einstein shot back that the young man couldn't possibly believe that *only* observable magnitudes should be part of a physical theory. This is when Heisenberg drew his famous comparison to Einstein's own work, pointing out that the revolutionary insight that enabled his relativity theory occurred when Einstein decided to disregard what everyone thought they knew about space and time, that they were absolute backdrops independent of any observer's specific attributes. Granting that he might have used a similar kind of reasoning, Einstein nonetheless rebuffed the comparison.[4]

As few and far between as their interactions were, the sparring between Einstein and Heisenberg has become a kind of shorthand for an extraordinary chasm that has challenged the advancement of physics over the past century. Einstein's theories of special and general relativity explain to a remarkable degree of accuracy the workings of the universe on the grandest of scales; they allow astronomers to understand the movement of stars and galaxies, to probe into the enigmatic depths of black holes, and to measure the age and rate of expansion of the cosmos itself. Quantum mechanics, for its part, has proven uncontested in its ability to probe the smallest constituents of matter and, in its later developments, has been capable of predicting with pinpoint precision the emergence of new fundamental particles. And yet, despite such independent proof of their validity, the two pillars of modern physics have also proven to be stubbornly incompatible.[5]

While the specifics underlying this incompatibility are highly complex, the overall reason lies in the very aspect of quantum mechanics that Einstein and Schrödinger found so distasteful, namely, its discovery that at subatomic levels reality cedes to the uncertainty principle; that, if you look closely enough at nature, the smooth continuity of matter's movement disappears and is replaced by violent quantum fluctuations; and that particles like electrons can't be said to follow distinct paths unless and until they are observed. In the final form Einstein gave it in 1916, when he successfully incorporated gravity, the space-time his theory described was a continuum; its equations describe the movements of objects across an admittedly complex and curved spatiotemporal fabric, but one that is ultimately smooth. Its equations cannot, in the words of the string theorist Brian Greene, "handle the roiling frenzy of quantum foam."[6]

Despite the popular narrative ascribing to each scientist a founding role in this dramatic schism, Heisenberg believed that his discovery had a spirit similar to that of Einstein's. He was not alone. Einstein's friend Philipp Frank also rebuked Einstein for his resistance to what he took to calling the "new fashion" in physics of refusing to ascribe reality to what cannot be measured or seen, reminding him that "the fashion you speak of was invented by you in 1905!" Einstein's sardonic reply, that a "good joke should not be repeated too often," would join many others in a posterity replete with his bons mots.[7]

For Heisenberg, Einstein's prior willingness to disregard what everyone knew about space and time in favor of what the data were telling him was the furthest thing from a joke. It embodied an approach to science and knowledge that he would defend for the rest of his career. It is also the best way for us to see how the realms claimed by relativity and quantum physics are, despite their history of conflict, profoundly related.

BY THE LATE NINETEENTH century scientists already had a pretty good measure of how fast light propagated in a vacuum. The puzzle Einstein set to unravel in his extraordinary 1905 paper was how to account for an apparent paradox. Strangely, light always clocked in at the same speed—no matter how fast the measurer travels relative to the light source and no matter who is doing the measuring.

To be clear, this is not how measurements of speed usually work. If you are moving on a train at 10 kilometers an hour and throw a baseball ahead of you at 20 kilometers an hour, you will measure the speed of the ball as 20 kilometers an hour, whereas your friend standing by the side of the road as you ride by will measure its speed as 30 kilometers an hour. Light behaves quite differently. If the crew of a rocket heading toward Mars were moving at 30,000 kilometers per second, or about 10 percent of the speed of light, and aimed a light beam toward Mars, they would measure the speed of that beam as 300,000 kilometers per second. Observers sitting on an asteroid as they zipped by, however, would measure the same light beam as moving *not* at 330,000 kilometers per second, but at light's normal clip of 300,000 kilometers per second.

Two observers who measure the same velocity for a light beam despite moving at vastly different velocities themselves couldn't *both* be right. Or could they?

By now we have learned to recognize situations in which two watertight conclusions are at loggerheads with each other, in which each statement *must* be true but both *cannot* be true. Kant called these antinomies, and it turns out Einstein's strategy for solving the antinomy of light's propagation was identical to Kant's. Just as Kant realized that resolving antinomies required removing the implicit assumption of a God's-eye perspective from how a particular problem had been presented and considered, Einstein now saw that the problem lay in a fundamental assumption about the "neutral" observers, principally that they have access to a universal, unchanging experience of time.

Newton had assumed that time was absolute. Einstein now realized that the apparent contradiction between expected and measured velocities emerged from this incorrect notion of time: "Before the advent of the theory of relativity it had always tacitly been assumed in physics that the statement of time had an absolute significance, *i.e.*, that it is independent of the state of motion of the body of reference . . . ; if we disregard this assumption, then the conflict between the law of the propagation of light *in vacuo* and the principle of relativity . . . disappears."[8]

In the case of our speedy voyagers to Mars and their neutral observers, each measures the same velocity for the light beam despite the vast differences between their respective velocities—*because their respective experience of time is different.* The observers on the asteroid imagine that the travelers must be measuring the beam's velocity at 270,000 kilometers per second, but the crew on the spaceship measure at 300,000 kilometers per second. Both measure the same velocity because the clock used by the crew is ticking away more slowly than the one used by the asteroid observers (their units for measuring distance are also shorter, but we can skip over that for now), thus allowing the light beam's velocity to remain exactly the same for both.

BY REMOVING NEWTON'S UNIVERSAL clock from the set of assumptions with which scientists approach the world, Einstein resolved a fundamental antinomy and provided physics with a new and highly accurate theory. But there was still something missing.

In the mid-seventeenth century Sir Isaac Newton worked out the equations that would, with extraordinary accuracy, be used for more than two hundred years to predict how large bodies moving in space influence one another. Each body in the universe attracts every other body in the universe with a force equal to the product of their masses divided by the square of the distance separating them. It's as simple as that. What Newton left untouched was the medium of that attraction. As he put it, the idea of bodies acting on one another across a vacuum without some medium connecting them "is to me so great an absurdity that I beleive [*sic*] no man who has in philosophical matters any competent faculty of thinking can ever fall into it." In fact, he refused to speculate what that medium might be, leaving that mystery "to ye consideration of my readers."[9] Moreover, Newton assumed the force of gravity acted instantaneously: thus, if the earth were suddenly to disappear, the moon would instantly alter its course, no longer under the sway of the earth's gravitational influence. But why? How would the moon know?

Newton's perfectly functioning explanation of gravitational effects, in other words, fell short as a theory. It left gaping holes of which Newton himself was fully aware. He illustrated another such hole with a particularly vivid thought experiment. If you hang a bucket half full of water from a string and then spin the bucket, the water inside will eventually start to rotate along with the walls of the bucket. As the speed of the rotation increases, the water will rise at the edges of the bucket, in a demonstration of what is known as centrifugal force. While this phenomenon is totally normal and to be expected, as Newton thought about it, he realized that under certain conditions it conflicted with Galileo's principle of relativity, which stated that the laws of physics apply equally to frames of reference in uniform motion relative to one another. What this means is that observers in one frame of reference, say, on board a moving ship, can't run any experiments that will privilege their own frame of reference over that of another ship so long as both are moving at constant rates. Neither can claim to be at rest while the other is moving.

At first glance, of course, this is not the case for the bucket. Because it moves in a circle, its motion is not uniform with respect to a neutral observer. And the lack of uniformity shows itself via the water climbing up the edges of the bucket. Even if we are walled off from the rest of the world, we know our bucket is spinning because the water *feels* the effect of the centrifugal force. But how does it feel it? Newton asked. What if the bucket floated in totally empty space, with nothing around it to determine that it is spinning? Would it still feel the centrifugal force? If so, why? Just like God trying to move Aristotle's cosmos without reference to a place in which to move it, what would it mean to spin a bucket in empty space?

Newton's presumptive answer was that the bucket could only know if it was spinning or not if the space in which it existed, like the time against which change is measured in the world, were a universal and stationary backdrop. Space and time both functioned as monumental and empty containers for anything that might pass through them. Just like his clock, Newton's model of universal, infinite, three-dimensional space lasted for a long time. But as often happens with science, resolving one problem popped open another. In this case, by denying absolute time and definitively showing that nothing could ever move faster than light, Einstein had also decimated Newton's provisional explanation of gravity, because according to the same theory there could be no neutral backdrop of space that can automatically and instantly tell the bucket if it is spinning or not. If the bucket feels something about its motion, this feeling must be conveyed from somewhere, and anything that is conveyed takes time. In short, having given up both space and time as absolute, rigid backdrops, Einstein would now need not a special theory, limited to cases of uniform motion, but a general one, one that would show how the laws of physics were interchangeable in all frames of reference, whether moving uniformly or not.

It was while struggling with this enormous problem that Einstein had what he would later call his happiest thought: "I was sitting in a chair in the patent office at Bern when all of a sudden a thought occurred to me. If a person falls freely, he will not feel his own weight."[10] What would become known as the equivalence principle of general relativity emerged from a combination of Newton's two open questions: What is gravity? And how does the bucket know it's spinning? As Einstein would later formulate it, a passenger in an enclosed chest being pulled along in empty space at a constant acceleration by some being would have no way to distinguish that feeling of acceleration from the feeling of being pulled by the earth's gravity.

As happy as the thought might have been, it would take another eight years to bring it to fruition. For one, Einstein had to grapple with a kind of mathematics that was new to him. While in his special relativity theory Einstein had already announced that space and time could no longer be considered independent of each other but would henceforth be aspects of a single overarching space-time, he now had to grapple with how to describe that four-dimensional space-time mathematically. He did so by turning to the geometry developed in the nineteenth century by the German mathematician Georg Friedrich Bernhard Riemann, which permitted geometrical calculations in multidimensional, curved spaces. This new math didn't come easily to Einstein. David Hilbert, a friend and competitor in the quest for a general theory of relativity, would later claim (somewhat hyperbolically) that "every boy in the streets of Göttingen understands more about four-dimensional geometry than

Einstein," before graciously acknowledging that, "in spite of that, Einstein did the work."[11]

With the math he borrowed from Riemann, Einstein was now able to propose experimental proofs for his contention that both gravity and acceleration were describable as the curving or warping of the four-dimensional space-time continuum. Specifically, he said that the light from a distant star would bend slightly as it passed around our sun. Using his theory, he worked out the angle of that curve and predicted that if astronomers could capture starlight as it came around our sun, the stars emitting that light "ought to appear to be displaced outwards from the sun by . . . 1.7 seconds of arc."[12]

Because of the brightness of the sun, such starlight is impossible to see—except during a full solar eclipse. So the world had to wait. A first proposed expedition to Ukraine in 1917 stalled under the pressure of the hostilities of World War I. Thus it was only in 1919, more than three years after Einstein announced his theory, that Arthur Eddington led an expedition to the Portuguese island of Príncipe off the coast of Africa to perform his observations of a total eclipse. The average of the images taken there and by a sister expedition off the coast of Brazil proved Einstein right. Back in Berlin, Einstein feigned nonchalance. "I knew the theory is correct," he told Ilse Schneider, the graduate student with whom he was meeting.[13] But what if the experiment had proved him wrong, she wanted to know. "Then I would have been sorry for the dear Lord," Einstein replied.[14]

WITH SPECIAL RELATIVITY, EINSTEIN set out to explain a contradiction that had been apparent to scientists since experiments that measured the speed of light in the late nineteenth century. A speeding traveler and a neutral observer will clock the same velocity for a light beam fired by the traveler, even though the neutral observer should be seeing the sum of the two velocities. So where did that extra velocity go? The brilliance of Einstein's insight was to realize that it hadn't gone anywhere at all. It was only our misunderstanding of the nature of time that made it seem as though there was a discrepancy. To get rid of the error, we must stop thinking about time as something in which we observe events and instead think of it as an aspect of how we observe those events that itself changes with our velocity relative to other observers.

With general relativity he had now made a similar move. Newton believed his bucket experiment pointed to the existence of absolute space. Einstein's new theory replaced that immobile and universal container with what he would call the gravitational field: the universally diffused gravitational influence of all bodies in the universe on all other bodies, which in turn creates the inertia that all objects in non-uniform motion feel. As he put it, "According to my theory, inertia is simply an interaction between masses, not an effect in which 'space' itself is involved, separate from the observed mass."[15] The water climbs the side of Newton's bucket when it spins because of the inertia imparted on it by the gravitational pulls of the rest of the objects in the universe. Without such objects, it makes no sense to say the bucket spins. Our inability to understand how gravity and acceleration were both expressions of the curvature of space-time resulted from thinking that space was an empty, infinitely extended, rigid backdrop in which we perceive events and movements, as opposed to being an aspect of how we measure and relate those events and movements.

Taken together, special and general relativity salvaged a picture of the physical world in which the same laws applied in the same ways no matter the situation of the one doing the observing, but at the cost of forever demolishing the idea of a privileged, neutral spot from which conflicting measurements—for instance, the length of an object or the time of an event—could be adjudicated.[16] At the core of this new understanding of reality lay a profound revision of the very notion of an observation. Observations, per Einstein, are nothing other than coincidences between measuring instruments, "the hands of a clock and points on the clock dial," and the events they are measuring.[17]

If we understand time not as a universal flow in which things happen but as one of the minimal conditions for observing things happening in the first place, we can see how time and space must be profoundly related. The classic line about time keeping everything from happening at once, while flippant, does clarify the strong link between time and observation. That events precede and follow on one another is a fundamental condition of their observability. For a human observer, at least, everything happening at once would be nothing short of an obscene mess.

But marking events as before and after also involves an aspect of spatial experience. Any clock I can imagine translates moments of time into something minimally spatial—the movement of a pendulum, a distinguishable alteration of a substance, "coincidences between the hands of a clock and points on the clock dial." Time cannot exist on its own but must partake in space. And exactly the same is true of space. The minimal condition for differentiating a here from a there—the dog of three fourteen seen in profile from the dog of three fifteen seen frontally—is the ability to compare the two markers for the time it takes an observer to span their distance and connect them. Just as clearly as time cannot exist without space, so space cannot exist without time.

The fact that time and space are observer dependent and inextricably connected also explains why there is a cosmic speed limit and how it works. Since the three dimensions of space are part of a larger four-dimensional space-time fabric, motion must always be shared among the four dimensions, and any measurement of time, being spatial, will be affected by observers' movements, as will any measurement of space, being temporal.

To better picture this, imagine a golf cart puttering along the right side of a field whose length represents time and whose width represents space. Let's say the fastest it can move overall is twenty-five kilometers an hour. Now, as long as it remains on the right sideline (that is, motionless in space), it can move forward on the field at a steady pace—which is to say, its clock ticks away at a normal pace. But there's a rub. Since space and time are interrelated measurements and the cart's total velocity on the field in any direction cannot surpass twenty-five kilometers an hour, if the cart veers to the left toward the other sideline (that is, starts moving in space), whatever velocity applied in that direction must detract from its progress toward the goal line, and the clock measuring its progress in time slows down accordingly. Indeed, if its driver wants to get from the right side of the field to the left as quickly as possible, the cart makes no progress down the length of the field at all—which is to say, its clock stops ticking so that it can turn all its velocity into spatial motion. Like a photon, the cart can traverse space at full speed, but only at the cost of coming to a complete stop in time.[18]

While Einstein abolished the idea of a privileged place in space from which to measure the movement of the rest of the cosmos, and a privileged standard against which to measure the ticking of time, he did find something absolute and constant: namely, that ultimate limit of observable change at the fulcrum of space and time, a fixed upper limit to how much space an entity can be observed to have crossed in a set amount of time. The velocity of light in a vacuum. Not twenty-five kilometers an hour, of course. But helpfully (for our experience of reality) much, much faster. This upper limit doesn't work like a legal speed limit, though. In the case of a speed limit, you *could* drive eighty kilometers an hour on your fifty-kilometer-an-hour-zoned local side street; not only would it be unsafe, however, but you could also be pulled over and issued an expensive ticket. In the case of the laws of physics, in contrast, as you push your ride up to the cosmic speed limit, the clock you use to measure time itself slows down relative to other observers. The closer you get to that limit, the more it slows down, until the clock you are carrying with you ceases to tick from the perspective of those not traveling with you. To be sure, you aren't noticing this slowing down. All you can observe from your perspective is that your journey through space seemed instantaneous. If you are traveling at the cosmic speed limit, your clock doesn't tick and you arrive at the same time you left, even if those you left behind have aged considerably in the time you were gone.

Of course, in our cosmos we can only imagine approaching that limit. Only photons and other massless electromagnetic radiation travel at light speed, and they, needless to say, don't experience anything. Still, from the perspective of a photon (that is, no perspective at all), time doesn't pass. For a photon that was emitted shortly after the origin of the universe that now happens to arrive through my office window, more than thirteen billion years have gone by in a flash. If time is what keeps everything from happening at once, those things can happen only because they have pulled back from a speed limit at which nothing happens at all.[19]

When we understand space-time not as an empty container in which all existence takes place but as an index for an observer to measure the interaction between two entities or events, intrinsic and necessary limits emerge: on the one hand, a lower limit on how small and how close together those events or entities can be before ceasing to be separate entities; and on the other hand, an upper limit on how far apart and how fast they are moving apart for a relation to exist at all. Indeed, we can quickly grasp the necessity of these limits by trying (and failing) to imagine the opposite, a universe without such limits on observation, a universe as experienced by the gods of very small and very large things. In such a universe "viewed" from such a vantage, nothing at all happens because everything, everywhere, is perceived at once. And no movement or change can happen because any given thing can only ever be identical to what it is here and now.

And it turns out that these limits—be they the upper limit on how much space can be traversed in a set time or how much time can be measured as elapsing by a timepiece moving in space, or the lower limit on how small or short the observation of a sliver of space-time can be—are subject to the very same irresolvable paradoxes that Kant discovered with his antinomies. Which is what Einstein found out when, in 1917, he tried to use his new theory to take the measure of the cosmos as a whole.

ON NOVEMBER 4, 1915, EINSTEIN arrived at the grand hall of the Prussian State Library to give the first of four previously scheduled lectures to the Prussian Academy of Science. Few knew that he had been racing down to the wire to finish his calculations, and indeed would continue to work on them throughout the month leading to his climactic delivery of the field equations of gravity on November 25. The results were nothing short of revolutionary. As his biographer Walter Isaacson has written, "The general theory of relativity was not merely the interpretation of some experimental data or the discovery of a more accurate set of laws. It was a whole new way of regarding reality."[20] Max Born would later dub it "the greatest feat of human thinking about nature" and "the most amazing combination of philosophical penetration, physical intuition, and mathematical skill."[21] Unsurprisingly, such a usurpation of the laws of physics would have profound ramifications for the study of the cosmos as a whole. In 1916, after briefly basking in the success of his grueling efforts, Einstein turned his attention to this most fundamental of all questions.

Newton had believed that the universe must be akin to a finite island of matter floating in an infinite void of space. That the island in question must be finite he deduced from the nature of gravity, for an infinite amount of matter in the universe would generate an infinite gravitational force at the surface of every sphere located in it, which is impossible. Einstein quickly saw that his theories of gravitation and light led to radically different conclusions.

To begin with, one of the outcomes of his theory of special relativity had been the equivalence of mass and energy (canonized in the most famous equation in history, $E = mc^2$). According to this understanding, any finite island of mass in an infinite sea of empty space would radiate energy, and hence lose mass over time, leaving it "to become gradually but systematically impoverished."[22] Moreover, it conflicted with general relativity as well. Newton had interpreted his bucket experiment as showing that objects must know where they are in absolute space. As we saw before, in Einstein's theory the inertial mass of objects in space depended on the diffusion throughout the universe of a gravitational field that could be expressed mathematically in the form of a curved space-time continuum. But a finite amount of stuff spread out in an infinite expanse of space would effectively produce no such field, and hence we'd be back to Newton's bucket not knowing if it was spinning.[23]

But solving this problem by making space itself finite raised the age-old problem of what it could possibly mean for an all-encompassing cosmos to have boundaries. If there are boundaries, what lies outside them? Moreover, the mere idea of a boundary to space completely violated the theory of relativity, since the assumption of specific boundaries to space itself imposes an absolute "where" from which any measurements or observations would have priority, thus restoring the very privileged positions of measurement that relativity had managed to remove in favor of the universal application of the laws of physics.

Faced yet again with an antinomy where both options seemed at once absolutely necessary and utterly impossible, Einstein used the very curvature of space-time that his theory had found to be real to propose a radical solution. He knew his solution was likely to elicit disbelief, and in fact wrote to his friend Paul Ehrenfest that he was tentative about sharing it because it would expose him "to the danger of being confined to a madhouse."[24] His radical solution was to propose a shape for the cosmos that was both finite and without boundaries, thus resolving the issue of where exactly the cosmos was supposed to be floating around and why its contents didn't just spread out into a further infinite emptiness around it: "The curvature of space is variable in time and place, according to the distribution of matter, but we may roughly approximate to it by means of a spherical space."[25]

By spherical Einstein specifically meant a 3-sphere, the space "discovered by Riemann" that we have already seen both in Dante's cosmos and in Borges's Library. Like those spaces, the sphere of this universe has no outer boundaries. As Einstein wrote, for anyone in such a cosmos moving out from a central point, "the circumference of a circle first increases with the radius until the 'circumference of the universe' is reached, and that it thenceforward gradually decreases to zero for still further increasing values of the radius."[26] Like Dante's cosmos, if you look outward from where you are, your line of sight eventually reaches a point where you start to look inward toward a central point. Like Dante's cosmos, its laws are the same everywhere; there is no place Dante could have stepped onto the primum mobile that would have made a difference to his route. Like in Borges's Library, there is no hexagonal cell that is any different from any other.

And yet Einstein's numbers didn't quite add up. According to his calculations, the universe as a whole must be changing in time, either shrinking or expanding. Unwilling to accept his own conclusions, Einstein fudged the numbers by inserting what he called a cosmological constant, a term he deemed "necessary only for the purpose of making possible a quasi-static distribution of matter"; in other words, the added number stabilized his calculations and allowed the universe to remain at a constant size. But remain that size the universe would not.

A few years after Einstein proposed his cosmological model, the Russian meteorologist Alexander Friedmann used the equations of general relativity to propose that the universe was in fact expanding. A decade later the astronomer Edwin Hubble performed observations of distant galaxies that proved this to be the case.[27] Einstein grudgingly accepted these findings and rued his addition of the cosmological constant as being his worst blunder ever. (Years later a new force pushing the expansion of the universe ever faster would be discovered, one that would be remarkably close in value to Einstein's blunder.)

Since Einstein's 3-sphere extends in four-dimensional space-time, it makes no sense to think of it exclusively in spatial terms. Rather, we need to take into account that information about one part of space always takes time to arrive at any other part of space. This means that as we aim our telescopes out into the night sky, we are not looking out, "like one looking out from the saloon entrance on to the dark Atlantic or from the lighted porch upon dark and lonely moors," but looking in. We are looking inward toward the origin of a universe that, as Augustine reminded us, began not in time but with time. The boundaries of the cosmos cannot be located in space and time; rather, its limits are intrinsic to space and time themselves.

This is what the astronomers Arno Penzias and Robert Wilson confirmed when they cleaned their radio telescopes of the pigeon droppings that had accumulated there in a futile attempt to get rid of the residue of static that was marring their readings of the distant cosmos. Their failure led them to deduce that they were detecting the cosmic microwave background radiation, the traces left over from the almost infinite density and temperatures of the earliest moments of the universe's existence. Like Dante's pilgrim, who, stepping onto the primum mobile, exclaimed its "nearest and most exalted parts are all so uniform, I cannot tell which Beatrice selected as my place," so uniform is the distribution of this radiation we can aim our telescopes in any direction we want and we will get the same readings.[28] Indeed, just like Dante's cosmos, a universe that expands in space-time must be contained by its own center: a point at the origin of space and time that envelops and enables all of existence. And just like in Borges's Library, where we are at any time determines that point. For this four-dimensional architecture implies an observer in the here and now, an observer who looks outward in space and simultaneously inward toward a singularity. An origin not in time but of time; not in space, but of space.

This architecture derives from the very principle that Einstein's relativity theories salvaged, the principle that there could be no privileged place in the universe from which to adjudicate different measurements. That no motion whatsoever, even that of the water in Newton's bucket, is motion in an absolute sense, but is always motion in respect to some other point of reference. That the universe is not located anywhere, but rather has no other *where* than here—not in the mind of God, but in the very minimum conditions that permit anything to be observed in the first place. For this extraordinary truth—that when gazing *out* into space, we are also gazing *in* toward the origin of all space and time—is not merely an interesting quirk of cosmology. It is what enables there to be cosmos in the first place.

HEISENBERG'S INVITATION TO SPEAK in Berlin in the spring of 1926 would have been daunting for anyone. Not only was the University of Berlin the citadel of physics, home to such luminaries as Einstein and Planck, but its physics colloquium was religiously attended by the entire faculty. Now the twenty-four-year-old research assistant had stood in front of this august assembly and explained why the fundamental assumptions of their worldview were wrong. In his typically understated way, Heisenberg would later recount that his "unconventional theory" managed to "arouse Einstein's interest."[29]

Back at Einstein's house after their walk from the institute, engaging in the requisite small talk along the way, Einstein launched into why supporting a theory only on observations is not enough. We are never in the presence of raw data, unadorned by theory, he told Heisenberg; rather, "it is the theory which decides what we can observe."[30] Where Heisenberg had drawn an analogy between his own discovery and what Einstein had done with Newton's concept of time, Einstein now drew a sharp distinction. With relativity he had redefined what counted as an observation. Two observers could no longer simply look at an event and agree that it had occurred at a specific time; instead, they would each synchronize their respective observations with a clock, and the time of the observed event would depend on the relative motion of the clocks. The "old descriptive language" for time thus needed replacing with a new theory.[31]

For quantum mechanics, the electron followed a path in the cloud chamber but appeared not to follow one inside the atom. In Einstein's view, by simply denying the continuity of its movement when in the atom, Heisenberg was setting himself up for failure, "moving on very thin ice," he told him, because he relied on the same old descriptive language.[32] Without a new theory to decide what to observe, Heisenberg would be stuck with observations that didn't make sense, because they didn't explain the reality of what happened between those observations.

The conversation with Einstein continued to haunt Heisenberg long after his visit to Berlin. Indeed, it would lurk in the recesses of his consciousness for almost a year before surfacing again during his stay at the institute in Copenhagen. There, finally relieved of Bohr's pestering presence by his decision to go skiing, Heisenberg's mind returned to the path of the electron in a cloud chamber, its trajectory clearly mapped for all to see. At the same time, his own mathematical framework proving the discontinuity of electrons inside the atom didn't lie. The contradiction appeared impossible to resolve.

And then, late one evening, he thought again of his conversation with Einstein.[33] Unable to sleep, Heisenberg pursued this thought as he walked out into the frigid night for a walk in Faelled Park. Einstein had pointed to the contradiction between his theory, which allowed for no path within atoms, and the clearly observable paths within cloud chambers. When Einstein said that the theory decides what we observe, he clearly meant that Heisenberg's math was clouding his observations. As he had said that day, "If your theory is right, you will have to tell me sooner or later what the atom does when it passes from one stationary state to the next."[34] He meant, in other words, that *in reality* the electron always moved as it does in the cloud chamber, even if Heisenberg's theory told him it didn't.

In the icy dark of his walk through the park, Heisenberg now realized that Einstein was right about the role theory played in directing his observations but he was wrong about which theory and which observations it was directing.

When scientists thought they observed a clear path in the cloud chamber, perhaps their theory told them what to see there. Perhaps they didn't see a path at all, but rather "a series of discrete and ill-defined spots through which an electron had passed." After all, the water droplets that formed the path in the chamber were far larger than the electron. Heisenberg rushed back to the institute and quickly scratched out a series of calculations that showed without a doubt that merely approximate values for an electron's place and velocity could easily account for the perceived path in a cloud chamber. Those calculations also put a lower limit on how exact the observation of either the position or the velocity could be. He had discovered the uncertainty principle.[35]

The theory guides the observation: this is a statement that might have been made by Kant. Every impression is informed; every intuition has a form, a condition of the possibility of its becoming an observation in the first place. Einstein reminded Heisenberg of this insight to dissuade him from undermining the basic sense of reality underlying our observations. For Einstein theory meant a "knowledge of natural laws" needed for reality to function in the first place.[36] When Heisenberg talked about observations without regard to theory, he was on thin ice because he was "suddenly speaking of what we know about nature and no longer about what nature really does."[37] He was failing to use his knowledge of natural laws to translate our *knowledge* of nature into the *reality* of nature.

Heisenberg took the lesson differently. What he realized is that *some* theory always accounts for our observations, and that precisely for this reason we are always limited to speaking of what we know about nature and not about what nature does in itself. We see the path of the electron in the cloud chamber because our theory tells us that particles travel continuously through space and time. But that continuity could also *not* be part of the electron's reality but rather be part of ours, because—like Funes recognizing himself in the mirror—the minimum requirement of any observation at all is that the observer span those space-time moments and create that continuity. This was what had led them astray. The observers and their theory, their way of seeing the world, the necessary forms of their intuition, sit at the heart of any observation, and there is no way to remove them from that place. The best we can do is account for their influence and understand that, when we push our observations to the limits of all possible experience, retaining the assumptions proper to our experience in space and time will lead us astray. This is precisely what cosmologists discovered when they turned their attention to the edge of the universe and to the primal moment of creation itself.

COSMOLOGY DEALS WITH THE largest of questions: the size and shape of the universe; its history over vast periods of time. Quantum mechanics, in contrast, confronts the unimaginably tiny and its eva-nescence in infinitesimal slivers of time. As such, the paradoxes of the quantum world, which don't affect our real-world experiences of planes and baseballs, would seem utterly trivial next to the incon-ceivable expanses of space and time.

The discovery that the universe is expanding changed all that. For if we trace an expanding universe back in time, we inevitably come to a moment when the unimaginably large becomes, well, imagin-able. And before that, rather small. And before that, unimaginably small. And all of a sudden we face the prospect that the discontinu-ous and probabilistic nature of the subatomic world must have had an enormous effect on our universe at the very first microseconds of its existence. Moreover, if we accept that particles have no single path until they are observed, or to put it another way, the path of particles is a quality of the observations we make of them and not of the particles themselves, we are stuck with the unsettling possibility that the same holds true for the universe.

The physicist John Wheeler proposed a thought experiment that would expand the apparatus involved in the two-slit experiment to cosmic scales. Light emitted from a powerful source like a quasar billions of light-years away can pass around a source of gravity like a galaxy and be refocused by the time it arrives at Earth, the very process predicted by Einstein and confirmed by Eddington that we now call gravitational lensing. In theory, each side of the galaxy acts like a slit in the experiment. Were we able to set up a vast array of detectors around Earth, we ought to be able to detect an interference pattern from the quasar's emissions. Furthermore, if we could position a device on the light's pathway toward Earth to detect which path the photons had taken, the pattern should disappear—even though the "choice" of which side of the galaxy the photon was taking would have been made eons earlier.[38]

Indeed, photons traversing the expanse of space-time must attend to the same rules that govern the behavior of photons passing through the slits in a tiny experimental device. Depending on one's interpretation of quantum mechanics, this can mean that our present-day observation determines the past trajectory; or that the photon has no path until it has been measured; or that the photon takes all possible paths until some measurement is performed that limits or removes some options; or that each measurement effectively splits the current universe into two, one for each "choice" the photon is forced to make. As Stephen Hawking and Leonard Mlodinow have argued, like the experimenter in a quantum experiment, our observations of the present state of the universe must determine its history.[39]

When we take the lessons we've learned from quantum mechanics and apply them to the universe as governed by Einstein's theory of relativity, an extraordinary thing happens. To begin with, as Einstein first resisted but eventually accepted, the universe's expansion is predicted by general relativity, but by the same laws the theory also predicts that moving backward in time, we must come to a moment when it was an infinitesimal point of infinite density and temperature,[40] a point much like that described by Dante, that sends forth "so acute / a light, that anyone who faced the force / with which it blazed would have to shut his eyes, / and any star that, seen from earth, would seem / to be the smallest, set beside that point, as star conjoined with star, would seem a moon."[41] And like this central point in Dante's cosmos, the singularity required by general relativity isn't located somewhere in space and time; rather, it has no other *where* because, as present-day cosmologists put it (echoing Augustine, whether consciously or not), the universe began not *in* space and time but *with* space and time, and thus asking what came before it is a meaningless question.[42] Like Dante's center, the infinitesimal point at the origin of space and time envelops all of creation; it is the horizon that we gaze out upon, only to realize we have been gazing inward all along.

Not only are we forced to reckon with the paradox of an edge to space and time when we attempt to conceive of the cosmos as a whole, but the fact that the singularity combines the conditions of infinite heat and density in an infinitesimally small space means that relativity no longer escapes the logic of the quantum world. As we have learned by now, the inescapable law of the macrocosm is the maximum amount of space that can be traversed by information relative to an observer in a given amount of time. Likewise, the law of the microcosm is nothing other than Heisenberg's uncertainty principle, which states that for an observer to reduce the uncertainty of the position of a particle to zero, its momentum becomes infinitely unknown, and vice versa, and for an observer to reduce the uncertainty of the time of an event to zero, its energy becomes infinitely unknown. Since conceiving of the origin of the universe by definition means focusing on a moment when time was nothing, uncertainty requires that the energy at that moment be literally anything. Uncertainty awaits us at the dawn of creation.[43]

.   .   .

THE RESULTS OF THE two-slit experiment seem paradoxical. How does merely observing a particle at one point cause the interference pattern elsewhere to disappear? The beauty of the Wheeler thought experiment is how it reveals that the two observations, the one at the slit (or galaxy) and the other at the screen (or array of detectors), are separate observations, the results of which can only ever be communicated at the speed of light—a fact obscured by the small size and easy communicability of observations in a laboratory. The weirdness that the two-slit experiment seems to showcase stems from believing that the observers are the same and that their observations are the same, but they are not. Just as with relativity, where observers in different frames of reference have different readings for what "now" means, these observers must have different descriptions of reality because their experiments measure the relations of points in space and time that are specific to the conditions of each measurement.

Like Achilles failing to overtake the tortoise, or the watched quantum pot failing to boil, the results seem paradoxical only because we project our expectation about reality—that it is single, consistent, and stable—onto observations that by definition relate different points in space-time, and then are surprised that reality behaves other than what we expect. We are surprised that the one observation seems to change the other because we assume, naturally, the unity of the reality in which those observations take place. They are part of, we believe, the same chunk of space-time, of reality stuff. But this shared reality stuff is of our own making. And thus our surprise is something like that of Funes at seeing his face in the mirror. Which should make us pause. For Funes's surprise depended on an illegitimate assumption.

Our observations always entail, require, a blurring of the now, a continuum of space-time. But then we turn that continuum into the thing we are trying to observe instead of the means of observing it and are surprised by the results. Funes is surprised at his own face because he thinks the continuity of space-time he brings with him to his observation pertains to the reality he is observing. It does not. The unity of his self is not a thing in reality; it is the means of his observing anything at all. We think we can home in on each moment of Achilles's path through space-time as he overtakes the tortoise, but we cannot. His path is not a thing in reality; it is the means of our observing his race. We think we should see the path of the particle, but we cannot. Its path is not a thing in reality; it is the means of our observing its place or momentum.

Because observations relate events in space and time, they are subject to the intrinsic limits of knowledge. As we stretch our minds to encompass everything, we inevitably encounter the very limits of what is capable of being comprehended, the limits inherent in observation itself. Space and time, as the cosmologist Marcelo Gleiser puts it, are "descriptive tools we create to quantify the transformations of the natural world."[44] At the scale of the universe, "we live in a spherical bubble of information."[45] Likewise, at the quantum scale we encounter a similarly unsurpassable limit on the information we can extract from the world. As Borges concluded so many years ago, we must suspect that there is no universe, at least in the organic sense we attribute to that word.[46] For all the reality we grant it, that universe is a human construct.

And how could it have been otherwise? This is where Einstein, so seldom wrong, failed. Heisenberg, he cautioned, was speaking of our knowledge of nature and no longer about what nature really does. But in science, the greatest scientist of all insisted, we ought to be concerned only with what nature does.[47] On this point Heisenberg would never agree, insisting until the end that what we observe is not nature itself but nature exposed to our method of questioning.[48]

Heisenberg was willing to face the consequences of his realization that our science is always an exploration of the world as it is revealed to us, in space and time. Indeed, the uncertainty principle tells us with enormous precision what the limits on that knowledge are in the world of the very small, just as relativity tells us with enormous precision that what we can know here and now about the larger universe around us is fundamentally limited by the speed of light. Those limits are baked into reality, yes, because our knowledge is also baked in. For what does "position" mean, what does "momentum" mean, outside a measurer, a knower who seeks to determine them? Likewise, what could the shape of the cosmos in space and time possibly mean independent of someone positioned in time and space, for whom the cosmos can assume a shape in the first place?

Like Heisenberg, Einstein had read Kant. He even brought Kant's *Prolegomena to Any Future Metaphysics* along for some light summer reading on the Baltic Sea in 1918, to help him come down from the herculean effort of formulating general relativity.[49] But on this point Einstein had missed the memo. If Kant was saying anything, and he was certainly saying a lot, it was this: we are *never* concerned solely with what nature does; we are *always* speaking of what we know about nature.

But Heisenberg grasped something else. Like Kant, he grasped what happens when we overlook that fundamental fact.[50] As we'll see in the next chapter, Kant's realization of the role reason has in creating the image we have of nature gives us the key to understanding the relationship of scientific knowledge to our experience of beauty; it also helps solve one of the most perplexing mysteries of modern cosmology: how the universe evolved to support life.

9

MADE TO MEASURE

B Y TURNING THEIR GAZES toward the deepest recesses of the past to understand the very origins of existence, cosmologists opened a Pandora's box of philosophical enigmas. Among these, one stands out: had the fundamental laws of nature diverged from their actual values by even vanishingly small degrees, the universe would not have evolved to sustain any kind of life resembling our own. In short, the cosmos appears made to measure, constructed with the purpose of producing beings like us who can in turn measure it, study its mysteries, and ask fundamental questions about their own origins.

The enigma of the improbability of human existence started to arise not long after it became clear that the universe expands and hence must have had a starting point in time. Already in 1951 the astronomer Fred Hoyle established that the forces holding together atomic nuclei had to be within a thousandth of their actual value for oxygen and carbon to be produced at the levels needed to sustain life.[1] In 1999 cosmologists discovered that if the early universe had been more homogeneous, galaxies and hence stars and planets might never have formed, but if it had been less homogeneous, with more prominent ripples of energy and matter, the resulting universe would have turned out so clumpy that today it would consist mostly of black holes—not the most hospitable home for life as we know it.

Another of the "dials" that had to be precisely set if life were to eventually emerge showed up when Einstein used general relativity to describe the whole of the universe. As we saw before, to ensure that a four-dimensional space-time sphere remained stable over time, as he believed any self-respecting universe must do, he slipped an extra number into his calculations, which he later regretted. And yet, years later, scientists discovered a mysterious force pushing the expansion of the universe that clocks in at just about the value that Einstein came up with—a little too large and the universe curves back into itself and crunches together; a little too small and it curves out from itself and tears itself apart.[2]

Estimates of the degree of fine-tuning the laws of nature must have had vary enormously, depending on what result one hopes to explain. Whereas a run-of-the-mill, could-sustain-some-kind-of-existence universe might cost us an improbability of one in a thousand or so, a made-to-order cosmos within shouting distance of our own comes with a price tag so steep that its zeros would outnumber all the atoms in the universe.[3]

The philosophical problem that emerged from the realization that our very existence as sentient beings owes a great deal to chance has led some scientists to what they call the anthropic principle. This principle takes two forms: a "weak" one that scientists often accept as likely true but not particularly mind-blowing as revelations go; and a "strong" one that comes across to most scientists like a lot of hocus-pocus. The strong anthropic principle also goes by the name of "design"—as in, to explain how something as wildly improbable as intelligent life emerged from such a potentially inhospitable set of possibilities requires us to presume that a being of vast power and intelligence planned it that way. The weak anthropic principle, in contrast, simply concedes that, as improbable as it may seem that the universe emerged to support intelligent life, it would be more improbable for life to find itself living in a universe that didn't support it.

While most scientists tend to harbor distaste for obviously metaphysical solutions such as presented by the strong anthropic principle, one cosmological theory that emerges from the weak principle has garnered some interest. This theory, known as the multiverse, posits that all possible universes in fact exist, and that our own is one in an innumerable set of universes of infinitely different sizes, shapes, and durations, each with its own set of laws and constants. If this were true, supporters say, it would solve the problem of the improbability of a life-supporting cosmos. As one proponent of this theory describes it, if you walked into a clothing store with only one suit on its racks, and it happened to fit, you would be rightfully surprised. If you walked into a store whose racks teemed with suits and one happened to fit, this would be considerably less surprising. The multiverse theory effectively turns a one-suit store into an infinite-suits store.[4]

Whether in its strong or weak versions, finding a suit that fits is a telling metaphor for the anthropic principle. The improbability of the laws of nature that would support our existence seems incommensurable with the fact of our existence. We feel a need to resolve this tension, to explain how such improbable laws came about. So, like Sherlock Holmes, we investigate and come up with a series of explanations. We desire to find the answer to the mystery, but we also desire it to end in a certain way; namely, we want to learn something new, but also something that makes sense, that fits into what we already know.

To find that the initial settings of the universe are a random set of numbers that could just as easily have been different seems clunky, infelicitous, something like plowing through a mystery novel, only to find out that the murderer is some random character we haven't even encountered yet. We yearn for a more aesthetically satisfying, even beautiful, answer. The anthropic principle in both its versions

seeks to respond to that yearning by showing us as an inevitable outcome of the initial settings. Either infinite universes exist and our
own existence selects for the conditions that support us, or a single
universe was created with purpose to sustain life. To put it another
way, either we take an idea, that the mathematical models we have
arrived at explain the universe, and grant it the privilege of really
existing in the form of the multiverse, or we elevate actual reality to
the level of the ultimate idea, namely, God's plan.

The belief in some element of design or intention in the forma-
tion of the universe has had a long history. The medieval theologian Thomas Aquinas deduced from the evidently ordered nature
of the world that "there is some intelligent being by whom everything in nature is directed to a goal, and this we call 'God.'"[5] The
key to Aquinas's deduction is the notion of purpose. Either things
happen without a purpose and hence occur by random chance, he
reasoned, or they are guided toward an end. Since it is evident that
something as extraordinary as life, and human life to boot, could
hardly come about by the random meanderings of blind chance, it
follows that the universe has purpose: the creation and sustenance of
human life.

The idea of purpose extends beyond the simple attribution of
the rigor we find in nature to a divine mind. In Kant's time, it had
become a philosophical commonplace to read the evidence coming
from organic life as a sign of a kind of causality that transcended the
merely mechanical. To a degree, Kant accepted these arguments. As
he reasoned in the last of his great works, whereas the various parts
of a watch are affected by encountering one another and imparting motion, organic matter, such as the seed that takes nourishment
from the earth and sun and turns it with time into a tremendous
oak, exhibits an entirely different kind of causal power.[6] As the seed
develops, Kant reasoned, the intricate causal links from cell to cell,
moment to moment of its growth, appear to be guided by the idea
of what the seed always had to be.

In Kant's time, the kind of extra causality he attributed to organic matter was widely thought to be at work in the world in general. Leibniz's thought, somewhat simplified and perhaps even degraded under the enormous influence of Christian Wolff's teaching, had its followers looking for an ultimate purpose pretty much everywhere. Sunlight, Wolff had proclaimed, exhibits purpose because with it "we can conveniently carry on our duties, which cannot be done in the evening at all, or at least not so handily and with difficulties."[7] For confirmation biases of this magnitude, Kant had little more than scorn. Indeed, he liked to respond by citing Voltaire's famous lampoon of Leibniz in his play *Candide*, whose titular character would claim with a straight face that God had obviously given men noses so as better to hold up their spectacles.[8]

Kant knew he was walking a fine line, on the one hand ridiculing the most obvious examples of imputing intelligent design to nature while, on the other, holding out the possibility of some other causality at work than the strictly mechanistic. What this other causality might be and how to understand its relation to the necessity of mechanistic causality would become the centerpiece of his last great work. It was in this book, which was ultimately about artistic creation as much as our understanding of the natural world, that Kant worked out the solution to a mystery that unites science and the arts, the mystery of what guided a genius like Einstein as he teased an explanation for gravity out of the subtle geometry of space and time, or one like Heisenberg when, in the dark of night on the windswept island of Heligoland, he saw spread before him the mathematics of nature in all its splendor. For as much as their discoveries differed, one and the same lodestar led both scientists to their insights. They knew their theories to be right because they perceived them to be beautiful.[9]

WHAT MAKES AN OBJECT, a person, an experience, beautiful? The ancients long had an answer for this question. Unless we resign ourselves to a concept of aesthetic appreciation as the mere expression of fleeting and meaningless pleasures, the perception of beauty must indicate a more noble, unchanging idea underlying it. For Plato, just as a person's beauty indicated the presence of a good and wise soul, the harmony of nature and the harmony of mathematics were signs that, in its transience, the physical world expressed permanent and perfect ideas that guide and form it. This was also the position of the rationalist philosophers who believed that the natural world expressed God's preestablished harmony, and it was the position that dominated Germany when, as he was wont to do, Immanuel Kant decided to step in.

In the spring of 1786, Kant was at the height of his intellectual powers. He had also become the academic equivalent of a rock star. Already a third book dedicated to his philosophy would appear that year; across Germany, university courses about his work were popping up; and the older generation's best-known philosopher, Moses Mendelssohn, had just laid on Kant the epithet of "all-crushing."[10] Perhaps most tellingly, people had started to wonder if Kant's philosophy just might be dangerous. A rumor quickly spread that his famously difficult writing had driven at least one student insane, and a popular psychologist inveighed against the study of Kant's writings, warning that they could "deaden the love of true learning" and "draw the attention away from the concerns of human life as well as from the works of art and nature which warm the heart and heighten the imagination." Reading Kant and his ilk, he grumbled, would "unsettle the powers of the understanding, spoil good principles, and poison the source of human happiness." Such sensationalism aside, Kant's writing might indeed have led to at least some risky behavior. At the University of Jena, one student insinuated that a colleague who had dared to make a comment about Kant would need thirty years of study to understand the thinker. For good measure he then added that thirty more would be in order before the fellow should open his mouth on the subject. Naturally, a duel ensued.[11]

Between engaging in debates, fending off critical reviews, and finishing the second edition of his masterwork, not to mention serving as rector of the university, Kant had his hands full. Yet his heart was not in it. For a large portion of his time had become absorbed by the waning health of his best friend, Joseph Green. Each afternoon he went to sit next to Green's sickbed, staying beside his ailing friend until the hour he would have left his house had they dined together. This lasted until the day of Green's death on June 27. Kant was devastated. From that moment he ceased to socialize in restaurants and cafés, and his social circles shrank. He would continue to visit a few friends in their homes, but for most of his meals Kant began to employ a cook and eat at home.[12]

The following year Kant decided to institutionalize this practice. So, with another friend and former student, Christian Jacob Kraus, he established a dining club that would regularly meet in his house. The ritual started slowly. On Easter Day 1787, Hamann went with his children to call on Kraus at his house, where they were told they could find him at Kant's house. When they arrived, they "found the two bachelors in a cold room, completely frozen."[13] Delighted to see them, Kant had some fine wine brought in, and the day brightened considerably.[14] From these inauspicious embers a crackling social fire grew. Many of the most prominent citizens of Königsberg would gather for meals at Kant's house, and many more would number among those visitors to the town who came to pay their respects to the great philosopher, only to end up, pleasantly surprised, sitting at his table.

Kant enjoyed these dinners immensely and would eagerly await the hour of his guests' arrival. Once the meal had started, he relished the role of host, personally handing out silverware and enchanting his guests with amusing patter. The meals materialized as if the order of the dishes were determined by an ethical maxim (in Kant's mind they likely were): "Only three dishes, but excellently prepared and very tasty, two bottles of wine, and when in season there was fruit and dessert."[15] If guests tried to say grace before dinner, Kant would cut them off, evincing an impatience with religiosity that would increasingly threaten to alienate him from the legal authorities. He would also interrupt and change the subject if diners of a philosophical inclination tried to talk shop. But he would happily dish out the juicy political gossip of the day alongside the tender roast he served with the best English mustard. The core group that attended these dinners became Kant's lifeline. By the time he died some seventeen years later, the two dozen or so who remained from this circle of dining friends would carry his coffin.[16]

Seventeen eighty-seven was also the year Kant published the second edition of his *Critique of Pure Reason.* He had put the time and effort into this task because he felt it necessary to clarify and, in some cases, modify his claims, but now he was eager to get on to his next project. As he wrote to a correspondent in June of that year, he needed to avoid taking on any further reviews or engaging in more debates about his prior work so he could devote his attention to bringing out a "Critique of the Foundations of Taste."

Applying his critical method to questions of aesthetic appreciation was not incidental. Kant saw in our ability to have rational discussions about beauty a linchpin without which his entire system would remain unstable. In the first *Critique,* Kant had shown that the condition of the possibility of our perceiving anything at all was our innate ability to translate an otherwise bewildering chaos of sensory input into ordered events in space and time whose causal relations could be objectively established. Such objectivity in turn required the presumption of a total unity of the physical world, a mechanistic chain of causality from past to future, just as our ability to stitch disparate moments in time together depended on the presumption of a unified seat of consciousness. Crucially, Kant realized that we must presuppose such unity even though we can never verify it in our experience—never see the universe as a coherent object in space and time; never see the self on its own, apart from the flow of experiences it sutures together. Similarly, Kant now realized, whenever we connect two or more specific claims as being examples of a more general truth, of an idea that contains them both, the very coherence of our judgments requires us to assume a web of connections that links each specific instance to the whole of creation, even though that whole can never itself be an object of our experience.

Here, Kant said, lay the harmony that the ancients had identified as the source of beauty. For when we perceive the chaos of data we receive about the world to be connected by an underlying unifying idea, we find that amalgam to be beautiful, harmonious, complete on its own. Our desire to explain further is disarmed, and we find ourselves enraptured in contemplating a scene that requires nothing more of us, something for which we need to supply no external purpose because it carries its purpose entirely in itself. This is a feeling Kant believed we experienced in the presence of great art. As the conductor Marin Alsop once said about a symphony of Gustav Mahler's, every note is there for a reason.[17] Each of its elements is situated exactly right and couldn't be elsewhere, hence the piece seems necessary, inevitable, yet in no way could we have come upon it on our own, in which case it would give us the sense of being hackneyed, clichéd.

Ancient philosophers were thus right in believing that we are attracted to and find beautiful those common principles that we discover underlying and unifying the bewildering diversity of nature. When Plato argued that we feel joy or pleasure upon discovering a mathematical rule expressed in nature, he touched on an essential faculty of our cognition that permits us to recognize and appreciate the purposiveness of nature—the purposiveness that expresses itself in the seed that grows to become a mighty oak, the purposiveness that seems to tell us this must have been designed this way.

While Kant agreed that we feel something is beautiful when we sense something like purposiveness in it, he believed the ancients erred in thinking such purposiveness was an essential aspect of nature itself. As he wrote, "In the necessity of that which is purposive and so constituted as if it were intentionally arranged for our use, but which nevertheless seems to pertain originally to the essence of things, without any regard to our use, lies the ground for the great admiration of nature."[18] Key here is the phrase "as if." The ground for our admiration, Kant insisted, lies not outside in the world but in our reason's relation to the picture we make of the world. So powerful is the draw of that picture's coherence that the ancients projected it outward into the world itself, transforming an inner sense of purposiveness into an actual purpose. There is indeed purposiveness, structure, rigor in our picture of nature, Kant replied, but it is supplied by our own reason.

Just as Kant showed that we must presuppose the existence of a whole, unified cosmos for our individual observations to cohere, even though we can never grasp that whole cosmos as an object, the harmony between parts of a system and its internal guiding principle is not an empirical fact that can be established for once and for all but a presumption necessary for deriving laws in the first place. We cannot see the oak tree in the seed, and yet we also cannot coherently grasp how seeds develop into oak trees without imagining them as being guided by a final purpose throughout their growth. Discovering such harmony ignites in us a feeling of beauty, and we are driven to it—not only in works of art or the appreciation of nature, but in science itself. Indeed, the standards that scientists report as guiding their preferences—the preference for the economy of nature's laws over their profligacy; the ideal of simplicity that guided science from Newton's discovery of the laws of motion to Einstein's gorgeous simplification and incorporation of gravity—make sense when we see them no longer as part of nature itself but as things we impose on nature to make sense of it.[19]

In this respect, our appreciation of artistic works provides us with a model for detecting purposiveness in nature. In artworks like Mahler's symphonies, we recognize a masterful hand that had a reason for placing each note where it was. We know there is a purpose there, and we hear it as we progress through the symphony; we marvel at its perfection. In nature we experience a similar marvel when we contemplate the towering oak that emerged from a tiny seed or realize that the movement of every massive object in the skies can be described and predicted by a few calculations. But whereas in nature we are attracted by the sense of a guiding hand even when there is none, in art the analogy is reversed: we are attracted to products of a guiding hand where the hand itself has become invisible. For a work of art whose artistry is too evident loses its ability to cause wonder; it becomes staid and predictable. In both art and nature, we see beauty in signs of purposiveness without purpose, natural artistry—but with an important difference. Whereas in nature we supply the artist, in art we supply the sense of its naturalness, that it was produced without evident artifice.

This structural analogy between the natural and the artistic both animates our appreciation of the products of the imagination and provides a standard for judgments about disputes of taste. The fact is, we do this all the time. Let's return to the example of a mystery novel. You make it through three-hundred-plus pages, and the culprit turns out to be a character you've never met before with no connection to the story so far. Surprising? Certainly, but no one in their right mind would judge this to be an excellent way to end the story. Now let's say that in the mystery you're reading, each clue led so inevitably to the final revelation that you could see it coming a hundred pages before the end. Clearly that would be unsatisfying as well. In the first case you would be faced with a random occurrence, an unmotivated insertion into the structure of the novel that destroyed any sense of its coherence, its purposiveness. The novel is certainly surprising, but there is nothing inevitable about it—the occurrences seem random, without purpose. In the second case, however, you've seen the author's handiwork the whole way through; it's all inevitability with no surprise, all artifice with no naturalness. Unlike with Mahler, our first reaction is that we could do that ourselves just by following a recipe. The result is a work of "art" that no one wants to spend their time on.

Purposiveness without purpose is thus a model for making claims about the aesthetic value of works of art, since we find art beautiful if it exhibits a harmony *as if* it had arisen there naturally.

In this way it releases us from the conundrum of radical subjectiv-ism, whereby all are entitled to their own opinion about a work's value and there are no rational bases for arguing about it. The irony of such subjectivism is that while it sounds coherent enough (how indeed can I trump someone's argument that, hey, this is beautiful because I find it beautiful?), no one in practice seems to believe it. As Kant puts it, in matters of taste there is a real difference between saying you like something and saying that it is beautiful. In the lat-ter case your statement implicitly demands concurrence, whereas in the former it does not.[20] Purposiveness without purpose provides an objective standard for arguing why one finds one work more beauti-ful than another.

But purposiveness without purpose is also a model for under-standing the appeal of scientific explanations of the natural world, since we are attracted by theories that reveal the harmony between specific observations and a general explanation *as if* that harmony had been put there by design. This fit between the knowability of the world and our ability to know it engenders aesthetic pleasure—not a fulfillment of personal benefit or the satisfaction of appetite, but the pure joy of experiencing, in a flash, how a single rule explains the functioning of seemingly disparate aspects of nature.

In a satisfying work of art, the ensemble of its elements con-forms to its internal principle, the idea that guides it. Thus, when we come to the end of a mystery novel, the solution appears inevitable, although we couldn't see it coming. Likewise, when we find a theo-retical explanation for the seemingly random events of the natural world, we feel the same aesthetic satisfaction as with a well-wrought plot or a masterfully composed symphony: we thrill to the diversity of nature expressing the idea of its order, its inherent rigor. That guiding principle that we read in nature or in art appears to us its purpose. But just as the work of art ignites our aesthetic judgment only when its creator has erased the signs of artifice, so our under-standing of the natural world is led by a silent conviction that the universe that unveils itself before our eyes works toward an end and purpose, one it expresses from the greatest cataclysms of galaxies down to the most intimate crevices of possible perception, and yet one that was never meant, never intended, never planned by angel, god, or human mind, other than our own.

AS A NEW DECADE dawned, Kant was feeling impatient. During the last, astoundingly productive ten years he had published more important, not to say world-changing, works of philosophy on a wider array of topics than pretty much anyone before him. But two of his most widely read works during that time, the *Groundwork for the Metaphysics of Morals* and *The Critique of Practical Reason*, had taken far longer to appear in print than he had anticipated. Now, eager to see the third major chapter of his critical philosophy in bookstores and sparking conversations, he decided to change publishers. Between January and March 1790, he sent his new editor in Berlin his manuscript of the *Critique of the Power of Judgment* in four batches as he finished them. The editor had clearly gotten the memo. By April, Kant was already grumbling about having to plow through page proofs, and the book would appear shortly thereafter.[21]

As busy as this period was, other tasks loomed. Kant was not getting any younger, and he had his philosophical legacy to attend to. Anyone getting the kind of attention he now found focused on him was bound to become the target of some negative reviews, and one managed to get under Kant's skin. The criticism, the work of one J. A. Eberhard, came out in four volumes over three years. Even as Kant was rushing to finish his third *Critique,* the tenor of the attack started to irk him. In essence, Eberhard accused Kant of not being original; he claimed that Leibniz had foreseen Kant and worked out a better system. Moreover, in the few ways they differed, Kant had simply gotten it wrong.[22]

Kant was not about to take this lying down. In the brief hiatus between sending in the preface and introduction of the third *Critique* to his editor on March 22 and receiving the proofs a month later, he published a small book in response. The title, *On a Discovery According to Which Any New Critique of Pure Reason Has Been Made Superfluous by an Earlier One*, would have made Borges proud for its temporal acrobatics and dripping irony. In "discovering" that Leibniz's philosophy was somehow a better critique of pure reason than Kant's even prior to Kant's dismantling of it, Eberhard had not only utterly failed to understand what Kant was doing; he had also pretty much mangled Leibniz in the process, exposing him "to ridicule just when he thinks he is providing him with an apology."[23]

Obviously, Kant's system agreed significantly with Leibniz's, Kant conceded. Specifically, both systems argued for a kind of harmony between the natural world and the moral one. The distinction, however, lay in how each thinker got there, and this distinction made all the difference. For Leibniz the very reason we could trust the laws of physics was the reason to trust the existence of an ultimate moral law, for just as surely as God's hand guided the one, it had to be guiding the other. The lawfulness of nature and of morality emerged from the programmer's code, and all we had to do was read it. Kant's critical philosophy had upended this way of thinking for good. Nature's ultimate lawfulness, the necessary link between cause and effect, the tendrils connecting genus and species—all of these could be derived as necessary presuppositions of our ability to perceive individual objects in time and space. They were aspects of our knowledge, to be sure, but also aspects with necessity and hence objectivity. Likewise, as we will see in greater detail in the next chapter, the ultimate freedom of the human subject to choose and the nature of its moral duty could not depend on any religious doctrine or earthly tradition, but was a necessary presupposition for a being who finds itself confronting moral choices, because a being that was truly unfree and merely adrift in the flow of causal connections could only ever do as it was inclined to do; the mere fact of being faced with choices required the postulate of freedom.

So, harmony exists between the natural world and the moral one, between empirical judgments of causality and free moral choices, but only if one understands, as Leibniz had not yet, that this harmony flows not from a divine code but as a necessary condition of the possibility of our ability to perceive and think about the movement of bodies in space and time and to make decisions in a social world. Kant's work could indeed be considered the real defense of Leibniz, Kant concluded—a defense, namely, against such ostensible defenders as Eberhard himself.[24]

Kant's review had eviscerated the hapless critic. If alternate philosophical paths to the Kantian revolution had held any attraction for young thinkers, this slap-down pretty much nipped those growths in the bud. As the last decade of the eighteenth century debuted, philosophy in Germany, for all intents and purposes, had become a footnote to the work of one man, a man who had attained the stature of, in the words of an admiring visitor, the king of Königsberg.

Kant trounced his critic so decisively in part because the book he had just finished writing, his *Critique of the Power of Judgment*, had finally clarified exactly how to salvage the lawfulness of nature without falling prey to the metaphysical grandiosity of claiming to discern its ultimate purpose. For the presumption of an invisible hand guiding nature is pervasive; we see it in how scientists choose one theory over another because of its economy, simplicity, or beauty; we see it when physicists lift the veil of nature and discover the mathematical laws that structure it; we see it at work in the greatest of minds, as when Einstein denied that the Old One plays dice with the universe.

Kant also saw this apparent guiding hand at work, especially in his approach to the organic world. Indeed, Kant seemed to presage Darwin by half a century when he wrote that a more fulsome natural history would "trace back a host of apparently diverse types of races to one and the same genus."[25] But where others would see such manifestations of teleological causality as evidence of a greater power at work in nature, Kant saw a conflict within our faculty of reason between two ways of ordering its impressions. The first of these modes correctly grasps the causal relations between events within space-time; however, when reason uses that mode to follow its investigations of space-time events to their extremes—when it inquires about those ultimate questions, such as the shortest sliver of space-time, the edge of the universe, the ultimate cause of everything, or the possibility of making a free choice—it arrives at a point where mechanistic explanations fall short. Such questions require a different mode of thinking, one that asks *why* this law, *why* this overall structure, *why* these initial conditions and not some others, *why* this choice and not that one.

Each mode of thinking—one concerned with mechanistic steps within and the other with the holistic question of purpose—is necessary and justified in its own sphere. When we confuse them, however, error and even fanaticism ensue. Perhaps we end up like Candide, blithely insisting that we inhabit the best of all possible worlds, for how else could God have chosen this one for us? Worse, we might become convinced the world is a manifestation of our idea of its ultimate purpose, that we are required to intervene with fire and fury to set things right. Or, as rational scientists, we might end up expressing amazement that the laws of nature would be so finely tuned as to permit our existence and feel forced to conjure rather less than parsimonious theories to account for the gratifying fit.

Our astonishment, however, belies the mere fact that what is, is; that the world as we find it must always be the starting point for our investigations; that to seek to account for the improbability of the universe existing is like expressing delight that out of eight billion possible souls you had the luck to be born as you. Just as there was no you before you were born to feel lucky for, we don't need to imagine the fate of all those universes that didn't evolve into ours. For such is the sleight of hand of both the Leibnizian rationalist and modern advocates of the multiverse, who transform the mathematical reasoning that allows us to explain the world as we find it in space and time into a vision of the cosmos as an unconditioned whole, planting it there in the desert before creation, only to then feel awe that it should have grown this way at all.

This, then, was Kant's insight: the deist who believes the universe came about by design and the atheist physicist who turns to theories like the multiverse to explain the extreme improbability of our own creation both err. They err by treating individual events in space-time as if they were guided by a ghost in the machine; they err, likewise, by conceiving of the entirety of existence as a thing in time and space, subject to the vicissitudes of cause and effect, a bauble in the hands of the god of very large things. But deists and scientists confronting the improbability of our existence do not err when they feel awe; their mistake lies in the source they attribute to that feeling and the scenarios they come up with to explain it away. For just as our power of judgment, when correctly understood and limited, sees beauty in nature's laws as in the well-constructed work of art, it supplies a different aesthetic feeling when faced with the incommensurability between what we can grasp with our limited senses and the absolutely great or overwhelmingly powerful, those cosmic phenomena that utterly outstrip the scale of our human perceptions.

Faced with the irreconcilability of our cognition and the whole of the cosmos, its origin and edge, or between that cognition and the most minute alterations in space and time, we are struck not by a feeling of beauty but by what Kant calls the sublime. The vertigo we feel in the face of the infinitesimal; the awe we succumb to when we face the inconceivable mathematics of the cosmos or the cataclysmic raging of black holes we can never grasp with our senses—confronted with these we are overcome with a sense of the overwhelming scope and force of nature. And yet, Kant specifies, at the source of this feeling, this scintillating mélange of pleasure and pain, lies not those objects themselves but a disposition of our souls. For at the very moment we engage with phenomena that outstrip our capacity to grasp them as a whole, we also witness the inexhaustibility of our cognitive means, which permit us to transcend our limited locales and stretch to the ends of the universe.[26] That science can calculate the density of black holes or the values of fundamental constants of nature is a strength beyond measure. Our feeling of nature's sublimity pays tribute to this: the force of our intellectual capacities.

The sublime, like the beautiful, does not reside in things in the world, whether natural or made; it emerges as a reaction of our judgment to the representations we make of the world. For our representations to cohere, we must assume a greater order to them that ultimately outstrips our ability to verify it. As we verify such order locally, our judgment gratifies us with a feeling of beauty, of the parts fitting an ideal of the whole, a center that seems to contain the astonishing variety of existence and give it sense or purpose. In contrast, whenever we engage phenomena that threaten to overwhelm our ability to grasp them with our senses, reason stretches in a vain attempt to comprehend the very edges of totality itself, the border conditions of the universe, small and large, and we are taken simultaneously by our inadequacy to the challenge and by the awesome power of reason that permits us to conceptualize that very impossibility in the first place.

The capillaries of coherence flowing from species to genus, from the particular to the universal, are the necessary presupposition that permits us to encounter and differentiate particulars in the first place. As we uncover those patterns of coherence, we experience their necessity and feel pleasure. Contemplating such purposiveness, we are lulled by its harmony, but we simultaneously strive toward a totality whose very incomprehensibility stokes that desire like an ever-present dissonance we desperately wish to resolve. Stretching out from ourselves to resolve that incompatibility, we ultimately realize what we are striving for lies inside us; we find ourselves in the world and the world in ourselves. For when Kant contemplated "the starry heavens above me and the moral law within me," he was filled with awe, an awe that sprang from the realization that, whether staring in or staring out, he was gazing into the same unfathomable abyss.[27]

KANT TOOK SERIOUSLY THE notion that the state of the physical world at any time flows directly from the position and momentum of its constituent particles at prior times. Any attempt to smuggle another kind of causality into that chain of events amounts to a "mental jugglery that only reads the conception of an end into the nature of the things."[28] A disembodied soul was not, for Kant, a plausible answer. Nonetheless, although Kant considered the causal chains that sustain our knowledge of the world in space and time to be necessary, as he used his reason to pry open the linkages of space-time, he encountered a roadblock there, an insurmountable impasse that would arise whenever human cognition would try to apply the logic of space and time beyond the limits of our ability to discern differences in space and time.

Precisely there, at the most minute points of continuity between one moment and the next, Kant saw an antinomy rear its head. On the one side, a perfectly mechanistic chain, with no room for willful intervention into the course of history. On the other, spontaneous freedom of choice, not only evidenced throughout history and every living moment, but also, Kant believed, required by the very nature of practical reason itself, a freedom inherent in the very acts of judging ourselves and others that lie at the basis of all social organization. Each side could be flawlessly argued: every action in space and time has an efficient cause, and nothing is spontaneous; or, any sequence of events must have an origin that is not caused, hence spontaneity must exist.

But like any antinomy, Kant could see that it did not arise from an error on one side; rather, the error lay in a failure to understand the basic structure and limits of human knowledge, and in our tendency to mix two ways of thinking about nature and the knowledge we have of it. On the one hand, our very ability to discern the most minimal change entails that our observation span at least two moments and hence elude total absorption in the event being observed. Thus, as we delve into each individual link in the causal chain, we find it relies on any two elements being related by a third, a mediator whose intervention must slip out unnoticed for the chain to appear unbroken—just as the beads of condensation require the physicist's theory to produce an electron's path in a cloud chamber.[29] On the other hand, even as our very act of analyzing the world seems to require it, we are unable to isolate that alien influence. No matter how deeply we dig into the space-time chain, we will never find a link put there by free choice; we can never find a particle of consciousness, a material embodiment of soul. For us to register the moment of change from one space-time cell to the next requires that there exist some anchor in the flow that can register differences, and hence a pivot from which to *choose* what to observe. But try as we may, we cannot find that anchor and turn it into an object of our cognition.

Faced with this antinomy between freedom and determinism, many modern scientists and thinkers have simply decided that one side, freedom, needs to fall out of the equation. If freedom conflicts with science, so much the worse for freedom. But this solution entirely misses the point. The antinomy between mechanistic causality and freedom is rife throughout scientific thinking and practice, even among scientists who are unaware they are postulating freedom at all. Freedom implies choice, implies selection. By denying it to individuals in time and space, scientists and philosophers who profess to believe exclusively in mechanistic causality reintroduce it elsewhere, namely, at the edge of existence, in the form of that magical set of conditions that allowed us to emerge, evolve, and eventually observe the universe that birthed us.

In the case of the strong anthropic principle, this move is obvious, but it pertains to the weak principle's concept of the multiverse as well, just more subtly. Because what is free will other than the presumption of something uncaused inserting itself in a causal chain?

In the case of the anthropic principle, we remove that uncaused cause from within time and space, from within the causal chain, and place it outside time and space, before the birth of the universe, so that we can say all initial settings give birth to all possible universes, and hence explain away the improbability of our existence. We implicitly imagine a choice of universes outside space and time awaiting their manifestation in space-time to be tested out for their livability—much like a shop filled with differently sized suits waiting to be tried on.

But uncaused causality doesn't belong outside time and space, certainly not as a cognizable object, namely, a specific universe with definable constants. Uncaused causality can never be found, never turned into an object. As we will see in the next chapter, it can only ever be, and in fact must be, presupposed in the context of human choices. For when we do not do so, we treat humans as calculable entities, as means to get from one causal link to another, and we make an untenable presumption about the ultimate causal chain, namely, that it is knowable from beginning to end.

The outermost border of all that exists and has existed coincides with the innermost point, a point where one moment slides into the next, where a here differs ever so slightly from a there, thus allowing something like an experience of the world to take form in the first place. Both are sites of the breakdown of causality because causality happens in time and space, and both the edge of space-time and the instant of change are ideal assumptions that cannot be found in space-time. Whenever we claim to encounter them from the outside, to encompass them as knowable objects, we commit metaphysical overreach, whether in the form of birthing phantom universes or obliterating human freedom.

This nexus between the edge of existence and the abyss of freedom was what Kant identified when he said that the two things that filled him with admiration and awe were the starry heavens above and the moral law within. In both cases we are faced with the sublime, the aesthetic feeling produced by our realization that we can conceive of something overwhelmingly absolute—the cosmos in all its magnitude, our implacable obligation to choose—from the confines of an existence hemmed in by space, time, and contingency. If beauty guides us toward the coherence of nature as grasped by our understanding, the sublime points to both the incommensurability of our abilities with that end and the inexhaustibility of the cognitive means at our disposal. Or, to say it again with Heisenberg, "The ability of human beings to understand is without limit. About the ultimate things we cannot speak."[30]

The antinomy between freedom and determinism thus emerges from the very tools we use to study and understand the cosmos. We don't escape it by assuming away freedom any more than we escape it by placing an all-knowing god at the origin of creation to guide our every decision throughout history. For when we believe that nature takes its orders from something akin to our reason, we project a choice there, a selection from among a random or even infinite field of options. We presume, in other words, the specter of an original free choice even as we deny that freedom in our selves.

We can make sense of the antinomy only when we understand and accept that our cognition has two modes of ordering the world as we encounter it and that both have their place. One pertains to explaining local and discrete changes in space-time; the other kicks in whenever we explore the edges of our knowledge, whenever we ask the big questions of where it all came from, what should I do, and am I making this choice freely or am I constrained. When we use the one in the domain of the other, when we think mechanistically about our obligations or the whole of creation, or when we apply teleological thinking as we drill down into the phenomena of nature, we fall into error.

Such was the case of Heisenberg's radical revelation. Driven by Einstein's conviction that the cosmos must have a final cause, that God does not play dice, he drilled down far indeed into the mechanisms mediating between tiny slivers of space-time, into the invisible spaces between the dots comprising an electron's path in a cloud chamber. But as Kant warned, "*human reason,* adhering to this maxim and proceeding on these lines, could never discover a particle of foundation" that would complete the picture of nature as we expect it to be.[31] Einstein and his followers would never tire of seeking such a particle, the one that would eradicate the troublesome quantum egg and put the world back on its expected footing. Heisenberg somehow intuited that such a final particle was, like the paradoxical edge of existence itself, a stitch holding together the fabric of the world we dream, a tenuous and eternal crevice of unreason that tells us it is false.

In the final section we will follow Kant, Borges, and Heisenberg as they delved into that final crevice of unreason that sprouts between freedom and determinism, and that condemned them to take responsibility for the choices that made them who they were.

Part IV

THE ABYSS OF
FREEDOM

10

FREE WILL

ANICIUS MANLIUS SEVERINUS BOETHIUS was thirteen years old when the man who would one day have him tortured and executed assumed control of the western Roman Empire. That man, the Ostrogoth king Theodoric the Great, initiated his long rule in typically violent style. After years of exchanging battlefield victories and defeats with Italy's longtime ruler, Flavius Odoacer, Theodoric stormed Ravenna, the seat of Italy's political power, and then surprised his rival by extending an offer of peace. On a fateful night in 493 CE, the two men and their retinues gathered for a feast to mend differences and divide the west between them. But when Theodoric stood to give a toast, instead of raising a goblet up, he brought his blade down on Odoacer's neck as his men fell upon the slain king's entourage, putting them to the sword before they could shake off their drunken stupor.

For the next thirty years Theodoric ruled the western empire, his Gothic fist wrapped in the satin glove of the civilized mores and institutions over which young Boethius, destined to become a senator, would preside. A scion of the Roman aristocracy, Boethius exemplified the patrician cult of learning while professing the Catholicism that by then had been widely embraced by the western church. But while he was willing to serve in political roles, his ambitions were intellectual, not worldly—to preserve and interpret the ancient sages, to unify the warring philosophical canons of Plato and Aristotle, to weigh in on theological controversies.

Boethius made his first major intellectual contribution by intervening in just such a religious debate. Should theologians, as the Arians held, understand God the Father as separate and superior to Jesus the Son? Or should they consider the two as identical, as one and the same God? Having absorbed Neoplatonic thought since a young age, Boethius now saw that for a statement of identity between two terms to have any meaning, the terms also had to exhibit some minimal difference. In other words, to say that God the Father and Christ the Son are the same necessarily implies that they also are in some way different. Thus did he forge a compromise between western and eastern theological positions: Christ could be, and in fact had to be, both identical to *and* discernible from the Father.

Boethius's foray into religious strife showcased his talent for making ancient learning pertinent for his own times. Sadly, that same talent also contributed to his demise. Theodoric had enforced religious toleration across his realm, allowing Jews as well as Catholics to freely practice their faiths. But now the ascension of a new emperor in the east, Justin I, had given him reason to rethink his policies. After several years of persecuting Arians in his realm, Justin had started to make overtures to Rome, threatening to upset the balance of power across the empire. In this fraught milieu, Boethius made his brilliant and original attempt to bridge the theological chasm. An act of peace in any other context now menaced the Ostrogoth king with the specter of a theologically united empire under an upstart eastern emperor.

Theodoric charged Boethius with treason, sentenced him to death, and imprisoned him in the town of Pavia to await his fate.

Unbeknownst to his executioners, by the time they arrived at his prison door, Boethius had engineered a kind of escape—in spirit if not in the flesh. During his days of waiting, he had composed another book. In it he recounted how philosophy had freed him from the mortal coils of dread and despair.

On the appointed day, the king's men entered his cell, wrapped thick wires around Boethius's temples and eyes, and slowly tightened them as he writhed and screamed in agony. They then finished the job by beating him to death with heavy wooden clubs. But as darkness fell over Boethius and the west, as Europe lost contact with the august literary traditions of the ancients, his *Consolation of Philosophy* lived on, conveying the lost treasures of Greek philosophy into the modern age. Dante would place Boethius in the fourth circle of heaven in his *Divine Comedy;* King Alfred the Great in the ninth century, Geoffrey Chaucer in the fourteenth century, and Queen Elizabeth I in the sixteenth century all tried their hand at translating his great book.

In his book Boethius recounts how, as he sat in his cell awaiting his fate, his anxiety gave way to perplexity. Would not an all-knowing God know in advance every choice a mere human such as himself would ever make? If so, how could he consider his choices free? In what sense could he claim responsibility for having made them? Trapped in this logical vortex, Boethius cries out in desperation, "There is no freedom in human actions or even intentions." Even worse, he laments, without such freedom the very idea of justice vanishes as well, "because to punish the wicked for what they couldn't help, or indeed to reward the good for deeds over which they had no control, makes no sense at all."[1]

Today we can hear echoes of the morose musings of a condemned Christian philosopher of late antiquity in the words of purported rationalists who consider free will an illusion we should reject along with outdated superstitions and religious beliefs. After recounting the horrific rape and murder of Jennifer Petit and her daughters by two strangers in 2007, the popular atheist writer and student of neuroscience Sam Harris questioned the inclination to morally judge the actions of the perpetrators. "As sickening as I find their behavior," he wrote, "I have to admit that if I were to trade places with one of these men, atom for atom, I would *be* him: There is no extra part of me that could decide to see the world differently or to resist the impulse to victimize other people."[2] The conclusion he draws from this realization is that "free will *is* an illusion."[3]

How curious that a fervent believer in sixth-century Italy and a convinced atheist and student of brain science of the twenty-first century would seem to agree on the issue of the illusory nature of free will. Except, crucially, Boethius's account doesn't stop there. On the brink of giving up all hope, Boethius receives a visitation—not from an angel, but from a pagan goddess. Philosophy, the condemned man's personified interlocutor, floats through his dungeon's stone walls to engage him in Socratic dialogue. During those brief exchanges, she reveals that his thinking suffers from an error, one that continues uncorrected in contemporary criticisms of free will.

Boethius, Philosophy explains, assumed that God's foreknowledge destroys freedom of choice because he failed to distinguish between human knowledge, congenitally trapped in space and time, and another kind of knowledge, proper only to God. If a human were to see into the future, that foresight would indeed contradict free will, because the things she foresees are yet to occur. But for God, for whom all space and time exist as a simultaneous here and now, knowledge of the future can't involve the distinction between something that has happened and something that remains to come. Just as I can know it is raining right now without that knowledge endowing the fact with even the slightest inevitability (it could also have *not* rained), a godlike knowledge can know everything that has happened or will happen without presuming any necessity that it had to happen that way. God can know every move and every decision I will ever make, and yet still I can choose freely.

In other words, that we can imagine a being who isn't constrained by having to live from one moment to the next is utterly irrelevant to what in fact happens in time. Some things happen purely by necessity; some things result from different degrees of choice. Whether we presume that all our decisions from now to our deaths are determined because God sees all of existence, all that happened, is happening, and will happen, in one eternal instant, or whether we presume that all our decisions from now to our deaths are determined because they stem from physical processes subject to the laws of mechanical causality, amounts to the same thing. But here's the crucial point: because they implicitly avoid the limitations of time, neither presumption undermines free choice.

To believe that either God or the chain of causality denies free will betrays an error in our thinking. It depends on the presumption that our knowledge of things equates to the things themselves, as opposed to being a picture separated from what we are trying to know by space and time. Indeed, Philosophy tells Boethius exactly this: "Things are known not according to their natures but according to the nature of the one who is comprehending them."[4] Ironically, the hard-nosed rationalists who denigrate belief in free will make precisely this error.

Like the materialist scientist expressing awe that out of billions of possible people I had the luck of being born as *me*, those who deny free will can only do so at the cost of assuming a godlike vantage neither they nor anyone else can ever occupy. When Harris asserts that if he were to trade places with one of these men he would *be* him entirely, without any supplemental remainder able to see the world differently, he is in fact *doing precisely what he disallows:* positing a secret extra part of himself able to clock those differences and report back. Just as Borges asked about the eternal return of the same, "Without a special archangel to keep track, what does it mean that we are going through the thirteen thousand five hundred and fourteenth cycle and not the first in the series or number three hundred twenty-two to the two thousandth power?" without just such a special archangel, Harris's replacement of himself with another would go entirely unnoticed by himself, by the other, or by anyone else in the universe, and hence his claim that he would act the same way—which is to say, that those actions are in some deep sense knowable and hence necessary and unfree—is as fanciful as that secret extra part of himself, that deciding soul he thinks he has banished.[5]

Such is the move made by all, materialists and predestinationists alike, who would claim to put an end to the illusion of freedom. They can make this claim only by occupying an impossible vantage, a vantage unlimited by temporal and spatial perspectives. In a word, they believe they can know nature itself instead of nature exposed to our methods of questioning. But to occupy this vantage they must forget that what is, is; that the world as we find it must always be the starting point for our investigations. Far from grasping the universe as a transparent whole, we are blind, groping seekers adrift in time and space. As such, free will isn't a metaphysical implant or delusion of grandeur but an admission of our fallibility in the face of an unknowable future.

IN 1792, KANT GOT around royal censors in Berlin by including an article they had banned in one of his books. Or so he thought. As it transpired, there would be serious repercussions for having disobeyed the royal decree not to intervene in matters of religious faith, repercussions that would strike at the heart of Kant's desire to live his own life according to the principles he had put down in his moral philosophy.

The conflict between Kant and the Prussian state began several years earlier, with the death of Frederick II, often referred to as Frederick the Great, the man Kant had (somewhat sycophantically) anointed as the epitome of the enlightened monarch. In his widely read 1784 "Answer to the Question: What Is Enlightenment?" Kant had claimed that his age, while not yet enlightened, was indeed "the age of enlightenment," before adding the shameless plug: "or the

century of Frederick." Kant based the designation in good measure
on Frederick's toleration of religious diversity. Frederick, in Kant's
view, was enlightened because he "considers it his *duty* not to pre-
scribe anything to human beings in religious matters but to leave
them complete freedom ... to make use of [their] own reason in all
matters of conscience."[6] Kant chose religious freedom as a kind of
test case, but really he wanted to defend the right of all to reason,
argue, and publicly express their opinions while obeying the laws of
the land.

Two years later, Frederick died without children and was succeeded by his nephew Frederick William II. The new king exhibited
a good deal fewer of the traits Kant had designated as enlightened
than his uncle. Right off he replaced the previous minister for cultural and educational affairs with a man named Johann Christoph
von Wöllner. The late king hadn't thought highly of Wöllner. In fact,
he had called him "a swindling, scheming parson."[7] Far more concerned with religious purity than his predecessor, the new minister
established a board of censors in Berlin to enforce a new religious
edict. While declaring toleration of subjects' religious beliefs the law
of the land, the new edict included a decisive caveat: "so long as each
quietly fulfills his duties as a good citizen of the state, but keeps his
particular opinion in every case to himself, and takes care not to
propagate it or to convert others and cause them to err or falter in
their faith."[8]

Such was the political atmosphere when Kant, in clear violation
of the 1788 edict, decided to publish his views on religion despite
the official censor's explicit denial of permission. At first, the state's
reply was tepid. Kant was, after all, the most famous philosopher in
the realm. The new king had gone so far as to assign to a courtier
who had studied with Kant the charge of tutoring his own children.[9] But then Kant followed his first misdemeanor with an even
more direct provocation.

In June 1794 he published an essay titled "The End of All Things"
in which he claimed that censorship of people's opinions directly

contradicted the essence of Christianity, which depended on its believers freely choosing to obey. Should the laws of Christian faith be supplemented by political mandate, he posed, that very core of free choice would vanish, leaving behind a husk of empty compliance. Thus, Kant concluded, "it is the *free* way of thinking . . . from which Christianity expects its teaching to be effective, by which it has the power to win over the hearts of men to itself, men whose understanding is already illuminated by the idea of the law of their duty."[10] With these words, plainly accusing the religious edict of damaging the cause of Christian faith, Kant had taken things too far.

In October of the same year, Kant received his reply directly from the king. Kant, the monarch said, had abused his position "for the distortion and debasing of many principal and basic teachings of Holy Scripture."[11] He would have to "give at once a most conscientious account"[12] of his actions and henceforth refrain from all such teaching and publications or "unfailingly expect, on continued recalcitrance, unpleasant consequences."[13] Kant certainly knew what such consequences could consist of. Having turned seventy, he was in no mood to lose his university position, forgo a pension in his old age, and possibly suffer banishment from the only home he had ever known. That said, he had staked a very public claim as defender of freedom of conscience and expression. He could hardly countenance a full-blown "retraction and betrayal of one's inward conviction." And yet, he reasoned, "even if everything one says is necessarily true, there is no duty to utter all truth publicly."[14]

Thus did Kant come down firmly on both sides of this most important question. On the one hand, he would strenuously deny the primary accusations against him, that he had denigrated religion and corrupted the youth. Rather, he had shown great respect for all religions, chiefly Christianity. And he could not have corrupted any youth, since teaching young people exceeded his job description and he had written the works for which he had been called to order as academic treatises intended for other philosophers. On the other hand, he fully acknowledged and submitted to the king's authority in this and all matters, and pledged *"as Your Majesty's most loyal subject, that I will hereafter refrain altogether from discoursing publicly, in lectures or writings, on religion, whether natural or revealed."*[15]

It would be fair to suspect some degree of plausible deniability in Kant's answer. His insertion of the phrase "as Your Majesty's most loyal subject," while certainly interpretable as a perfunctory honorific, could also easily function in Kant's mind as a caveat, namely, "I pledge to refrain from so doing *as long as I am your subject.*"

Sly caveat or not, at first it looked as though Kant would keep his word. Shortly after sending his response to the king, he wrote to an editor who had requested a piece from him that he had indeed finished a new essay on religion, but because of the censors in Berlin he would refrain from publishing it. Nevertheless, although Kant showed some restraint in withholding that work—which he would only publish the year after Frederick William's death, hence ostensibly keeping his promise—he plowed ahead with the publication of his last great work of ethics, the long-promised *Metaphysics of Morals*. And that book in no way steered clear of religious questions.

In its pages Kant continued the verboten ideas from *Religion Within the Limits of Reason Alone*, even citing the censored argument and doubling down on it. Religious duty, he proclaimed, following dictates of doctrine or tradition, should not determine the course of ethical duty, which a person owes to herself, not to any external force. To the extent that we at times couch our true ethical duty as a duty to serve God, this is because we've clothed the inner, ethical duty in the historical garb of a religion as a kind of heuristic device for those cases in which "we cannot very well make obligation (moral constraint) intuitive for ourselves."[16]

Fortunately for Kant, Frederick William II died shortly after the publication of these words, and no official response to the violation of his pledge ever came. The following year Kant would also publish the book he had put on hold, *The Conflict of the Faculties*, whose first part consisted of a response to the censorship that had initiated his own conflict with royal authority. Not only, Kant declared, was he justified in publishing his thoughts on religion, but it was wrong in principle for the state to require a philosopher to uphold biblical faith. Philosophy, which holds no political sway or actual authority over people's lives, must always be free from "the government's command with regard to its teachings."[17]

Kant's conflict with his government during the last years of his life raises questions about the concept of freedom his philosophy exposited. He had spent a career arguing that freedom of expression was the essential political good, because its violation would amount to a negation of that core autonomy that defined all rational beings. And yet here Kant squirmed in the vise of a dilemma. When responding to the king's injunction, did he display judiciousness or cowardice? Did he undermine his own defense of the freedom of expression by refraining from publishing his book until the king's death? Did he violate his duty and hence his autonomous self-legislation by breaking his promise not to discuss religion while still ostensibly His Majesty's loyal subject? Had Kant, in other words, undermined his own philosophical defense of freedom by succumbing to coercion?

WHEN DISCUSSING HUMAN CHOICE in the introductory pages to his last great work on ethics, Kant writes that it "can indeed be *affected* but not *determined* by impulses." Freedom of choice, he continues, "is this independence from being *determined* by sensible impulses."[18] Those who argue for the illusory status of free will all make some version of the claim that this independence from determination by sensible impulses simply doesn't exist. We are sensible beings; we react in certain ways to stimuli; and to think that we harbor some agency that escapes that chain of command is mere fantasy. Indeed, the data from contemporary brain science would seem to support this conclusion. Studies have demonstrated that when we make decisions, the neural activity accompanying the decision precedes our conscious awareness of making that choice and, in some cases, can even be detected by a third party.[19] But if a scientist monitoring a PET scan of our neural activity can know what our decision is before we consciously decide it, doesn't that pretty much skewer any talk about freedom from impulses? Indeed, doesn't it show that the very mechanics of making a choice consists of nothing but impulses?

In fact, such experiments tell us nothing that we couldn't already intuit, namely, that, however fast it is, making decisions takes time and that our current technology may allow us to get a glimpse of that activity faster than subjects can report on their own awareness of it. The dystopian specter of such technology reading all the impulses and responses of our entire lives—the implicit extension of the argument that the visibility of our neural processes contradicts our freedom of choice—merely recycles Boethius's concern that God's foreknowledge undermines human choice. But just as Philosophy quickly extinguished that worry for Boethius, here Kant's thought should do the same.

Boethius, Philosophy taught him, had confused knowability with inevitability, when in fact the two have nothing to do with each other. Just as my knowledge of something that just happened or is happening right now confers not an iota of necessity to it, supposed knowledge that something is about to happen or will happen eight months from now has nothing to do with whether rational choice provoked it. All of this stems from confusing decisions and occurrences in time with a picture of the world from outside space and time, one that implicitly incorporates all time in a single moment. We fall into this confusion, as Philosophy explained to Boethius, because we project our way of knowing things onto the things themselves.

This confusion is rampant whether you are a hard-nosed rationalist or a dyed-in-the-wool deist. Harris shows this overlap when he writes, "Even if you believe that every human being harbors an immortal soul, the problem of responsibility remains: I cannot take credit for the fact that I do not have the soul of a psychopath."[20] This reasoning has a broad following. The influential British philosopher

Galen Strawson finds the same infinite regress in any attempt to account for "how one is," the description of that total state, mental and physical, that someone is in when she makes a decision. As he writes, "Ultimate responsibility for how one is is impossible, because it requires the actual completion of an infinite series of choices."[21] I cannot be responsible for any given choice I make now, because I cannot be responsible for having become the person who made that choice.

Those who use the infinite regress of "how I am" to argue away responsibility, however, fail to grasp something that Kant saw clearly: the infinite regress of responsibility, just like the infinite regress of causality, engenders an antinomy. Whether I am what I am because of my circumstances, because of my parents' genes, or because God gave me a soul at the beginning of time that was just going to turn out this way, the very same arguments that lead us to refute responsibility for our actions can equally be used to support a claim of ultimate responsibility, be it of "the buck stops here" sort, where I am responsible for every choice I make, or the sort that says I, God, or evolution hold that responsibility. And this antinomy arises because we have taken something always located in time and space, namely, choices, and projected them out to the limits of time and space, as if the sum total of their determinations could become an object of cognition.

The conviction that we contain an immortal soul and the conviction that we are mechanistically determined represent two sides of an antinomy that arises from a move common to both religious zealots and materialist free-will deniers: extending judgments about causality in space and time to something not sensible but intelligible, namely, the ultimate reason someone chooses to do something. We can see Strawson do this explicitly in this passage: "To be ultimately responsible for how one is, in any mental respect, one must have brought it about that one is the way one is, in that respect. And it's not merely that one must have caused oneself to be the way one is, in that respect. One must also have consciously and explicitly chosen to be the way one is, in that respect, and one must also have succeeded in bringing it about that one is that way."[22] While the passage offers a shining example of philosophical academese replete with the amusing if head-scratching repetitions, the tricky work gets done right at the outset, with the word "ultimately." Since one cannot have brought about the way one is, one cannot be "ultimately" responsible for one's decisions. But the sleight of hand took place right there, with the presumption of a total and unknowable history of causes as being the sine qua non of responsibility.

Both sides of the antinomy imagine an ideal, ultimate cause, outside space and time, as a precondition for either assigning or denying responsibility. In an analogous way, those favoring either of the anthropic answers to the question of the initial settings of the universe imagine an ideal, ultimate cause, outside space and time. One version imagines a conscious intent to that cause in the form of God's design, the other an infinite store of real universes so as to deny design. In both anthropic principles, the otherworldly scenarios are invoked to avoid the embarrassment of accounting for the existential fact that we find ourselves in this universe and these are the values that we derive from our measurements. Likewise, otherworldly scenarios to implant a free soul into a mechanistic world or to deny all responsibility to human agents fall on the same strategy. They create an uncaused cause outside space and time and then pretend it has real purchase on the here and now. They also do so for the same reason—to avoid the embarrassment of accounting for an existential fact. We are physical beings whose every move occurs in the mechanistic flow of space-time, *and* we are rational agents who can visualize options and choose which one to take.

That free-will denial and the anthropic principle share the same logic becomes clear in Harris's counterfactual scenario of exchanging all his atoms with those of a killer. The implication of the scenario is relief, as in, "How lucky I am not to have turned out that way!" Such relief makes sense if and only if the "I" in question preexisted the "way" it ended up and then were thrown into a cosmic lottery with a tiny chance of ending up virtuous. But the innumerable ways I could have turned out, just like the innumerable settings that the dials of the universe could have been tuned to, result from reason's tendency to overstep its bounds, to garb its ideas with the space-time fabric of its sensible reality and extend to space-time measurements the eternal dignity of an ideal.

For Kant, in contrast, free will, like the seemingly astonishing purposiveness of existence, is a necessary postulate of reason. As he begins his famous discussion of free will in the *Groundwork of the Metaphysics of Morals,* "All human beings think of themselves as having free will."[23] Without this postulate, there would be no way of explaining counterfactual thinking, the fact that we consider opposite courses of action from those we ultimately take and then regret or approve of those. In Harris's account, Steven Hayes and Joshua Komisarjevsky, the men who raped Jennifer Petit and then set her house on fire, murdering her and her daughters, "briefly considered what they should do," before proceeding with their atrocities.[24] Later, Komisarjevsky professed to have been "stunned" by his actions.[25]

It should be utterly clear by now that Kant's position has nothing to do with the straw-man version of free will that the deniers (rightfully) criticize. As Brian Greene has put it, "All particle motion—whether in a brain, a body, or a baseball—is controlled by physics and so is fully dictated by mathematical decree. The equations determine the state of our particles today based on their state yesterday, with no opportunity for any of us to end-run the mathematics and freely shape, or mold, or change, the lawful unfolding."[26] Indeed, for Kant, the fact that we consider and choose among options coincides with the fact that our entire being, atom for atom, exists in the physical world of appearance and bows to the conditions of causality in time and space. To put this in Kant's words, "It is equally necessary that everything which takes place should be determined without exception in accordance with laws of nature."[27]

It is also crucial to add that this defense of freedom has nothing to do with some attempts that have been made to use quantum indeterminacy as a reason for thinking the human brain might be exempt from the determinacy of the physical world. Max Born rejected determinism in favor of a probabilistic range of outcomes; nothing here saves a voluntaristic notion of free will. Nor does Heisenberg's claim that our perfect knowledge of the future is impossible because we cannot perfectly measure the present. Again, nothing here salvages a deciding ghost in the machine. As Greene writes, "Whether the laws are deterministic (as in classical physics) or probabilistic (as in quantum physics) is of deep significance to how reality evolves and to the kinds of predictions science can make. But for assessing free will, the distinction is irrelevant."[28]

And yet where free-will deniers err is in the absurdity of the very scenarios they conjure to undermine free will and in inferring any real-world consequences from those scenarios. Just as Harris imagines an atom for atom exchange with a killer, Greene posits a "superhuman vision" capable of analyzing "everyday reality at the level of its fundamental constituents"[29] in order to establish the impossibility of free will. But their conclusions overlook Kant's fundamental insight.[30] Free will is not the illusion. The illusion, or delusion, is that something so matter of fact, so everyday, and so real as having to make choices is in any way affected by an impossible God's-eye view dreamed up by our most grandiose metaphysical pretensions. For as Boethius learned, even God himself knowing all our actions in all their unfolding has no effect on either our ability or our obligation to make decisions in time. When we attribute free will and hence responsibility to a choice, we are doing so in response to a different question: not what chemical reaction or set of particle collisions led you to do something, but rather, *why did you choose to do this and was it the right thing to choose?*

Freedom is an idea of reason that can never be confirmed or denied by experience. And yet we must presuppose it. For whenever the arrogance of our knowledge suggests to us that we can dispense with it, that we can erase the difference between ourselves as physical objects in the sensible world and ourselves as deciding subjects in the intelligible world, antinomy raises its bewildering head.

In fact, like Boethius revealing that even as we identify God and the Son as one, we simultaneously distinguish between them, we can and must think of ourselves as physical beings determined by the laws of nature and as free deciding agents *at the same time, without contradiction.* Only then do we see that different standards and different questions apply when we view ourselves as objects affected through the senses, and when we view ourselves as intelligences who need to make decisions in the world, and that to say we are both "contains not the least contradiction."[31]

As Kant considered the consequences of violating the king's edict, he knew he would have to account for his decision before the court of his own moral judgment. He knew that he could act in accordance with his duty as a free, self-legislating rational being, or in violation of it. But there was something else he knew. The constraints that bind our freedom as political subjects do not extend to the freedom of our will. We may experience greater or lesser freedom to pursue our desires and inclinations in different settings and under different political regimes. None of this, however, changes our basic moral constitution. Kant could choose to obey the king or choose to defy him. He could fear the outcome of his decision. But whether he obeyed or rebelled, whether he conformed to pressure or risked the king's displeasure, both would be the actions of a free will.

IN GABRIEL GARCÍA MÁRQUEZ's renowned novel *One Hundred Years of Solitude,* the town of Macondo receives a visit from a woman called, appropriately, Visitación. Unbeknownst to the town's inhabitants, she brings with her a plague. As the plague spreads, the townspeople first lose their ability to sleep; they fritter away countless wakeful hours on repetitive games in the vain hope that their boredom will lull them into a long-desired slumber. But a far worse scourge follows on the heels of insomnia. Soon the villagers realize they have started to forget the identity of the objects around them. Faced with the prospect of a total memory collapse, they begin to label the things they come into everyday contact with, reminding themselves of their purpose. On one animal they pin a sign that reads, "This is a cow." Soon they realize they have no idea what to do with a cow, so they add another note elaborating, "You milk her." Because they don't know what to do with the milk, a further clarification is called for. "You mix it with coffee and make coffee with milk." Toward the nadir of this regressive spiral, signs start popping up reminding the villagers that "God exists." As the narrator explains, "In that way they continued to live a sifting reality, momentarily captured by words, but that was to flee irremediably when they forgot the meaning of the written letters."[32]

It is one of the sad ironies of intellectual history that as he entered the last years of his life, one of the most capacious intellects of all time would suffer a fate similar to that of the residents of García Márquez's fictional town.

By 1796, at seventy-two years old, Kant reported having to refrain from lecturing, "because of age and indisposition."[33] Still, his morning routine continued as before. Up at 5:00 a.m., two cups of strong tea, a pipeful of tobacco. Kant liked this time very much, telling a visiting friend it was "one of my happiest times. Then I am not yet strained, and I try gradually to collect myself, and in the end it becomes clear what and how I will spend my day."[34]

Not burdened by lecturing and administration, Kant would spend much of those days trying to complete the ambitious portfolio of philosophical projects he had laid out for himself. He published *The Metaphysics of Morals* in 1797 and *The Conflict of the Faculties* the following year, along with a collection of his edited lectures on anthropology. In his own mind, Kant was primarily at work on his crowning oeuvre, a book that would tie his system together into one expansive package. Given the diminished state of his intellectual powers, no one expected it would turn into much. As a friend of his wrote, "I do not believe that he will live to see the end. It cannot be published as is under any circumstances."[35] His good friend Kraus was even more pessimistic, later saying of "the last scribblings over which Kant died" that "no sense or understanding wants to enter into them."[36]

Kant's physical and mental decline hung out like knickers on a line for all to see. He still took his daily strolls. But now frail and afraid of falling, he developed a curious style of walking that involved stamping flat-footed, which he believed would help keep him stable. It didn't. He soon enough fell, and shortly after his accident stopped going on walks altogether. As he trundled around his house, his short-term recall began to fail him. So, like the residents of Macondo, he started writing notes to remind himself of basic things. As a friend recalled, "In the end he wrote down every little detail that others told him or that came to him."[37]

Kant's notes to himself display a mind adrift in an undifferentiated morass of memory and perception, a mind using words to momentarily capture a rapidly sifting reality. One note remarks that his students should avoid blowing their noses and coughing. Another insists that the word we use for "footprint" is wrong. Still another reads, "Nitrogen azote is the basis of nitrate and has acidic powers."[38] For some reason Kant needed to remind himself about the downy fluff found under the winter coat of angora sheep and even some pigs.

Kant's friend and executor Ehregott Wasianski, who dutifully gathered and compiled these notes, eventually supplied the philosopher with notebooks to carry with him so that he could dispense with the errant pieces of paper that flooded his residence. Wasianski would also arrive to rescue Kant when he lay in a helpless puddle beside his chair after slipping off it while reading. He eventually insisted Kant keep a glass of water next to that reading chair. Not to drink, but to put out the flames that three times had already jumped from his candle to his nightcap, risking life and house.[39] On February 11, 1804, Wasianski mixed water and wine together and gave it to his friend and mentor. *Es ist gut,* Kant muttered. "I've had enough."[40] His last words.

The loss of memory that comes to some with old age or, more acutely, what we now recognize as a severe brain ailment, Alzheimer's disease, is a cruelty beyond measure for any rational being. That Kant's philosophy did more than any other to focus attention on the essence of rationality only highlights that cruelty. As he aged and lost his memory, Kant lost his ability to connect and systematize impressions. He lost, in other words, the very faculty that, according to his own philosophy, permits us to synthesize the manifold of sensible input under concepts and makes sense of the world. Strangely, in losing his memory, Kant was slowly approximating the world as experienced by another, fictional man—one who suffered from an inability not to remember but to forget.

Like Funes, Kant in his last years had lost his ability to abstract from his absorption in the world. Memories failed to distinguish themselves from current input. With his perfect memory, Funes suffered from the same shortcoming. "He had effortlessly learned English, French, Portuguese, Latin," Borges writes. "I suspect, nevertheless, that he was not very good at thinking. To think is to ignore (or forget) differences, to generalize, to abstract."[41] Likewise Kant, the great thinker, had, in Wasianski's words, "stopped thinking."[42]

Perfect memory could also become a disability, as Alexander Luria realized in the case of Solomon Shereshevsky, whose brain, he wrote, was "lacking . . . the capacity to convert encounters with the particular into instances of the general."[43] Indeed, at their extremes, perfect memory and total forgetting would converge; the result, a being adrift in the here and now, with no ability to synthesize disparate impressions into a flow of time, a fabric of space. Such a being, perhaps moving through the world by instinct, perhaps driven exclusively by mechanistic impulses, would also lack the capacity of reflection that Kant identified as the very heart of practical reason. A being that lacks free will. Indeed, in this regard the same could be said of a stone or a god. For facing a choice and not knowing which option one should or will take doesn't just involve freedom; that moment of indecision, of abstraction from total saturation in the flow of impressions, *is* freedom. This much Kant had seen before time and age smothered him in the blanket of the world. To reason is to be free. There is no way around it.

Kant believed that humans, like every other being that appears in nature, flow with the causal mechanisms of the laws of physics. At the same time, a minimal abstraction from absorption in the natural world endowed those same beings with freedom, with the ability and even the necessity of seeing themselves in that world, deciding on a course of action, and judging their choice. The brilliance of Kant was to see what others did not and have since forgotten: that the horns of this dilemma come into contradiction only if we presuppose something false about the world, if we believe that the space-time continuum—in which we experience the world and decide among our options—constitutes the ultimate nature of reality.

As Borges would show, and as we explore in the next chapter, failure to grasp this point would lead humanity into the greatest extravagances of thought and the deepest paradoxes of the imagination. As Heisenberg would discover, even as his fellow scientists would continue to prefer any flight of fancy over accepting this fact, there is no way to extirpate the moment of choice from our knowledge of the world; observation inserts freedom into nature; we are, and ever will be, active participants in the universe we discover.

11

FORKING PATHS

FOR ALL ITS ASTONISHING, mind-bending complexity—for all its blurry cats, entangled particles, buckyballs, and Bell's inequalities—quantum mechanics ultimately boils down to one core mystery. This mystery found its best expression in the letter Heisenberg wrote to Pauli in the fevered throes of his discovery. The path a particle takes "only comes into existence through this, that we observe it." This single, stunning expression underlies all the rest: the wave/particle duality (interference patterns emerge when the particles have not yet been observed and hence their possible paths interfere with one another); the apparently absurd liminal state of Schrödinger's cat (the cat seems to remain blurred between life and death because atoms don't release a particle until observed); the temporal paradox (observing a particle seems to retroactively determine the path it chose to get here); and, the one that really got to Einstein, if the observation of a particle at one place and time instantaneously changes something about the rest of reality, then locality, the cornerstone of relativity and guarantee that the laws of physics are invariable through the universe, vanishes like fog on a warming windowpane.

If the act of observation somehow instantaneously conjures a particle's path, the foundations not only of classical physics but also of what we widely regard as physical reality crumble before our eyes. This fact explains why Einstein held fast to another interpretation. The particle's path doesn't come into existence when we observe it. The path exists, but we just can't see it. Like the parable of the ball in the box he described in his letter to Schrödinger, a 50 percent chance of finding a ball in any one of two boxes does not complete the description of the ball's reality before we open the box. It merely states our lack of knowledge about the ball's whereabouts.

And yet, as experiment after experiment has proven, the balls simply aren't there before the observation. We can separate entangled particles, seemingly to any conceivable distance, and by observing one simultaneously come to know something about the other—*something that wasn't the case until the exact moment of observing it.* Like the beer and whiskey twins, we can maintain total randomness up to a nanosecond before one of them orders, and still what the one decides to order will determine the other's drink, on the spot, even light-years away.

The ineluctable fact of entanglement tells us something profound about reality and our relation to it. Imagine you are one of the twins about to order a drink (this should be more imaginable than being an entangled particle about to be observed, but the idea is the same). From your perspective you can order either a whiskey or a beer: it's a fifty-fifty choice; nothing is forcing your hand. Unbeknownst to you, however, in a galaxy far, far away, your twin has just made the choice for you. Your twin can't tell you this or signal it in any way, but what you perceive to be a perfectly random set of possibilities, an open choice, is entirely constrained. You have no idea if you will order beer or whiskey, but when you order it, it will be the one or the other all the same. If your twin is, say, one light-year away, the time in which you make this decision doesn't even exist over there yet. Any signals your sibling gets from you, or any signals you send, will take another year to arrive. And still, as of this moment, you each know. Neither will get confirmation for another year, but you can be confident, you can bet your life's savings on it—a random coin toss in another galaxy, and you already know the outcome.

The riddles that arise from Heisenberg's starting point would seem to constitute the most vital questions of existence. And yet one of the curious side effects of quantum mechanics' extraordinary success has been a kind of quietism in the face of those very questions. The interpretation of quantum mechanics, deciding what all this means, has tended to go unnoticed by serious physics departments and the granting agencies that support them in favor of the "shut up and calculate" school, leading the former to take hold mainly in philosophy departments, as a subfield of the philosophy of science called foundations of physics. Nevertheless, despite such siloing, a few physicists persisted in exploring possible solutions to the quantum riddles. Some of their ideas have been literally otherworldly.

In the 1950s, a small group of graduate students working with John Wheeler at Princeton University became fascinated with these problems and kept returning to them in late-night, sherry-fueled rap sessions.[1] Chief among this group was Hugh Everett III, a young man with classic 1950s-style nerd glasses and a looming forehead. Everett found himself chafing at the growing no-question zone that proponents of the Copenhagen interpretation had built around their science. Why should we accept that in one quantum reality, observations somehow cause nature to take shape out of a probabilistic range of options, whereas on this side of some arbitrary line in the sand we inhabit a different, classical reality where observations meekly bow to the world out there? What exactly determines when this change takes place? "Let me mention a few more irritating features of the Copenhagen Interpretation," Everett would write to its proponents: "You talk of the massiveness of macro systems allowing one to neglect further quantum effects ... but never give any justification for this flatly asserted dogma."[2]

Everett wrote those words to defend—futilely, it would turn out—his own interpretation, one he had started to dream up during those late-night symposia. What if our assumptions about what happens when we perform a measurement on a quantum event are just wrong? What if it's not the case that the particle was everywhere at once and then suddenly in one place, just because we measured it to be there? Imagine that what an observation does is not retroactively send a ball into a box depending on where it was observed, but instead creates two entirely separate universes, one in which the observer finds a ball and the other in which there is no ball in the box. In such a scenario it would seem to the observers that they had caused the ball to materialize retroactively by observing it, or caused a blurred ball to decide where to be, but in the world they now inhabit, no such magic is required. Depending on their world, the ball was either always in that box or always not.

If that was the case, Everett speculated, the apparent paradoxes of the quantum world disappear. Observations don't retroactively determine paths and have superluminal effects; cats are not both alive and dead. Rather, observations entail new entanglements that then exclude a host of other possibilities, effectively creating a different world. When we see one twin order a beer, she doesn't *cause* the other to order a whiskey. Rather, our observation of her ordering that beer decides what world we are in, namely, the one where this twin had beer and the other had whiskey. The other world, where this twin ordered whiskey and her sister beer, still exists, but it has forever escaped our grasp.

The same can be said of Schrödinger's cat and Einstein's ball in the box. It's not that our observation resolved a blurry cat or that half balls waited for us to open the box before turning into whole balls. Rather, our observation merely entangles us in such a way that we now definitively inhabit a world in which the cat is alive, the ball is here, and those other options have slammed the door on us forever.

When we make our observation and become so entangled, the world that peels off from our own becomes like a ghost world to ours, one that has, as the physicist Sean Carroll, one of Everett's most prominent contemporary adherents, puts it, "absolutely no bearing on what happens in our world."[3] Of course, we've seen ghosts in this story before. The electrons we don't detect, but somehow still manage to interfere with each other in the two-slit experiment. Except in Everett's interpretation, all those possible interactions between wavelike particles vanish and cease to have bearing on our world once a particle has become entangled with one of our devices. Our world, our device, the particle, and we have branched off into a separate existence; we can no longer see the results of all that wavelike interference; the pattern disappears.

In 1957, a disgruntled Everett handed in a much-redacted version of his ideas as his doctoral thesis and then left academia to take a job with the U.S. Department of Defense. Unbeknownst to him, a decade earlier a story appeared in the genre journal *Ellery Queen's Mystery Magazine*.[4] It was the first translation into English of an Argentine writer who was still largely unknown in the United States. He had published it in 1941 as the title tale in his first landmark collection. It had drawn positive comments from critics because, unlike so many of his other stories, it actually contained a plot. What no one could know at the time was that, with "The Garden of Forking Paths," Borges had previewed, almost verbatim, Everett's solution to the mysteries of quantum mechanics.

BORGES BEGINS HIS SPY story in a typical way—for him: a snippet of text in a history book, an overlooked mystery, some missing pages. In what remains of the text, a certain Yu Tsun relates his shock at recognizing a voice on the phone: a captain in the English army named Richard Madden. Madden is a notorious spy hunter, a bloodhound on the scent of Prussian agents in England, where Yu Tsun works and lives. Yu Tsun is just such an agent. When he hangs up the phone, the clock has started to count down the hours and minutes of his life. Madden knows he is here, and nothing stops Madden.

Yu Tsun has one card left to play. He knows the location where the British have installed a new artillery park. If he can get this information to his German leaders in the next few hours, he will at least draw some of the enemy's blood before Madden cuts him down. In a few minutes and with the help of a telephone book, he conceives of a plan. To complete it, he needs to find a man named Stephen Albert.

As Yu Tsun races against Richard Madden to reach the town where Albert lives, he reflects on his ancestor Ts'ui Pen, a governor in Yunnan who stepped out of the public eye to write a novel and build a labyrinth. After thirteen years working in solitude, Ts'ui Pen was murdered. His novel was massive and incomprehensible, his labyrinth never found. When Yu Tsun finally arrives at the gate to Stephen Albert's house, he is astonished to find out that Albert is a sinologist who has reconstructed the work of his ancestor Ts'ui Pen, the famed yet never recovered Garden of Forking Paths.

In the scant hour he reckons he has before Madden tracks him down, Yu Tsun learns from Stephen Albert that the labyrinth Ts'ui Pen set out to build and the incomprehensible novel he left behind are, in fact, one and the same thing. Ts'ui Pen's novel is a labyrinth in time. In life as in most fictions, characters who face "diverse alternatives" must choose one and eliminate the others; in Ts'ui Pen's textual garden, in contrast, they simultaneously choose all of them, creating "an infinite series of times, a growing, dizzying web of divergent, convergent, and parallel times," a fabric of times that "contains *all* possibilities."[5]

As he listens to Albert, Yu Tsun feels around and within him "an invisible, intangible pullulation."[6] He senses that the house is "saturated, infinitely, with invisible persons," other versions of Albert and himself "in other dimensions of time."[7] His reverie fades away at the arrival of Madden. Quietly, resolutely, Yu Tsun kills Albert, the man he had come to revere in the short time he knew him. He had found in the pages of the phone book a listing for a man whose last name was that of the town where the artillery barrage lies in wait. The news of that man's murder by a Chinese resident of England will give the Prussian command the information they need to attack the park and set back the British advance.

Captured by Madden, he is sentenced to hang while the Prussian army successfully stalls the British advance by a few paltry days. Left to face a fate he now longs for, Yu Tsun reflects how the very leaders he aided cannot know, because no one can know, his endless contrition.[8]

If Borges remained virtually unknown during the years that Everett worked up his many-worlds interpretation of quantum mechanics, a few years later this would decisively change. In 1961 a group of major publishing houses in Europe and New York came together to create the International Publishers' Prize, which came with a cash award of ten thousand dollars and translation deals with each of the presses involved. After much toggling among the six committees established to choose a winner, the judges opted for both finalists, Samuel Beckett and Jorge Luis Borges. Borges was at Bioy's house for Sunday breakfast when the call came. Naturally, he hadn't heard of the prize and thought it was a prank.[9] Within a very short time, this obscure writer of genre literature from deep in the Southern Cone became a household name.

While the Publishers' Prize lit the fuse, it had been fueled by growing enthusiasm for his work in France over the prior decade. The famous critic Roger Caillois had translated a collection of his stories under the title *Labyrinthes*, and the same year a review of his *Ficciones* appeared in Jean-Paul Sartre's journal *Les Temps Modernes*. Translations quickly followed in Germany, Italy, and Spain, where the publisher of the leading press Seix Barral proposed Borges for the Publishers' Prize, noting his influence on the generation of writers emerging from Latin America, such as Gabriel García Márquez and Mario Vargas Llosa, who themselves were taking the literary world by storm.

While his work had not yet begun to be widely translated in the English-speaking world, in 1961 Borges would receive his first of countless invitations to travel to the States to lecture and serve as guest professor. This time his gig was with the University of Texas at Austin, but during the six months of his stay, accompanied as usual by his mother, he made pilgrimages to the homes of writers he admired: Longfellow's mansion in Cambridge and Emerson's house in Concord. He would continue the practice in his many travels to come.[10] When he visited Johns Hopkins and Baltimore toward the end of his life, the philosopher Stephen Vicchio, then a graduate student, took him downtown to the grave of Edgar Allan Poe. The blind man stood in rapt contemplation as he caressed the contours of the statue's face. "This is the Poe I know," he whispered.[11]

Back at home in Buenos Aires, Borges had become Argentina's most famous native son. The days of a long commute by tram to a municipal library were long gone. Now he held the prestigious post of director of the National Library and a chair in literature at the University of Buenos Aires. He had received literary knighthoods from France, England, and Italy. Harvard University named him its Charles Eliot Norton Professor of Poetry for the 1967–68 academic year. In short, shy Georgie had become a big deal.

The allure of international travel came with some challenges for a blind, absurdly impractical man in his late sixties. For some time, Borges's mother had served admirably as his travel companion and guide. But as she had turned ninety, the specter was rising of a time when Borges could no longer rely on her to play that essential role. And thus did the issue of marriage rise with it, though not for the romantic reasons Borges had always dreamed of. Rather than creating a barrier to her son's eventual match, Leonor led the charge, pushing her Georgie to get in touch with Elsa Astete, a woman he had known and briefly wooed in his twenties who had recently been widowed.

Borges vacillated. He had in the meantime developed another of his poetic crushes, this time on a student named María Kodama, the daughter of a Japanese businessman who had attended his courses at the university. But Kodama was far too young for Borges, even for a time when relations between aging professors and young students didn't raise the eyebrows they do today. So, he put aside his fantasies and eventually made a choice. He proposed to Elsa in the summer of 1967. She accepted, and in the same year they were married, first in a civil ceremony and shortly thereafter in church, only a week before the planned departure for Harvard. The plan of a small, private ceremony quickly succumbed as the press, having caught wind of the impending wedding, thronged the church, stretching their necks to catch glimpses and photos of the most famous man in Argentina finally tying the knot.[12]

The troubles in Borges's marriage started almost as soon as the wedding bells stopped ringing. Stressed over the preparations for their impending voyage, Elsa failed to show up at the party Leonor threw for the newlyweds. Once they arrived in Cambridge, she complained about the apartment Harvard had rented for them and insisted on changing addresses. Knowing only Spanish, she felt out of sorts in Borges's literary and academic orbits, and quickly retreated from view. Though the marriage had always been conceived in practical terms as a way of placing a caretaker in Borges's life, in the end Harvard assigned a graduate student to guide the aging poet to his lectures.[13] Back in Buenos Aires after the visiting professorship, things didn't improve. Elsa felt as much out of place in the literary circles at home as she had among the professors at Harvard. The upper-crust ladies in Leonor's own social circles looked down on her provinciality as well, and she eventually retreated from Buenos Aires social life altogether.

By 1969 the situation had become close to unbearable for Borges, who confessed to a friend his desire to leave his wife. When asked if he had informed Elsa of his intentions, however, he demurred, citing his dislike of conflict. In May of that year, he finally consulted with a lawyer, again unbeknownst to his wife, and worked out the steps toward a legal separation—in secret. So it was that in July, her husband ostensibly on a trip but in truth hiding from her to avoid a scene, Elsa opened the door of her apartment to a lawyer presenting her with Borges's application for separation. She accepted and kept the apartment. Borges went back to his mother.[14]

IN A SENSE, THE cowardice exhibited by Borges in the face of a confrontation with his wife seems out of character. Where was the irascible adventurer who risked his own and his friends' lives insulting roughnecks in the back streets of shady neighborhoods? Where was the inveterate verbal brawler who faced down the changing political winds bringing fascism to his country in the 1940s? In fact, if Borges erred on the side of timidity in affairs of the heart, in public life his stridency would prove the most destructive.

Abhorrence for fascism had long guided the course of Borges's politics. In 1939, as the war broke out in Europe, he had written that victory for Germany would lead to the "ruin and degradation of the entire globe" and called for the "annihilation of Adolf Hitler."[15] Four years later he reacted with defiance to the rise of Juan Domingo Perón, the charismatic leader of the military coup that brought the nationalists to power in Argentina. In 1945, at the celebratory dinner for his award of the Grand Prize of literature by the Argentine Society of Writers, he stood to speak and lambasted the military leaders and the Nazi ideology they admired in Europe, calling it a perverse sect.[16]

Now, some thirty years later, Borges would have a chance to double down on those impulses. In 1970 a group of Peronists started an armed rebellion against the Argentine state. One of their early actions was the kidnapping and murder of a general who had played a part in Perón's downfall and exile some fifteen years earlier. As the reigning junta scrambled to compose a sense of order, negotiations began with the Peronists that, it was rumored, might lead to the return of Perón himself. Outraged, Borges joined a group calling itself the Committee for the Promotion of Civic Involvement in Support of the Republic and released a statement calling Perón's Argentina a "vernacular imitation of fascism."[17]

Despite his efforts, two years later the Peronists took the presidency, setting the stage for Perón's return from Spain. Contemptuous as ever, Borges remarked in an interview with the Italian press that his party had won because of the votes of "six million idiots."[18] Perón, for his part, when asked about Borges's invectives, was circumspect, saying, "If we put up with him for ten years when we were in government, there is all the more reason to do so now that he is an old man."[19]

As it turned out, the government went to considerable lengths not to appear to be persecuting the old man. When rumors circulated that Borges was considering resigning from his post as director of the National Library, officials rushed to assure him that they had no intention to interfere with his work there. Undeterred, Borges resigned. Soon thereafter Perón did return, winning election to the presidency in a landslide. It turned out that calling Borges old had been a classic case of calling the kettle black. Several years Borges's senior, Perón died less than a year after taking office, leaving a void in his wake that quickly devolved into political chaos.

In the wake of Perón's death and the subsequent power vacuum, a new military junta took control under the leadership of one General Jorge Videla. Back in Buenos Aires after another international trip, Borges accepted a lunch invitation from the general, at which he praised him for "what he had done for the *patria*, having saved it from chaos, from the abject state we were in, and, above all, from idiocy."[20] Shortly after his lunch with Videla, he was invited to Chile to receive an honorary degree. Chile's dictator, Augusto Pinochet, had deposed the democratically elected Salvador Allende's government in a violent coup that resulted in the president's assassination. Warned not to accept by friends who were concerned that showing support for a pariah regime like that of Pinochet would scuttle his chances of winning the Nobel Prize that year, Borges was defiant, telling them that their very admonitions now obliged him to go.[21] Not only did he leave for Santiago, but he also dined in private with Pinochet, who personally knighted him with Chile's highest honor. True to his friends' fears, such public endorsement of one of the world's most notorious human rights abusers would ensure that Borges would never receive the world's highest literary honor.

THE IMAGE OF FORKING paths or roads is a powerful one. We are drawn to imagining time as a line, a path we travel down, with moments of bifurcating decisions forcing us to choose between different futures. When, in Robert Frost's evocative image, two roads diverge in a wood, we tend to conjure alternative presents for ourselves. In Frost's famous poem, the walker laments that he "could not travel both / And be one traveler," and decides to keep "the first for another day." Yet he also grasps, knowing how "way leads on to way," that he will most likely never come back for it.[22]

Early in his life Borges had gravitated to such images and noted that realizing one set of possibilities in life "would have excluded or put off the others."[23] *What if* the flow of an afternoon in life had taken a different turn? *What if* he hadn't bowed to the pressure to marry a woman he didn't love? *What if* he had been more circumspect about endorsing generals who would turn out to be torturers, killers, war criminals?

For all his headstrong, even petty contrariness, Borges could show humility when the circumstances demanded it. In 1980, the track record long clear, he expressed sincere regret for his prior political stances. In Spain to receive the Cervantes Prize, he was questioned by the press on his support of the generals and their now wellknown Dirty War. Back in Argentina he would say that the Spanish reporters "interrogated me a good deal," that "they also taught me a lot."[24] An old acquaintance who regularly protested the disappearance of her daughter with the Mothers of the Plaza de Mayo—a group of women who lost children and grandchildren to the Dirty War—visited him in his apartment. As she would later report, "Borges listened to me very carefully and with great respect . . . and he was able to get a sense of the full extent of a mother's grief."[25] Later that year Borges would sign the first of several open letters decrying the fate of the disappeared. He could call for an "investigation into the economic ruin, the disappearances, the war."[26] He called Argentina a land of "wise but desperate people in the hands of madmen."[27] The shift in his public position quickly resulted in a change in the military government's treatment of him. Copies of an interview he did in *Newsweek* were banned in Argentina; the nationalist paper excoriated him with a headline accusing him of being a "grotesque traitor."[28]

But while he could feel regret and change his position, he could not go back and take that other path. It's hard not to read in "The Garden of Forking Paths" a philosophical rumination on precisely that mode of regret. Yu Tsun senses the pullulation of invisible competing versions of himself—all those roads not taken because we cannot travel both and be one traveler. But what if we could?

To reflect on a past decision, a fork in the road, a road not taken, may occasion regret. It may occasion remorse. These feelings reflect personal responsibility. They imply freedom: I could have chosen otherwise. But if at every fork in the road we travel both roads, what does that entail for freedom, for responsibility? Faced with an invitation from a controversial dictator in Chile, Borges had a decision to make. His friends counseled him not to go. He would ruin his chances to win the Nobel Prize. They were right, but their arguments backfired. Borges found such bet hedging execrable and decided to accept. In the universe described by Ts'ui Pen's novel, Borges also declines the invitation. That Borges decries human rights abuses from early on. And yes, that Borges wins the Nobel Prize for Literature. But—and here's the crucial point—if Borges takes both roads, would either Borges be responsible for that choice?

Clearly the answer is no. If having taken a tough decision results merely from a previous version of you not deciding at all, but rather spawning two versions of yourself, then neither of those versions chose freely and neither can claim responsibility or credit for the outcome. To live in the Garden of Forking Paths is to cease to be a rational agent at all, since all possibilities are taken by all actors, and any one of us at any time embodies the reality of one path, itself soon to bifurcate again.

This imaginary situation relates to the thought experiment of the entangled twins. In that case, each twin will believe she has made a free choice. If one chooses whiskey and later gets a hangover, that one may feel responsible for the choice, and perhaps regret it. But that regret, that feeling of responsibility, will be misplaced. For if the one's order of whiskey was required by the other's simultaneous order of beer, even light-years away and with no possibility of communication between the two of them, in what sense was the decision a free one?

The scenario is repeated in Sam Harris's fanciful musing of replacing himself, atom for atom, with the person of a killer and then denying the existence of an extra part of him "that could ... resist the impulse to victimize other people."[29] In fact, just like in that case, *each of these scenarios that appears to deny us any agency is misleading, because it depends on an impossible presupposition about knowledge.*

Just as Boethius realized in his prison cell, a millennium and a half before Borges dreamed his garden and Everett conjured his many-worlds solution to the measurement problem of quantum mechanics, timeless knowledge can never obliterate choice, because choice takes place in time. Entanglement is real, but its reality says absolutely nothing about the randomness of what a measurement reveals or, for that matter, about freedom. While it is undeniably true that the measurement of one entangled particle's spin decides that of the other, that information can never be communicated in time for the new measurement to be affected. It only ever exists in an ideal way, like the foreknowledge Boethius was concerned about. And like that knowledge, it is a projection outside time and space and hence has no effect on either randomness or freedom.

Likewise, Hugh Everett's model for explaining how measurements seem to simultaneously affect other places in space-time works as mathematics, but it requires a presumption of godlike knowledge for us to assume its reality. The invisible pullulations of those infinite other worlds can remain only that, shadows, impossible to discover, alternate realities conjured to assuage the discomfit caused by the inconsistencies of our own.

Only, what if those inconsistencies are only apparent? What if there is a better explanation than an infinite proliferation of worlds? This is what Borges intuited, in a move that, remarkably, will bring us back to Heisenberg.

MARÍA KODAMA WAS A child when she first saw Borges. According to her recollection, she had accompanied her father to one of Borges's lectures and ventured up to talk to him afterward. He was fifty. She was twelve. Later she took a class on Icelandic literature with him at the University of Buenos Aires, after which she joined his weekly class at the National Library on Anglo-Saxon language and literature.[30] Some two decades after that first meeting, María Kodama began to come regularly to the apartment he shared with Elsa Astete, assisting the now blind writer by reading to him and working through texts composed in Anglo-Saxon.

Racked by unhappiness and loneliness in his failed marriage, Borges had clearly started to develop feelings for Kodama during this time but resisted acknowledging them given the difference in their ages: she was now in her early thirties; he was nearing seventy. In December 1969, after a reading at the Ninety-Second Street Y in New York, the Borgeses were invited to a party, but Elsa refused to go. María Kodama was in New York and did attend. As she would later tell Borges's biographer Edwin Williamson, after this meeting and after seeing Borges in such distress, Kodama realized that the tenderness and pity she felt for him manifested something deeper.[31]

The following summer Borges and Elsa Astete separated, but another year would pass before the occasion arose where Borges and María Kodama would consummate their hidden passion. In March 1971, Borges's American translator arranged a stopover for him in Iceland. María joined him there. Iceland, Borges said, was a "dream come true."[32] There, overwhelmed by emotion to be in the land of the Eddas and sagas he loved so dearly, they confessed their feelings for each other. At seventy-one years old, the rueful and abandoned man finally found requited love.[33]

María Kodama initially refused to marry him, citing her distaste for the institution, but would eventually do so on his deathbed. Borges's love for her, but also for Iceland and its ancient culture, provided him with inspiration for several stories. One of these tells the tale of a medieval Icelander named Ulf Sigurdarson who goes on a quest for a mythical people known as the Urns. Upon entering their land, Sigurdarson learns the name of the Urnish king, Gunnlaug. Despite being told of the king's unpleasant habit of crucifying foreigners, he composes a poem about his deeds and commits it to memory, at which point two men appear as if on cue to convey him to meet the king. They take him on a journey along which he encounters mystical, Christological objects—a fish on a yellow stake, a disk on a red stake—each of which, his guides tell him, "is the Word."[34]

When Sigurdarson enters in the presence of Gunnlaug, who lies dying of a "great affliction," a harp is presented to him.[35] He takes it up and sings the poem he composed. The king appears pleased and gifts him with an iron ring. Then an onlooker takes the harp from him and sings a song composed of a single word, which Sigurdarson is not able to make out. As all those present file out, someone touches Sigurdarson on the shoulder and tells him he will soon die, because he has heard the Word. But, he adds, because he is a poet of the same lineage as Sigurdarson, he will endeavor to save him.

The poet, Bjiarni Thorkelsson, explains to Sigurdarson that while his song told of many things, the poetry of the Urns encodes all things into a single word. He cannot reveal the Word to him, though; Sigurdarson must seek it on his own. He promises to hide him for the night, and the next day Sigurdarson sails south. He travels for many years and lives the equivalent of many lives, but, as he says, "the essential thing was always the Word."[36]

When he finally returns to the Urns, Sigurdarson finds again the house of Thorkelsson, who is now dying himself. When he sees his old friend has returned, Thorkelsson takes up the harp to sing. This time, Sigurdarson hears the Word. The dying poet, he recounts, "spoke the word *Undr,* which means *wonder.*" Here Sigurdarson ends his narrative, and Borges his story, in this way:

> I was overwhelmed by the song of the man who lay dying, but in his song, and in his chord, I saw my own labors, the slave girl who had given me her first love, the men I had killed, the cold dawns, the northern lights over the water, the oars. I took up the harp and sang—a different word.
>
> "Hmm," said the poet, and I had to draw close to hear him. "You have understood me."[37]

In this story, dreamed up in the land of his dreams, surrounded by the fire and ice, the Eddas and sagas of a distant past, Borges distilled the poetic answer to the riddle he conjured thirty-five years prior. Imprisoned in the here and now, siloed by an ever-narrowing thresher of choices, we combine and connect experiences and create a story of ourselves, a timeline of our lives. At the same time, though, we imagine a story of our unlived lives, potentially infinite ramifications of worlds and meanings exceeding the grasp of anything but our imaginations. In identifying what we are, we close off those pathways we didn't take, turn them into ghosts, pullulations that haunt the garden of our dreams.

But what is it that permits this flight of the self? What connects disparate moments in space and time while also projecting us to places unseen? The Word, the Aleph—these are Borges's names for that minimal abstraction from absorption in the world, that synthesis of one moment in space-time to another that permits such moments to be moments at all. This Word is language, yes, but it is also something deeper than that. We find it in the power of poetry, to combine multiple meanings in one sign. But beyond even poetry it forms the essence of knowledge, the condition of the possibility of perception, the active ingredient in anything we could call, citing Einstein, an observation—the coincidence in space and time between an instrument and the hands on a clock.

Indeed, the Word and all those mystical entities in Borges's long oeuvre stand in for something he teased out already in his story about a man who couldn't forget. We seek to know the world, to know it perfectly, but the very power of that knowledge, the very source of its drive, stems from its imperfection, its inability to be identical to what it knows. This is what the poet understood when he took the harp of a dying man and said another word. To experience anything at all, to grasp any one thing, to observe a particle, to hold on to the flow of an afternoon in life, is also to experience something else, and to open the imagination toward what could have been, but wasn't.

The very fact that we can conceive of roads not taken but cannot actually take them means that, for all the best efforts of religion and science alike to speak in the name of God, our freedom remains ineradicable. In a short story he published in 1960, the year before his meteoric rise but when he was already the best-known writer in Argentina, Borges describes his relationship to another Borges, the public intellectual and author. He relates how, bit by bit, he has been passing more of himself over to this other Borges, the one who has, Borges says, a perverse way "of distorting and magnifying every-thing." He confesses that, years ago, he tried to free himself from this other Borges by moving on "from the mythologies of the slums and outskirts of the city to games with time and infinity." But those games, he concedes, "belong to Borges now, and I shall have to think up other things." Naturally, by the end of the page, which is the length of the story, the narrator admits he is not sure "which of us it is that's writing this page."[38]

Of course, he cannot know, for the very same reason that neither Borges, nor Yu Tsun, nor for that matter you or I, or any of us can ever experience those infinite roads not taken. It is because I cannot take both roads and still be the same traveler that I imagine them and, in imagining them, and in choosing, am condemned to that very freedom that the godlike knowledge of a mechanistic universe seeks to absolve me of. We seek to render that godlike knowledge real; we contort our imagination and make myths out of math; we brew bubbling Kandinsky multiverses[39] and grow gardens of infi-nitely forking paths. But the intimate rifts, the interstices of unrea-son that those models seek to obliterate, are indelible. They inhabit us. They make us what we are.

Which is exactly what Heisenberg's greatest discovery revealed.

12

PUTTING THE
DEMON TO REST

ON A COOL SUNDAY in late April 1934, the Washington Senators' catcher Morris Berg made a fielding error. That error
broke what had been an American League record of 117
consecutive error-free games—a high point in an otherwise average
baseball career. After leaving the Senators later that summer, Berg
played for the Cleveland Indians and then joined the American all-
star team as their third-string catcher for a trip to Japan before moving to Boston, where he played his last five seasons with the Red Sox.

While mostly unremarkable on the baseball diamond, Moe Berg
earned fame and respect for what he did outside the ballpark. A
graduate of Princeton and Columbia, he was known for his smarts
and his ability to speak multiple languages, a trait his teammates
shrugged off with the practiced nonchalance of the bullpen. As the
Senators' outfielder Dave Harris quipped when asked about the
seven languages his teammate reportedly spoke, "Yeah, I know, . . .
and he can't hit in any of them."[1] When he appeared on the popular quiz show *Information Please* in 1939, Berg essentially broke the
radio, spouting disquisitions ranging from the meaning of words

in ancient languages to dates of obscure events in history. After that star turn, Kenesaw Mountain Landis, the league's first commissioner, told him he had done more for baseball in half an hour than Landis himself had done in his entire tenure. But Moe Berg's most important service was yet to come.

In 1942, General William Donovan, head of the Office of Strategic Services, started assembling a team of spies dedicated to ferreting out information about the state of Germany's atomic research. He appointed Moe Berg to lead the team. By 1944, Berg, now posted in Switzerland, picked up the scent of his number one quarry: the head of Germany's nuclear research project, Werner Heisenberg. Concerned that Heisenberg could be working on an atomic bomb, Berg joined forces with an experimental physicist at Zurich's Polytechnic University, Paul Scherrer, a committed anti-Nazi, and persuaded him to invite Heisenberg to give a lecture. While they prioritized detaining and questioning Heisenberg and his fellow physicists, the Allies didn't exclude more drastic options, should the need arise. Berg attended the talk and sat next to Heisenberg at the dinner Scherrer hosted after the event, a loaded pistol under his jacket. He never had to use his firearm that evening. Heisenberg spoke about an obscure new attempt at creating a unified field theory. He didn't mention atomic weapons once.[2]

Because Berlin had increasingly been leveled by Allied bombing, all scientific operations, including Heisenberg's atomic research facility located in the ominously (and deliberately) named Virus House on the grounds of the Kaiser Wilhelm Research Institute, had been forced to seek alternate quarters in the small town of Hechingen, in Germany's Black Forest. There, in the hectic last months of the war, Heisenberg had come closer than ever before to producing a sustained fission reactor. Having decided that killing Heisenberg wasn't warranted, Berg next coordinated his capture. From the postmark on an intercepted letter to a Swiss colleague, Berg now knew the location of Heisenberg's new lab.

On April 19, as Allied forces closed in on Hechingen, Heisenberg mounted the sole form of transportation left to him, a bicycle, and headed east, his only thought to rejoin his wife, Elisabeth, and their six children. Heisenberg's family had been living out the war's last months suffering from cold and hunger in a mountain lodge in Urfeld, in the Bavarian mountains, to which they had decamped when their house in Leipzig had been razed by bombs. Urfeld was 250 kilometers from Hechingen. Heisenberg pedaled by night to avoid being shot by American aircraft or by roving German commandos, desperately fulfilling their führer's final orders to kill any Germans seen fleeing the enemy.[3]

On the day that Adolf Hitler and Eva Braun committed suicide in Berlin, the U.S. command in Heidelberg sent a team in search of Heisenberg. The team's leader, Colonel Boris T. Pash, driven by the urgency of what he believed to be "the most important single intelligence mission of the war," was relentless in his pursuit.[4] Arriving in the nearby town of Kochel on May 1, 1945, Pash's troops reported that the bridge on the only road leading up the mountain to Urfeld had been demolished and the road was impassable. Not to be deterred, Pash and a few men climbed the still snow-covered mountain by foot. Upon reaching the tiny town, they exchanged fire with some of the German battalion that occupied the town. During a pause in the firefight, Pash saw two officers approaching on scooters. While discussing terms with them, he realized that the Germans believed him to have far more than the few soldiers who had hiked up with him. Deciding it would be unwise to correct this impression, he ordered the Germans to assemble their men in the town the next day for an organized surrender. Once the scooters drove off again, he and his party hurried back down the mountain and used the bought time to repair the bridge in the night, allowing the rest of his trucks and men to pull in to town the following morning just in time to accept the Germans' surrender.

Only after taking charge of his prisoners did Pash turn to the pressing business at hand. Accompanied by two soldiers, he hiked the remaining way up the mountain to the front steps of Heisenberg's mountain retreat, where he found the great physicist awaiting him on his veranda. Heisenberg politely invited Pash in, introduced him to his wife and children, and then gathered his belongings and accompanied the colonel into custody.[5]

Given the nature of their quarry, it was natural that Pash's team would include a scientist. The one chosen for the job was Samuel Goudsmit, a Dutch experimental physicist who had immigrated to the United States to take up a position at the University of Michigan long before the war broke out. Goudsmit had met Heisenberg as a young man and had been duly awed by the genius who had founded the field of quantum mechanics. He had enjoyed conversations with him again when Heisenberg lectured at the University of Michigan in 1939.

During the early years of the war Goudsmit had become increasingly alarmed for the safety of his aging parents. After the Nazis occupied the Netherlands, he set to work obtaining visas for them. Tragically, they had only just received their papers when the deportation of Dutch Jews began in earnest in 1943. Before they could escape, they were rounded up and delivered to Auschwitz. Heisenberg received an appeal through common friends to advocate for the Goudsmits, to which he responded by writing a letter touting his own experience of their hospitality to him and other Germans during visits to Holland. It was to no avail. By the time he had written the letter, the Goudsmits had met their end in the gas chambers. Not long after the death of his parents, Samuel Goudsmit, now a U.S. agent in charge of tracking down Germany's atomic researchers, wept over the ruins of his childhood home, overcome "by that shattering emotion all of us have felt who have lost family and relatives and friends at the hands of the murderous Nazis."[6]

Back in Urfeld, his bags packed and tearful farewells exchanged with his wife and children, Heisenberg departed with Colonel Pash and his team for a long, bumpy journey by truck to his first detention site, the American base in Heidelberg. There he was brought into an interrogation room. As he looked across the table, he found

himself staring into the angry eyes of his former friend and colleague Samuel Goudsmit. The conversation that followed wouldn't
end that day. Instead, it metastasized into years of accusations and
rebuttals, recriminations and rehabilitations, all swirling around the
question of Werner Heisenberg's responsibility in working for the
most despicable regime the world had ever seen.

TWENTY YEARS EARLIER, LATE at night in a sparsely appointed room
on a barren island in the North Sea, when the fog of hay fever lifted
from his brain, what Heisenberg saw spread out in mathematical
script before his mind's eye had changed humanity's most basic
assumptions about nature and our relation to it. Since Newton had
derived the fundamental laws determining how objects move, scientists had become convinced that the physical reality we inhabit must
follow those rules at all levels and in all ways. No matter how tiny
the objects in question, or how small the distances, knowing the
mass of an object, its exact place in the universe, and every force acting upon it, one could know everything about that object's future.
The only limit was on the part of the knower. Those of us observing
the object might be constrained in how far or how small we could
focus our gazes or instruments, but as far as the object was concerned, its fate was sealed.

On the island of Heligoland, two years even before he wrote his
uncertainty paper, the abstruse mathematics Heisenberg invented
to account for the before and after measurements of electrons decisively undermined that premise. The problem was that Heisenberg's
math didn't commute. For those who haven't had to think about
math since high school, the commutative property means that what
you can do in one direction, you can also do in the other. It's the
same if you multiply two times eight as if you multiply eight times
two. But the commutative property that held for operations in normal mathematics no longer worked in Heisenberg's matrices. It was

as if carrying out the operation in one order undid the possibility of doing it in reverse, such that the answer one got from multiplying two and eight depended on whether one decided to start with two or start with eight.

In the specific case Heisenberg was working on, the numbers were sets of numbers—these were the matrices in question—that represented either the momentum or the position of an electron as measured in an experiment. The non-commutability of his equations signified one astounding fact: the product of an electron's observed momentum multiplied by its observed position will always be different from the product of its observed position multiplied by its observed momentum.[7] In other words, it makes a difference whether one measures the momentum and then the position or the position and then the momentum, *because what one chooses to start with changes the result for the next measurement.*

While it took Heisenberg another two years to formulate the uncertainty principle, in some ways it, too, flows from this original discovery. For if the fundamental insight of quantum mechanics is that one must choose to measure position or momentum first, and what one chooses affects what one will come up with when one measures the next value, this necessarily leads to a fundamental limit on the amount of information we can have about the world. As we drill down into the most basic presumption of Newton's classical world—namely, that knowing everything about a particle's position and momentum and the forces acting on it means knowing its past and future—we run into an impenetrable barrier. Perfect precision in our knowledge of the one creates radical indeterminacy in our knowledge of the other.

Once we accept the truth of Heisenberg's discovery, the hard part becomes jettisoning the assumptions we hold about what reality is or must be like. In fact, all the paradoxes associated with quantum mechanics, even the very idea made popular by Richard Feynman that "nobody understands quantum mechanics," stem from our resistance to letting go of these assumptions.[8] Indeed, letting go is hard. After all, if geniuses like Einstein couldn't do it, if swaths of top-notch physicists seem willing to go to any length to avoid letting go of it, that's because the "it" in question contains one of our most basic beliefs about reality, namely, that it is, in Borges's words, "ubiquitous in space and durable in time."[9]

But what if it is not? What if reality is not extended smoothly in space and time, but something fundamentally different? What if space and time are themselves nothing but, as Einstein himself so brilliantly saw, the indexes of measurements, coincidences between two events noticed by a third party. In fact, if we fully, radically accept this premise as our starting point, the paradoxes of quantum mechanics dissipate like warm breath on a cold day. We quickly see that the strangeness sprang from what we expected to see, rather than from what we in fact observe.

Let's take the measurement problem itself. How can it be, we wonder, that what we decide to measure, here and now, determines the path the electron has taken through time and space to reach us? How can the electron "know" that we detected it going through one slit, and thereby "decide," instantly, not to have gone through the other, thus violating relativity's ban on the superluminal transfer of information? How can one particle of an entangled pair instantaneously "tell" its other what spin it chose, no matter how far the distance has grown between them? The answer is simple. It can't. The electron doesn't know anything; the particle doesn't communicate anything. We do. But what we now know in that moment pertains to us, period. We cannot transfer that knowledge anywhere else, to anyone else, other than by good, old-fashioned subluminal communication. We may now know that since our particle has a down spin, its pair will be measured as up, but until we can communicate it, this knowledge is as irrelevant to anyone else's knowledge of the world as is Sam Harris's imaginary speculation of what he would be like if he swapped all the atoms in his body for those of a serial killer. Only the gods of small and large things can know this, and those gods don't talk.

Like Frost's walker in the woods, when I look back at my life, the path I am on is the one I have taken, no other. This is what I measured; this is what I found. I may now infer what I would have found on that other path, but other walkers won't know until they walk down it themselves.

If we accept this simple premise, we can also see the monumental metaphysical effort made by those alternative approaches to avoid this simple understanding, all because they want to salvage a specific, sacred idea of reality. Their resistance to the fundamental non-commutability that Heisenberg discovered (when they insist that our observation can't change reality), their resistance to the fundamental limitation in how much of reality one can know (when they insist that there must have been a path there, between the observations), all comes down to this: reality is something out there, independent of us, ubiquitous in space and durable in time. But again, perhaps it's not. Perhaps, rather, what constitutes the reality for any single entity is nothing other than the *relation* it has with something else, in Carlo Rovelli's words, "*the way in which one part of nature manifests itself to any other single part of nature.*"[10] Vitally, as that renowned physicist and creator of the relational interpretation of quantum mechanics has also put it, far from conflicting with relativity, this understanding is a continuation of its most important insight, the "discovery that *all* the properties (variables) of *all* objects are relational, just as in the case of speed."[11]

The twenty-four-year-old hiking on Heligoland, the twenty-six-year-old walking at night in Copenhagen's Faelled Park, they didn't reflect too deeply on this problem. Those two respective moments in the life path that would be Werner Heisenberg's were too busy sloughing off the blinders of expectations to consciously construct a new interpretation of reality. But soon, as a newly anointed professor started gathering his students around him, that man did start to ask those questions. And one of the ways he did so was by reading, discussing, and writing about the works of Immanuel Kant.

ONE OF THE STANDOUTS among the group of physicists who rushed to Leipzig to work with Werner Heisenberg when he assumed his professorship there was a young nobleman, Baron Carl Friedrich von Weizsäcker. Weizsäcker would go on to work with Heisenberg in the German atomic program as well as make important discoveries in the science of nuclear fusion, but as a young man he had studied philosophy before opting for physics, and he brought these interests with him to Leipzig. For his part, Heisenberg had already made clear the challenge that his discoveries, in particular the uncertainty principle, posed for the dominant philosophical understanding of reality. As he had written, uncertainty demolishes the law of causality that both science and philosophy presume sacrosanct, because that law depends on the premise that we can know the present fully, which uncertainty showed we cannot.

The demise of causality was not something that either scientists or philosophers were going to swallow without a fight. And so it was that in his first years as a full professor in charge of his own institute Heisenberg took that fight to the philosophers. He began with a lecture at home in Leipzig, attended by the philosophy department and interested members of a broader audience. Soon he would develop those ideas and bring them out in the form of a paper called "Causal Law and Quantum Mechanics," which he delivered in Vienna, then the world capital of the scientifically oriented branch of philosophy known as logical positivism.[12]

In challenging the philosophers, Heisenberg knew that he would also have to take on the greatest of them all, Immanuel Kant. In his lectures and papers Heisenberg remained respectful of Kant's awesome imprint on intellectual history, but he didn't shy from claiming that quantum mechanics posed such enormous challenges to the critical system that, he feared, philosophers would now face the "very difficult task of rolling out the Kantian basic problem of epistemology once again and, so to speak, starting all over again."[13]

The "basic problem" Heisenberg identified was the demarcation in Kant's system between a priori and a posteriori knowledge, that is, the portion of our knowledge that must be true, independent of all experience, and that portion we learn by interacting with the world through our senses. Kant had taught that space and time and the causal relation of events in space and time were not aspects of the world that we picked up through living in it, as Hume had argued, but rather the necessary conditions of possibility of our picking up anything at all about the world. Kant had gone further than merely positing some notion of space, time, and causality as a priori, however. In the first section of *The Critique of Pure Reason* he had extrapolated from the necessarily spatial and temporal form of our intuition to the basic rules of geometry itself. In other words, since space is one of the a priori forms governing our very ability to perceive the world, what we can derive about such ideal shapes as triangles and rectangles and the mathematical rules that govern them must also be a priori true. We know that the area of a triangle is one half the product of its height and its base, and this knowledge doesn't depend on our ever having encountered or measured a triangle in our daily lives.

But this idea of geometry and the model of space and time that informed it, Heisenberg argued, had already been sidelined by Einstein's general relativity paper, which not only had incorporated Riemann's non-Euclidean geometry but also had made that geometry central to the very functioning of the cosmos. In the Riemannian spaces needed to understand how gravity warps space-time and ultimately the shape of the cosmos itself, the long-standing truth of a triangle's area simply no longer held true, and hence the rules of Euclid couldn't be considered a priori at all.

To make matters worse, if Einstein had done a number on space-time, Heisenberg had put the kibosh on causality. The Kantian idea of causality depended on an observer isolating an object in space and time and determining the directly preceding cause to its present situation (its position and momentum). As Heisenberg explained it, "Whereas beforehand the spatiotemporal description could be applied to an isolated object, it is now essentially linked to the interaction between the subject and its observer or its apparatus. *The object in total isolation no longer has, in essence, any describable properties.*"[14] Heisenberg still believed the essence of Kant's position was right; namely, that some aspect of our knowledge of the world had to come from us and not from the world. Nevertheless, that line would have to move. He had made his challenge, and it was time for the philosophers to respond.

Respond they did. But while papers abounded and some of the top thinkers in the world weighed in on the influence of quantum mechanics on Kantian thought and on philosophy in general, the most direct and ultimately effective intervention came from a rising star in neo-Kantian circles named Grete Hermann. Exercised by the challenge posed by the new physics, Hermann came to Leipzig in 1932 for a series of discussions with Heisenberg and his circle, discussions in which his newest acolyte, the aristocratic philosopher-physicist Weizsäcker, played a prominent role.

In her opening salvo, Hermann presented the challenge in precise Kantian terms. Causality can't depend on experience, because it's "the very basis of all experience."[15] How can experiments, which proposed to say something meaningful about the world by hypothesizing claims and testing them with apparatuses and observed results, produce knowledge of the world that undermines the very presuppositions on which our inferences are then based? In other words, if our results tell us that the most basic presuppositions for obtaining those results aren't true, then don't we need to be rethinking the conclusions we are drawing? If quantum mechanics has led people to believe that observable effects, such as the decay of a radium atom and emission of an electron, happen without a cause, isn't it far more reasonable to assume the cause exists and we just haven't delved deeply enough to find it?[16]

Heisenberg responded by describing a version of the two-slit experiment. If a detection apparatus such as a screen beyond two slits registers the behavior of electronic emissions passing through those slits, it will show them interfering with each other, just as waves do when passing through two sluices. But if we add an apparatus at one of the slits to determine which direction an electron went, its other possible direction is "extinguished," and the pattern ceases to show up. If the indeterminacy of the direction of emission were simply a matter of our not knowing enough, we could presumably position monitors more closely to the sources and figure out which direction the emissions are taking. But we can't, because when we do that, no interference occurs. The very phenomenon we are trying to learn more about disappears when we try to learn more about it. Which is to say, it's simply not the case that our original detector doesn't tell us the whole story and that a more precise measurement will tell us more. A particle is in multiple places until it is measured; we cannot assume a determinate time, place, or cause for its movement prior to our intervention.[17]

Hermann, clearly unsettled by this evidence, continued to insist that atoms and particles must be objects and hence determined by such categories as substance and causality. But while the two sides failed to bridge the chasm, Heisenberg and Weizsäcker learned something from the encounter. Before Hermann took her leave of them, Weizsäcker spelled out the position that would continue to be Heisenberg's for the rest of his career. Space, time, and causality must indeed be treated as a priori, even for relativity and quantum theory. However, these new theories decisively changed their content.[18] In what way? Kant simply could not have foreseen the development of an experimental realm "so far beyond daily experience."[19] He could therefore not foresee that atoms, simply put, *aren't objects.*[20]

Strangely, given Heisenberg's original position that uncertainty had in some definitive sense overturned one of Kant's essential principles, Weizsäcker would eventually maintain that he and Heisenberg remained closer to Kant than did many of the generation of

Kantian thinkers who preceded them.[21] In Heisenberg's final words on the subject, he averred that Kant's a priori concepts formed an essential part of modern physics, albeit "in a somewhat different sense": specifically, space, time, and causality could at one and the same time be the very conditions of science and have "only a limited range of applicability." For, on the one hand, without the assumption of the tightly linked causal chain of events, "nothing can be known about the atomic event."[22] On the other, by following that chain we come to a point that undermines those very preconditions.[23]

But, of course, this is exactly the paradox Kant foresaw. For all Heisenberg's attempts to distance himself, as Weizsäcker suspected, he was moving closer to the Sage of Königsberg all the time. Heisenberg had focused on Kant's assertions in the first part of *The Critique of Pure Reason* that because space and time were necessary forms of intuition and causality, they must remain unchanged for all time. In so doing, however, he overlooked the second part of the book, the part in which Kant laid out in detail the heuristic nature of these provisions and the *paradoxes* that would emerge whenever one overstepped and treated them as possible objects of knowledge. There, and later in his third *Critique,* Kant had stipulated that the continuity of all existence in space and time and the causal chain linking all events were *both* necessary presumptions *and* ultimately unknowable. Whether drilling down into the tightest crevices of space-time or pulling back to contemplate the whole of existence, a scientist could not avoid the abyss that awaited there, an abyss that haunts the limits approached by ever more accurate measurements just as it hovers at the borders of the universe itself.[24]

Despite appearances to the contrary, we can and must *both* presume causality (to draw inferences from our observations) *and* accept the uncertainty those observations lead to, for even though the extremity of measurements enabled by modern physics was not available to him, Kant knew this: there must be a point at which the minute analysis of causal chains breaks down, not because it lands on one or the other side of the antinomy that lies there, but because that antinomy cannot be solved as long as we treat as real the heuristic assumptions needed to make inferences in the first place. Indeed, just as the universe as a whole must in some sense be contained by its center, so must our attempts to plumb the depths of analysis, to arrive at "an experimental realm so far beyond daily experience," reveal to us the embodied antinomy of what constitutes the very essence of a thing in the world. The atoms, the particles we seek there, "are neither things nor objects."[25]

"In that case what are they?" Grete Hermann asked Heisenberg and Weizsäcker that day in Leipzig. "We lack the right term," Heisenberg responded, "for our language is based on daily experience, and atoms are not." Atoms, he went on, are the words we use to describe "parts of observational situations." They are the marker of a relation that pertains to only that relation, "since all the terms with which we describe experience apply to a limited realm only."[26] In other words, the paradoxes of quantum mechanics, like those of the antinomies Kant traced from Zeno to his own time, didn't emerge from Heisenberg's discovery. They were born of the attempt to make that discovery conform to a God's-eye view on nature that was never ours to have in the first place.

AT 8:15 IN THE morning of August 6, 1945, the United States dropped an atomic bomb on the city of Hiroshima, leveling most of its buildings, enveloping it in a cloud of radioactivity, and killing well over a hundred thousand civilians. On the other side of the world Werner Heisenberg was having dinner with his team of German scientists at an estate called Farm Hall, in Godmanchester, England. Soon after his detention and interrogation in Heidelberg by Samuel Goudsmit, Heisenberg had been moved to France and then ultimately to Farm Hall, where he and his team would be interned for the next six months. When the news came on the radio that evening, it cast a pall over the room. The scientists were stunned. As the group slowly came to and started to converse again, Heisenberg told the others, "I was absolutely convinced of the possibility of our making a uranium engine but I never thought that we would make a bomb and at the bottom of my heart I was really glad that it was to be an engine and not a bomb."[27]

Heisenberg and his team had been working on nuclear fission for several years. In 1942, Heisenberg had reported to the Nazi government that while it was theoretically possible to weaponize uranium 235, the quantities needed to produce a bomb made it impractical to do so. Had he been wrong? Or had he feared the overwhelming moral implications of harnessing for violent ends the power his own discoveries had played such a large role in uncovering? A year earlier Heisenberg traveled to occupied Denmark and met in private with Niels Bohr. Their respective accounts of that conversation differ significantly, have led to decades of speculation about the purpose of the visit, and even inspired a Tony Award–winning play. Did Heisenberg go to Copenhagen to extract information from Bohr, to learn something about the Allies' intentions and potential progress with regard to an atomic weapon? Or did he go to Copenhagen to try to arrive at a tacit agreement with Bohr not to use their knowledge for such destructive purposes? As they walked alone, with no third party to hear them, did he really pose the question he later claimed to have asked Bohr during their much-disputed meeting, "if as a physicist one had the moral right to work on the practical exploitation of atomic energy"?[28]

According to his recollections, as he listened in horror to the reports from Japan, Heisenberg felt devastated. He had thought that Bohr, that the great Einstein, so vocal in his opposition to war and violence, would have entertained the same qualms he had. One week later, Heisenberg lectured to his colleagues and explained to them exactly how the bombs over Hiroshima and Nagasaki had worked. Perhaps he had miscalculated, but there's almost no doubt that Heisenberg could have worked it out, had he truly wished to do so.

The response formulated by the group the night they learned of the destruction of Hiroshima would become the basis of Heisenberg's own version of the role he played in Germany's atomic project: namely, the German atomic team had concluded early in 1942 that, while possible, producing an atomic bomb would be so costly as to be impractical. That the scientists were, furthermore, unconvinced of the moral rectitude of such work. That Heisenberg had used the prospect of weaponization to keep the Nazi regime interested enough in his work to continue funding and supporting it even while secretly having decided that "an energy-producing uranium burner for powering machines"[29] was the "only goal attainable."[30] And that his group had tacitly decided it would not work toward the production of a weapon. In 1946 he went so far as to claim that, given their scientific assessment of the impracticality of pursuing a weapon, the German scientists had been spared "the difficult moral decision" taken by their American counterparts.[31]

For the Americans, such public pronouncements by Germany's most famous scientist and one of the founders of their field were nearly unbearable. Robert Oppenheimer, for instance, who had led the Manhattan Project and even had a hand in selecting the Japanese targets, suffered enormous feelings of guilt in the years after the war's cataclysmic end. The outrage he and his fellows felt now, to be implicitly lectured by colleagues who had chosen to continue to work for a regime like that of the Nazis, was palpable. As one American physicist put it, just as the U.S. team had, the "German scientists worked for the military as best their circumstances allowed." The unforgivable difference, he added, was that "they worked for the cause of Himmler and Auschwitz, for the burners of books and the takers of hostages."[32]

The debate over the culpability for the development of nuclear weapons would extend for many years, and for many years Heisenberg would embody the German side. The face of the other side would be the same one Heisenberg had gazed into when he was ushered into the interrogation room in Heidelberg: Samuel Goudsmit. Goudsmit had been chosen for his role in tracking down and interrogating German scientists both for his knowledge and for his lack of it. On the one hand, he had deep reserves of expertise in theoretical and atomic physics; on the other, he was not a part of the top secret Manhattan Project and knew nothing of his colleagues' progress. For Heisenberg's part, once captured and sitting across the table from his former colleague, he felt the war was lost and seemed at peace with that and ready to move on to a more promising future. As he recalled their conversations in Heidelberg, he told Goudsmit of the German determination not to pursue a bomb and asked him point-blank about the American team's position. Goudsmit responded that they had "made no efforts in that direction" and that they had "more important things to do."[33] Years later Heisenberg would confess to Elisabeth his shock when he realized that Goudsmit had lied to him.[34]

From Goudsmit's perspective, made public in a best-selling book, Heisenberg and the Germans were disingenuous at best, highly complicit at worst. Where Heisenberg protested that his team knew a bomb was possible but decided not to pursue it for both practical and moral reasons, Goudsmit drew the exact opposite interpretation: the Germans under Heisenberg's leadership were too incompetent to realize its feasibility and had covered that incompetence with false moralization, made even more heinous by their willingness to work for an evil regime. Heisenberg became for Goudsmit the face of the complacent incompetence that permitted German physics, once the pride of the world, to be overtaken by the upstart Americans. Trapped by their ideology of racial superiority and besotted by what he called "the smug Heisenberg clique," the Germans simply couldn't imagine that the Americans could succeed where they had failed.[35]

Heisenberg aired his own umbrage just as publicly. In a series of letters published in Nature, The New York Times, and elsewhere, he defended the scientific and moral integrity of his colleagues. In his telling, the Germans knew the theoretical steps involved in runaway fission; they simply lacked the resources of the American technological and industrial machine. Not to be deterred, Goudsmit in his response hewed to the central theme of his book: German science failed because of its totalitarian regime, and Heisenberg, while no doubt resisting the Nazis, did so "not because they were bad, but because they were bad for Germany, or at least for German science."[36]

The day after the news of the destruction of Hiroshima reached Farm Hall, the detainees gathered to discuss and draft what would become their official statement. Max von Laue was there and would openly support the statement for many years. Still, later in his life he distanced himself, noting that the position the Germans took that day had been largely orchestrated by Carl Friedrich von Weizsäcker and that during the discussions "I did not hear the mention of any ethical point of view." Heisenberg, he went on to add, emphasizing the point with italics, "*was mostly silent.*"[37]

Whether Heisenberg truly felt the ethical qualms he later claimed; or whether these were concocted over time to hide his complicity; or, as is also possible, whether he genuinely came to believe he had more concerns than he had at the time: these questions are profoundly difficult to decide. That difficulty in part springs from the challenge that always faces historians: that our object of study, the past, is divided from us by an ever-thickening veil of time that obscures our vision of the events we strive to understand. But this very true limitation on our historical knowledge smuggles with it an assumption about our knowledge of the present. It implies that, were we to pierce that veil of time, were we to be present for certain conversations or even to inhabit the consciousness of the persons whose intentions we wish to understand, our vision would be crystal clear, and we would have our answer. But what if our assumption is wrong? What if the obscurity inherent in viewing the past lurks in the present as well?

In 1949, a scant four years after the end of the war, the Allies lifted their prohibition on nuclear research in Germany. Heisenberg and his colleagues immediately set to work, and within less than ten years the Federal Republic of Germany had become one of the world's leading producers and exporters of atomic energy. Heisenberg's personal investment in nuclear as a source of power, however, accompanied a fierce conviction that his own country should never be trusted with nuclear weapons. Whether genuine or politically motivated or some mixture of the two, the horror he had expressed in Farm Hall and the worry he had evinced in Copenhagen led Heisenberg to militate against the weaponization of atomic power. When NATO proposed a plan to equip the German army with tactical nuclear weapons in 1955, Heisenberg and his circle openly opposed it and mobilized the German populace in their support. Germany's ban on nuclear weapons has lasted to this day.

Likewise, he was convinced that science could best remain peaceful by being an international concern, and to this end he lobbied for the centralization of atomic research at the European level, becoming an early advocate for the foundation of CERN, the fabled pan-European nuclear research center located in Geneva, now the home of the Large Hadron Collider, the most massive machine ever built by humankind. In 1952 he also took the helm of the Alexander von Humboldt Foundation, Germany's government-sponsored program to send its postdoctoral students around the world to collaborate and share knowledge. He held this position for more than two decades, until illness prevented him from continuing his work.[38]

On February 1, 1976, Werner Heisenberg died after a long battle with kidney cancer. A few years earlier, enjoying the twilight of his years in his mountain cabin in Urfeld, the aging physicist had reflected on his early readings of Plato, when he had become captivated by the idea that geometrical shapes and mathematical relations could hold the secret to the universe. Today, he concluded, the "particles of modern physics are representations of symmetry groups and to that extent they resemble the symmetrical bodies of Plato's philosophy."[39] Plato's fundamental questions, he mused, had perhaps found their answer in "the contemporary physics of elementary particles."[40]

Back in the United States, a physicist and Nazi hunter who had known him since the golden years, when the young man who looked like a simple farm boy had revolutionized physics, volunteered to pen his obituary. Spent of his vitriol over so many years, Samuel Goudsmit would write of his onetime idol, onetime enemy, that he was "a very great physicist, a deep thinker, a fine human being, and also a courageous person."[41] The man who had lost his parents to the Nazis, who had spent half his life investigating their murderers, had found the grace to rise above his rage.

WHEN HEISENBERG DECIDED TO stay in Germany; when he decided initially to ignore or overlook the Nazis' brutish policies; when he saw what they were doing but decided to focus on the beauty of the science he was doing; when he cooperated with an evil regime in order to protect his work and that of his team—in some ways he was demonstrating precisely the cautious, wait-and-see attitude that served him so well as a scientist. Heisenberg was never one to let prior beliefs, or indeed deeply held principles, get in the way of evidence. And yet, if there was ever a time to jettison such a predilection, it was Germany in the 1930s. That he didn't do so invites our scrutiny, perhaps even our opprobrium, just as it did Goudsmit's. But Goudsmit changed his mind.

Which Samuel Goudsmit was right? The one who judged Heisenberg a hypocrite who later covered over his own incompetence with moral superiority, or the one who forgave Germany's greatest scientist and praised his courage? This question, the very idea that Goudsmit was right at one time and wrong at another, has the virtue of laying bare an assumption common to both science and morality. That assumption is that things happen independently of our knowledge of them and that people's decisions and actions have a moral value in their own right.

Thankfully, for many of our practical purposes this assumption works just fine. David Mermin's witticism notwithstanding, we can be confident that the moon does not vanish when we cease to look at it. The *Spirit of St. Louis* most certainly did take a path after leaving New York and before being sighted again in the skies over Europe. Likewise, if you embezzle from your company or cheat on your spouse, your responsibility for those crimes or betrayals does not depend on their learning about it. And just as the uncertainty Heisenberg discovered at the edges of scientific perception is utterly irrelevant to our tracing a plane's path on a map, we can and should brush aside any facile reference to his ideas when talking about, say, the reality of an accused person's actions and intents, or the meaning of a work of art.

The trouble comes when we take our common and perfectly acceptable image of reality as an independent space-time in which things are happening in blissful disregard of our knowledge and start applying it where it doesn't belong: below the limits of observability or beyond the very borders of existence itself; between the links of the mechanistic causal chain enabling a human action; or to the very sense of self underlying that action. When we do so, we sacrifice the core of what has made the scientific method so extraordinarily successful: its profound humility; its awareness that our knowledge is always subject to revision, to improvement. Moreover, when we do this, we err profoundly about human agency and freedom, either erasing it along with all responsibility in a vain attempt to understand humans "scientifically" or projecting at the core of all decisions a purely rational agent, utterly transparent to itself as it navigates life's choices.

As we steer a course through the river of our lives, we are affected by innumerable forces, the vast majority unknown to us. By some accounts this makes of our freedom an illusion, for how can we purport to freely choose when we can't even see a fraction of the legion of influences acting on us, limiting our movements, sparking our appetites? The threat this picture poses to traditional notions of agency suggests a counternarrative. There must be some part of us that floats above the river, untouched by its waters and therefore utterly free and totally responsible for our every turn. But both these pictures are misleading, and for the same reason. Our freedom, and hence our responsibility for the choices we make, is neither a thing to look for in our material existence nor some ghostlike essence unmoored from that existence. Rather, it is a necessary postulate for a being who can imagine having chosen differently, the condition of the possibility of conceiving of that life as one possible path among many.

As Goudsmit sat across the table from Heisenberg at his first debriefing in Heidelberg, he looked into the eyes of a man he believed had chosen poorly. This man had an opportunity to leave, an opportunity not to serve a regime that killed millions of people, that murdered Goudsmit's own parents. Over the years as the two men engaged in heated debate, Goudsmit must have felt he knew the path of Heisenberg's soul, felt he could see his fear of losing his position, see his willingness to make a bomb, if only he could. But he couldn't see these things.

When we judge the actions or intentions of another person, we never have access to their thoughts, never actually see the world from their eyes. We construct an image of their intentions, and then forget we made it. But like an experimenter measuring an event, what we find out pertains to us. It is the product of a relation, the way some part of nature manifests itself to us.

Ultimately, to judge the guilt or rectitude of another's choices is not to know the secrets of that person's heart; it is to consider what I would have done, what I should have done, had I been in that person's shoes. Indeed, to judge another person is to raise for oneself the question of the path not taken. It is to imagine another life and compare it with one's own. It is nothing more, and nothing less, than the existential burden of one who is free to choose, and to regret those choices. As he sat down to write his obituary, Samuel Goudsmit couldn't know how Werner Heisenberg judged his own life and choices, but in the end he seemed to realize that such knowledge was not his goal. The absolution he gave wasn't for Heisenberg. It was for himself.

POSTSCRIPT

QUANTUM THEORY IS THE victory of science over the presuppositions that make science possible. That its findings still register such shock manifests how deeply those presuppositions take root. The physicist Carlo Rovelli puts it this way as he outlines what he calls the relational interpretation of quantum mechanics: "If we imagine the totality of things, we are imagining being *outside* the universe, looking at it from out there. But there is no 'outside' to the totality of things.... [W]hat exists are only internal perspectives on the world which are partial and reflect one another. The world *is* this reciprocal reflection of perspectives."[1] Indeed, the alternative interpretations of quantum mechanics I have discussed here—from objective collapse to many worlds—are, in his words again, "efforts to squeeze the discoveries of quantum physics into the canons of metaphysical prejudice."[2] Those canons of metaphysical prejudice work in mysterious ways. Even as they guide how scientists think about the meaning of their most significant discoveries, they also affect the lives those scientists lead, how they judge their lives, how we *all* judge our lives.

By the end of their respective lives, Goudsmit's interpretation of Heisenberg's choices had changed. But had Heisenberg changed? Had the person who made those decisions—to stay in Germany; to work for the Nazis; to do his best for German science; to produce, or not to produce, a weapon—changed as well? We tend to imagine the series of choices an individual makes through the course of her life as if they were the conscious decisions of a completed person, taken in full knowledge of all the options and their respective consequences, both in the present and as they will eventually play out. We do so because what we think about our own and others' choices always and by necessity emerges from and takes place in a present from which we look back on those moments, reading them as a path through time leading to the here and now. Even when we might consider such a vision naive, we nonetheless imagine it as the more fulsome picture, how things must have happened even if our limited knowledge in the here and now cannot fully reconstruct it.

But perhaps—just as Heisenberg put it when explaining electron emissions during those long arguments with Grete Hermann— perhaps our vision of an ultimately knowable *human* path through space and time isn't merely problematic because it is incomplete. Perhaps it is per se impossible. Like Funes reconstructing a day in his memory but needing a full day to do so; like the cosmos repeating itself after an unimaginable time but needing a special archangel to notice it; like a man asking if, were he to replace himself, atom for atom, with the person of a murderer, he too would become such a murderer: a perfectly knowable path through space-time utterly contradicts its own presuppositions. Because to register something, anything at all, one must be minimally different from it; one must be in a *relation* with it.

What Borges's stories, Heisenberg's discovery, and Kant's system all reveal is that the assumption underlying this fantasy, the full coincidence of knowing and being, self-destructs on closer examination. On the one hand, to measure something is to differ from it in some minimal but irreducible way, and hence the very condition of knowing anything about the world demolishes the possibility of doing so perfectly. On the other hand, full presence, being truly and completely a part of the flow, requires eradicating such difference, and hence makes knowledge impossible. One can imagine *knowing* the world perfectly, but only at the cost of *being* what one knows; or one can imagine *being* identical with the world, but only at the cost of *knowing* it. Like what Heisenberg's most famous principle revealed about momentum and place, we can't have both.

Far from a weakness, however, this fundamental limitation on our knowledge empowers what we have come to call the scientific method. Science works not despite the limitations of our knowledge but because of our willingness to test our theories and accept the results, whether they affirm or contradict what we hope or expect to see. This means that a theory endures only as long as observation and experiment continue to support it. Science can always come up with a new explanation for the world; no knowledge is dogma. And yet, while all scientists accept this fact in principle, unconscious bias abounds. One such bias is what Rovelli called metaphysical prejudice, the belief that reality exists, out there, independent of our interactions with it, and does so in ways that correspond to how we experience human life on Earth: smoothly extended in space and successive in time. And this belief, this desire that the world confirm our expectations, is so strong no construct is too wild if it manages to uphold it.

The radical incompatibility of being and knowledge also has massive ramifications for our understanding of choice and responsibility. For the scientific dismissal of free will has always depended on the presumption that somewhere, beyond the natural limits on our ability to know, lies a more complete picture in which each particle of our being is determined by its place and momentum in the causal flow of matter through space-time. If we imagined a being in this flow who was perfectly aware of its place, knowing everything down to the atomic level, that being could, in theory, see everything, but it could not choose. Choices happen in space and time. But for such a being—a being at one with the world and aware of it, simultaneously from beginning to end, like the Aleph under the basement stairs—time and space, which require distance, difference, relations to something else, don't exist.

But we are, evidently, not such beings. Unlike such beings we are trapped in what Shakespeare called "the dark backward and abysm of time," blind to all that hides from us behind spatial and temporal horizons. And as beings thus trapped in the flow, we may simultaneously presume ourselves determined by it and yet still make choices, still be held responsible. Like Robert Frost's walker in the yellow woods, we pause where the paths fork and peer down one as far as we can, only to lose sight of it as it bends through the underbrush. We feel sorry that we cannot travel both and be one traveler. Indeed, in blatant contradiction to what materialist or religious attacks on freedom conclude, the assumption of mechanistic causality is utterly at peace with the existential blindness that allows for responsibility, for freedom.

So, freedom is just ignorance, and nothing else? Not in the slightest. For as Boethius realized as he stared his impending death in the face, his assumption of an omniscient god who knows every step of the path Boethius would take through life emphatically failed to deprive him of his freedom, failed to absolve him of responsibility or credit for his choices, bad or good. The assumption of such knowledge dissolves the very space-time medium in which we swim, and hence for that impossible perspective my future choices take place in an eternal now in which knowing for certain what path I will choose has no more effect on the freedom of my choices than does someone witnessing me as I make those choices. In the same way, the famed paradoxes born of entanglement lose their sting, because my knowledge of a particle's yet-to-be-measured spin, or of a twin's choice of beer or whiskey in a galaxy far, far away, has no more effect on either its randomness or the twin's choice than would the lingering eyes of the god of things on the particles or people who play out their paths and lives in the eternal present of that limitless mind.

In some cases, one knows what one does. In the Garden of Forking Paths, you may pull the trigger knowing full well which path you are choosing. In other cases, even the one deciding doesn't know why. One physicist leaves; another stays. Those decisions are made and replayed, over and over, as an ever-changing self evolves. To say so isn't to invite infinite apology, to grant clemency to all acts. It is, rather, to grasp that the very nature of an entity in time, from the evanescences we call particles up to those massive collections of particles known as humans, always and only exists as a relation. Just as every measurement involves an interaction and creates a reality exclusive to those parties involved, every individual creates a life that comprises myriad relations. The relations don't bloom between previously pristine individuals; rather, like the particles our measurements detect, the individuals spring forth from the relations themselves.

In short, despite our dearest desires and most desperate dreams, we are finite. That we can only ever understand things in relation to one another means that understanding will always stem from a limited perspective. Our reason propels us to incredible heights—understanding the fundamental components of matter and laws of the universe, seeing almost to the edges of the cosmos and the beginning of time. But it also leads us woefully astray. For the very ability we have to map our world and hence see our way through the dark also treats that map as though it were the world, and hence drapes a new veil over our enlightened eyes.

"Metaphysical prejudice": the perfect term to describe that magical thinking that Borges, Heisenberg, and Kant each explored, engaged with, and ultimately undid. Quantum theory may not gird us against metaphysical prejudice, but we cannot fully grasp its meaning while maintaining that prejudice. And thus, the persistence of its apparent paradoxes serves as a powerful reminder of how deeply set, how necessary to our thinking those prejudices are.

When we see an effect, we reach for a cause, out there, in a world that is ubiquitous in space and durable in time, because we know, just know, that is how the world must be. We know so, but we are wrong. There is rigor there, indeed. But to see that we are the chess masters who made it, we must let the angels go. And that, it seems, is the hardest task of all.

ACKNOWLEDGMENTS

This book is the product of more than twenty-five years of thinking, teaching, and writing about cosmology, literature, and philosophy. I first started thinking about Dante's cosmos in a seminar at Stanford taught by Jeffrey Schnapp during which I read Bob Osserman's book *Poetry of the Universe* and Mark Peterson's article "Dante and the 3-Sphere" and was inspired to start studying medieval conceptions of curved space. Since then I have taught some version of a course called The Cosmic Imagination to my students at Johns Hopkins on several occasions, most recently in the fall of 2022 to a marvelous group of freshmen. I am grateful to all of them for their ever-present curiosity. I am also grateful to the many friends and colleagues who looked at all or some of the manuscript during its gestation or interacted with me at conferences or lectures I have given. These include Robert Davidson, Marcelo Gleiser, Brian Greene, Robert Pogue Harrison, Virginia Jewiss, Robert Leheny, Karen ní Mheallaigh, Yi-Ping Ong, Gordon Rubenfeld, and Robert Rynasiewicz. My wife, Bernadette Wegenstein, played an outsize role in commenting on the manuscript and helped scour the archives for details that helped bring the characters to life. Special thanks go to my agent, Michael Carlisle, whose early guidance helped me form the conception for the book, and to my editor, Edward Kastenmeier, who always knew just the right questions to ask. I also want to thank Andrew Weber, who, along with the late and greatly missed Dan Frank, acquired the book for Pantheon. Additionally, Michael Mungiello gave me valuable feedback as I worked on formulating the book's structure, and Chris Howard-Woods provided a steady hand during the editing and production schedule. As always I owe a great debt of thanks to Troy Tower, whose meticulous eye and gargantuan research abilities helped assemble the back matter stemming from multiple disciplines and more than ten languages. Finally, I am forever grateful to a friend, among the truest, who read every word, often multiple times. At his own request he remains unnamed.

NOTES

INTRODUCTION: WHERE DID IT GO?

1. Bryson, *One Summer*, 96–98.
2. Gleiser, *Island of Knowledge*, 169–70. Very recent research has shown that changes in quanta can be continuous and predictable. Vitally, however, the experimental conditions for this to happen require "continuous observation," and hence allow for "the reconciliation of the discreteness of countable events, such as jumps, with the continuity of the deterministic Schrödinger's equation"; see Minev et al., "To Catch and Reverse a Quantum Jump Mid-flight," 203.
3. Williamson, *Borges*, 143, 507n21.
4. Ibid., 143.
5. Williamson, "Borges in Context," 208.
6. Borges, *El tamaño de mi esperanza*, 130, translation from Williamson, *Borges*, ix.
7. Borges, *El idioma de los argentinos*, 47, translation from Williamson, *Borges*, 148.
8. Andrés, *Palabras con Leopoldo Marechal*, 24, translation from Williamson, *Borges*, 149.
9. Schlosser, *Kleine Schriften*, 1:29, translation from Epstein, *Genesis of German Conservatism*, 79.
10. Hamann, *Briefwechsel*, 4:196, translation altered from Kuehn, *Kant*, 241.
11. Translation from Williamson, *Borges*, 156.
12. Borges, *El idioma de los argentinos*, 24, 20, 23, translation from Williamson, *Borges*, 157.
13. Borges, *El idioma de los argentinos*, 24, translation from Williamson, *Borges*, 158.
14. Pauli, *Wissenschaftlicher Briefwechsel*, 1:347, translation altered from Lindley, *Uncertainty*, 145.

15. W. Heisenberg, *Gesammelte Werke*, C1:21, translation from Cassidy, *Uncertainty*, 228.

16. W. Heisenberg, *Gesammelte Werke*, C1:21, translation altered from Cassidy, *Uncertainty*, 228.

17. Borges, *Obras*, 1:245, translation from Borges, "Perpetual Race of Achilles and the Tortoise," 44.

18. Borges, *Obras*, 1:248, translation from Borges, "Perpetual Race of Achilles and the Tortoise," 47.

19. Borges, *Obras*, 1:273, translation from Borges, "Avatars of the Tortoise," 202.

20. Borges, *Obras*, 1:258, translation from Borges, "Avatars of the Tortoise," 202.

21. Kant, *Gesammelte Schriften*, 4:260, translation from Anderson, *Kant, Hume, and the Interruption of Dogmatic Slumber*, xi.

22. W. Heisenberg, *Gesammelte Werke*, C1:379, translation from Cassidy, *Uncertainty*, 236.

23. W. Heisenberg, *Gesammelte Werke*, C3:92, translation from Isaacson, *Einstein*, 332.

24. See Isaacson, *Einstein*, 389, 326, 609n45.

25. Borges, *Obras*, 1:442, translation from Borges, *Collected Fictions*, 81.

26. The order of my sections does not match Kant's antinomies precisely. I begin with his second, the mathematical antinomy of atomism; then pass to his fourth, the dynamical antinomy of necessity; then to his first, the mathematical antinomy of space and time; and, finally, to his third, the dynamical antinomy of causality.

1. UNFORGETTABLE

1. Luria, *Romanticheskie ésse*, 17, translation from Luria, *Mind of a Mnemonist*, 11.

2. Johnson, "Mystery of S."

3. Luria, *Romanticheskie ésse*, 25, translation from Luria, *Mind of a Mnemonist*, 31.

4. Bruner, "Foreword," xxii.

5. Luria, *Romanticheskie ésse*, 72, translation from Luria, *Mind of a Mnemonist*, 118–19.

6. Bruner, "Foreword," xvii.

7. Johnson, "Mystery of S."

8. Williamson, *Borges*, 166.

9. García Márquez and Mendoza, *El olor de la guayaba*, 52, translation from García Márquez and Mendoza, *Fragrance of Guava*, 49.

10. Williamson, *Borges*, 195.

11. Borges, *Obras*, 1:293. While he never revealed the identity of I.J., "English" and "Angel" most likely would have been enough to cement Norah as the addressee. That the protagonist of *45 Days and 30 Sailors* is called Ingrid Julia merely seals the deal. Williamson cites the 1935 edition but then

notes the change to the "equally mysterious S.D." that appears in the 1954 edition I cite here. Williamson, *Borges*, 514n23.

12. Borges, *Inquisiciones*, 85–86, translation from Borges, "Nothingness of Personality," 4.

13. Borges, "Historia de la eternidad," in *Obras*, 1:364, translation from Williamson, *Borges*, 214.

14. Williamson, *Borges*, 168, 510n13.

15. Borges and Carrizo, *Borges el memorioso*, 118, translation from Williamson, *Borges*, 241.

16. This marvelous phrase is from Williamson, *Borges*, 242.

17. Borges, *Inquisiciones*, 93, translation from Williamson, *Borges*, 98.

18. Unamuno, *Obras*, 10:281–82, translation from Unamuno, *Tragic Sense of Life*, 49.

19. Homer, *Odyssey*, 23.240–45.

20. Geier, *Kants Welt*, 40–41.

21. Kant, *Gesammelte Schriften*, 10:70–71, translation from Kuehn, *Kant*, 179.

22. Kant, *Gesammelte Schriften*, 2:383.

23. Kuehn, *Kant*, 198.

24. Hume, *Treatise of Human Nature*, 264.

25. Mendelssohn, *Saemmtliche Werke*, 6:vi, translation from Kuehn, *Kant*, 251.

26. Hume, *Treatise of Human Nature*, 252.

27. Ibid., 269.

28. Borges, *Obras*, 1:487–88, translation from Borges, *Collected Fictions*, 134–35.

29. Borges, *Obras*, 1:489, translation from Borges, *Collected Fictions*, 136.

30. Borges, *Obras*, 1:489, translation from Borges, *Collected Fictions*, 136.

31. Luria, *Romanticheskie ésse*, 72, translation from Luria, *Mind of a Mnemonist*, 118–19.

32. Borges, *Obras*, 1:489, translation from Borges, *Collected Fictions*, 136.

33. Hume, *Treatise of Human Nature*, 252.

34. Kant, *Gesammelte Schriften*, 4:77, translation from Kant, *Critique of Pure Reason*, 228–29.

35. Mermin, "What's Wrong with This Pillow?," 9.

36. Mermin, "Can You Help Your Team Tonight by Watching on TV?," 50.

37. Henderson, "Rebel Physicist on the Hunt for a Better Story Than Quantum Mechanics."

38. Wittgenstein, *Tractatus*, 188–89.

39. Henderson, "Rebel Physicist on the Hunt for a Better Story Than Quantum Mechanics."

40. W. Heisenberg, *Gesammelte Werke*, C1:224, translation from W. Heisenberg, *Reality and Its Order*, 27.

41. W. Heisenberg, *Gesammelte Werke*, C1:224, translation from W. Heisenberg, *Reality and Its Order*, 26.

42. Kant, *Gesammelte Schriften*, 4:77, translation from Kant, *Critique of Pure Reason*, 228.

43. Kant, *Gesammelte Schriften*, 4:77, translation from Kant, *Critique of Pure Reason*, 228–29.

44. Kant, *Gesammelte Schriften*, 10:70–71, my translation.

45. W. Heisenberg, *Gesammelte Werke*, C1:226, translation from W. Heisenberg, *Reality and Its Order*, 29.

2. A BRIEF HISTORY OF THIS VERY INSTANT

1. Geier, *Kants Welt*, 28.

2. Ibid., 59.

3. Kant, *Briefwechsel*, 2, my translation.

4. Borowski, *Darstellung des Lebens und Charakters Immanuel Kants*, 32, translation altered from Cassirer, *Kant's Life and Thought*, 40.

5. Borowski, *Darstellung des Lebens und Charakters Immanuel Kants*, 185, translation from Cassirer, *Kant's Life and Thought*, 39.

6. Borowski, *Darstellung des Lebens und Charakters Immanuel Kants*, 186, translation from Cassirer, *Kant's Life and Thought*, 39.

7. See Cassirer, *Kant's Life and Thought*, 40, 41n5.

8. Rink, *Ansichten aus Immanuel Kant's Leben*, 14, translation from Cassirer, *Kant's Life and Thought*, 18.

9. Geier, *Kants Welt*, 30.

10. Hippel, *Biographie des Königl. Preuss*, 79, translation from Cassirer, *Kant's Life and Thought*, 15.

11. Kant, *Gesammelte Schriften*, 7:133, translation from Cassirer, *Kant's Life and Thought*, 18.

12. Kant, *Gesammelte Schriften*, 10:41, translation from Kuehn, *Kant*, 171.

13. Swedenborg, *De caelo et ejus mirabilibus et de inferno*, 265; Swedenborg, *Heaven and Hell*, 261.

14. Swedenborg, *De caelo et ejus mirabilibus et de inferno*, 265–66; Swedenborg, *Heaven and Hell*, 261.

15. Kant, *Gesammelte Schriften*, 10:66, translation from Kuehn, *Kant*, 172.

16. Kant, *Gesammelte Schriften*, 2:348, translation altered from Kant, *Theoretical Philosophy*, 335–36.

17. Kant, *Gesammelte Schriften*, 2:307, translation from Kuehn, *Kant*, 160.

18. Kant, *Gesammelte Schriften*, 20:175, translation from Kuehn, *Kant*, 464n65.

19. Plato, *Opera*, 2:129c–d, translation from Plato, *Parmenides*, 363.

20. Plato, *Opera*, 2:131b, translation altered from Plato, *Parmenides*, 365.

21. Plato, *Opera*, 2:131c, translation altered from Plato, *Parmenides*, 365.

22. Jachmann, *Immanuel Kant geschildert in Briefen an einen Freund*, 155–56, translation altered from Kuehn, *Kant*, 115–16.

23. Hamann, *Briefwechsel*, 2:234, translation from Kuehn, *Kant*, 134.

24. Kant, *Gesammelte Schriften*, 2:41–42, translation from Kuehn, *Kant*, 126.

25. Kant, *Gesammelte Schriften*, 7:58, translation from Kuehn, *Kant*, 150.

26. Kuehn, *Kant*, 155.

27. Kant, *Gesammelte Schriften*, 20:46, translation from Schilpp, *Kant's Precritical Ethics*, 73.

28. Plato, *Opera*, 2:156d, translation from Plato, *Parmenides*, 388.

29. Plato, *Opera*, 2:156e, translation from Plato, *Parmenides*, 388. In fact, it is a stunned Aristotle who is left to reply, "It looks that way." While it's not possible that the Aristotle we know today was present for the meeting of Socrates with Zeno and Parmenides, Plato gives that name to the young student who agrees to be Parmenides's foil, and adds, "the man who would later be one of the Thirty," referring to his own academy; Plato, *Opera*, 2:127d, translation from Plato, *Parmenides*, 361. It is probable that Plato did this in part because he noticed how struck his own student Aristotle was by Zeno's arguments. Indeed, while Zeno's book itself is lost, we know about it and his paradoxes because Aristotle deals with them in great detail in his *Physics*, which would go on to become one of the central sources for Scholastic science.

30. Aristotle, *Physics*, 180 (bk. 6.9, col. 239b), as quoted in Hegel, *Vorlesungen über die Geschichte der Philosophie*, 1:296; the rather loose translation is from Hegel, *Greek Philosophy to Plato*, 274.

31. Plato, *Opera*, 2:152b, translation from Plato, *Parmenides*, 384.

32. Plato, *Opera*, 2:152c–d, translation from Plato, *Parmenides*, 385.

33. Kant, *Gesammelte Schriften*, 4:221, translation from Kant, *Critique of Pure Reason*, 417.

34. Kant, *Gesammelte Schriften*, 3:345, translation from Kant, *Critique of Pure Reason*, 517 (A502): "I do not find that this charge can be justly lodged against him."

35. Hegel, *Vorlesungen über die Geschichte der Philosophie*, 1:292, translation from Hegel, *Greek Philosophy to Plato*, 271.

36. Hegel, *Vorlesungen über die Geschichte der Philosophie*, 1:297, translation from Hegel, *Greek Philosophy to Plato*, 275.

37. Hegel, *Greek Philosophy to Plato*, 263, recalling Diogenes Laertes (bk. 9).

38. The philosophically inclined reader might have realized by now that my interpretation is deeply indebted to the thought of Martin Heidegger and Jacques Derrida, even if neither plays a starring role in this account.

39. See Martin Hägglund's brilliant exposition of this idea in *This Life*.

3. VISUALIZE THIS!

1. Mehra and Rechenberg, *Historical Development of Quantum Theory*, 1.1:345.

2. Born, *My Life*, 212.

3. W. Heisenberg, *Gesammelte Werke*, C5:399, translation from Cassidy, *Uncertainty*, 40.

4. Cassidy, *Uncertainty*, 563n4, 42.

5. Heisenberg, *Teil und Ganze*, 9.

6. Ibid., my translation.

7. Ibid., 16.

8. Plato, *Opera*, 4:53b, translation from Plato, *Timaeus*, 1256.

9. Plato, *Opera*, 4:56a–b, translation from Plato, *Timaeus*, 1258.

10. W. Heisenberg, *Gesammelte Werke*, C3:20–21, translation from W. Heisenberg, *Physics and Beyond*, 8.

11. W. Heisenberg, *Gesammelte Werke*, C5:102, translation from Cassidy, *Uncertainty*, 47.

12. Heisenberg, *Teil und Ganze*, 13.

13. Ibid., 20, my translation.

14. Cassidy, *Uncertainty*, 83.

15. See Kirchhoff, "Ueber das Verhältniss zwischen dem Emissionsvermögen und dem Absorptionsvermögen der Körper für Wärme und Licht," 277; and Kirchhoff, "On the Relation Between the Emissive and the Absorptive Power of Bodies for Heat and Light," 76.

16. Gribbin, *In Search of Schrödinger's Cat*, 37, 41–42.

17. Hermann, *Frühgeschichte der Quantentheorie*, 31–32, translation from Mehra and Rechenberg, *Historical Development of Quantum Theory*, 1.1:49–50.

18. W. Heisenberg, *Physics and Philosophy*, 5.

19. Einstein, *Swiss Years*, 150, translation from Einstein, "On a Heuristic Point of View About the Creation and Conversion of Light," 91.

20. Isaacson, *Einstein*, 94.

21. Planck, "Zur Theorie des Gesetzes der Energieverteilung im Normalspectrum," 239, translation from Isaacson, *Einstein*, 96.

22. Einstein, "Autobiographisches," 44, translation from Isaacson, *Einstein*, 96.

23. Bohr, *Foundations of Quantum Physics I*, 415, 38.

24. Gribbin, *In Search of Schrödinger's Cat*, 65.

25. W. Heisenberg, *Gesammelte Werke*, C3:44, translation from W. Heisenberg, *Physics and Beyond*, 26.

26. Forman, "Alfred Landé and the Anomalous Zeeman Effect," 261, translation from Cassidy, *Uncertainty*, 119.

27. W. Heisenberg, *Gesammelte Werke*, C3:63, translation from W. Heisenberg, *Physics and Beyond*, 41.

28. Eddington, *Nature of the Physical World*, 290–91.

29. Ibid., 291.

30. Van der Waerden, *Sources of Quantum Mechanics*, 168.

31. Lindley, *Uncertainty*, 103–4.

32. Ibid., 106–7.

33. W. Heisenberg, *Physics and Philosophy*, 13.

34. W. Heisenberg, *Gesammelte Werke*, C3:89–90, translation from W. Heisenberg, *Physics and Beyond*, 61.

35. Gribbin, *In Search of Schrödinger's Cat*, 87–88.

36. Einstein, "Quantentheorie des einatomigen idealen Gases," 9, translation from Hentschel and James, *Berlin Years*, 377.

37. Lindley, *Uncertainty*, 120.

38. Schrödinger, "Undulatory Theory of the Mechanics of Atoms and Molecules," 1058.

39. Dresden, *H. A. Kramers*, 82n84, 51.

40. W. Heisenberg, "Development of the Interpretation of the Quantum Theory," 14.

41. Born, "Zur Quantenmechanik der Stoßvorgänge," 866, translation from Lindley, *Uncertainty*, 136.

42. Einstein, *Berlin Years*, 403.

43. W. Heisenberg, *Gesammelte Werke*, A1:382, translation from Lindley, *Uncertainty*, 115.

44. W. Heisenberg, *Physics and Philosophy*, 32.

4. ENTANGLEMENTS

1. Cassidy, *Uncertainty*, 240.

2. Hermann, *Werner Heisenberg in Selbstzeugnissen und Bilddokumenten*, 36, my translation.

3. Ibid., my translation.

4. Ibid., 37, my translation.

5. Ibid., 39, my translation.

6. Cassidy, *Uncertainty*, 242; Lindley, *Uncertainty*, 147–48.

7. W. Heisenberg, *Gesammelte Werke*, A1:503, translation from Lindley, *Uncertainty*, 243.

8. Cassidy, *Uncertainty*, 243–44.

9. Ibid., 244.

10. Lindley, *Uncertainty*, 154.

11. Ibid., 155.

12. "New Problems in Quantum Theory," *Nature*, 579.

13. See Isaacson, *Einstein*, 345, 611n26.

14. Lindley, *Uncertainty*, 157.

15. Born and Heisenberg, "La mécanique des quanta," 178, translation from Cassidy, *Uncertainty*, 250.

16. Born and Heisenberg, "La mécanique des quanta," 143, 178, translation from Cassidy, *Uncertainty*, 250.

17. Born and Heisenberg, "La mécanique des quanta," 178, translation from Cassidy, *Uncertainty*, 250.

18. Isaacson, *Einstein*, 346.

19. Cassidy, *Uncertainty*, 252–53.

20. Lindley, *Uncertainty*, 161.

21. Lorentz et al., "Discussion générale des idées nouvelles émises," 256, translation from Isaacson, *Einstein*, 347.

22. Gribbin, *In Search of Schrödinger's Cat*, 170–71.

23. Lindley, *Uncertainty*, 169.

24. Einstein, "Remarks," 674.

25. "Stimson Says Law Required Action," *New York Times*, 3.

26. See Isaacson, *Einstein*, 404, 619n26.

27. See Rosenfeld, "Niels Bohr in the Thirties," 127.

28. Ibid., 128.

29. Pauli, *Wissenschaftlicher Briefwechsel*, 2:402, translation from Lindley, *Uncertainty*, 191.

30. Rosenfeld, "Niels Bohr in the Thirties," 128.

31. Gleiser, *Island of Knowledge*, 196.

32. Bohr, "Can Quantum-Mechanical Description of Physical Reality Be Considered Complete?," 696–97.

33. Schrödinger, "Die gegenwärtige Situation in der Quantenmechanik," 812, translation from Jauch, *Foundations of Quantum Mechanics*, 185.

34. Schrödinger, "Die gegenwärtige Situation in der Quantenmechanik," 812, translation from Isaacson, *Einstein*, 457.

35. Schrödinger, "Die gegenwärtige Situation in der Quantenmechanik," 827, translation from Isaacson, *Einstein*, 454.

36. See Isaacson, *Einstein*, 455, 626n19.

37. Bernstein, *Quantum Profiles*, 84.

38. Gleiser, *Island of Knowledge*, 214.

39. Ibid., 211.

40. Knight, "Entangled Photons Secure Money Transfer."

41. Gleiser, *Island of Knowledge*, 215–16.

42. Feynman, Leighton, and Sands, *Feynman Lectures on Physics*, 3:18.3.

43. Cassidy, *Uncertainty*, 295.

44. *Verfassung des Deutschen Reiches vom 11. August 1919*, 89 (article 9.2), translation from Kaes, Jay, and Dimendberg, *Weimar Republic Sourcebook*, 48.

45. Cassidy, *Uncertainty*, 150.

46. See Cassidy, *Uncertainty*, 303, 599n20.

47. Pauli, *Wissenschaftlicher Briefwechsel*, 2:168, translation from Cassidy, *Uncertainty*, 307.

48. Cassidy, *Uncertainty*, 307.

49. Lindley, *Uncertainty*, 173.

50. See Cassidy, *Uncertainty*, 310, 601n52.

51. Ibid., 310, 602n53.

52. Cassidy, *Uncertainty*, 324.

53. Ibid., 330, 606n75.

54. Born, *Born-Einstein Letters*, 158.

55. Greene, *Fabric of the Cosmos*, 117.

56. Gribbin, *Schrödinger's Kittens and the Search for Reality*, 132.

57. Ibid., 135.

5. SUB SPECIE AETERNITATIS

1. Kuehn, *Kant*, 222.

2. Ibid., 205.

3. See ibid., 206.

4. Reicke, *Kantiana*, 19, translation from Kuehn, *Kant*, 206.

5. Kuehn, *Kant*, 215.

6. Kant, *Gesammelte Schriften*, 10:231, translation from Kuehn, *Kant*, 219.

7. See Kuehn, *Kant*, 221, 476n125.

8. Ibid., 222.

9. Kant, *Gesammelte Schriften*, 10:97, translation from Kant, *Correspondence*, 107–8.

10. Kant, *Briefwechsel*, 110.

11. Kant, *Gesammelte Schriften*, 10:149, translation altered from Cassirer, *Kant's Life and Thought*, 134.

12. Kant, *Reflexionen*, 2:4, translation from Cassirer, *Kant's Life and Thought*, 112.

13. Geier, *Kants Welt*, 148.

14. Kant, *Gesammelte Schriften*, 10:123, translation from Kuehn, *Kant*, 232.

15. Cassirer, *Kant's Life and Thought*, 132.

16. Hume, *Enquiry Concerning the Principles of Morals*, 77.

17. Ibid., 117.

18. Kant, *Gesammelte Schriften*, 19:116–17, translation from Kuehn, *Kant*, 201.

19. Kant, *Gesammelte Schriften*, 19:103, translation from Kuehn, *Kant*, 202.

20. Geier, *Kants Welt*, 159.

21. Kant, *Gesammelte Schriften*, 10:130, translation from Cassirer, *Kant's Life and Thought*, 127.

22. Kant, *Gesammelte Schriften*, 10:130–31, translation from Cassirer, *Kant's Life and Thought*, 128.

23. Hume, *Enquiry Concerning the Principles of Morals*, 117.

24. Kant, *Gesammelte Schriften*, 10:131, translation from Cassirer, *Kant's Life and Thought*, 129.

25. Geier, *Kants Welt*, 161.

26. Kant, *Gesammelte Schriften*, 10:123, translation from Cassirer, *Kant's Life and Thought*, 130.

27. Geier, *Kants Welt*, 170.

28. Kant, *Gesammelte Schriften*, 3:181, translation from Kant, *Critique of Pure Reason*, 317 (B258).

29. Borges, *Obras*, 1:91, translation from Borges, "John Wilkins' Analytical Language," 231.

30. As Kant puts it in the *Critique,* this overstepping of reason "passes off the constant logical subject of thinking as the cognition of a real subject of inherence, with which we do not and cannot have the least acquaintance." Kant, *Gesammelte Schriften*, 4:221, translation from Kant, *Critique of Pure Reason*, 417 (A350).

31. Kant, *Gesammelte Schriften*, 3:392, translation from Kant, *Critique of Pure Reason*, 559 (A582/B610).

32. Kant, *Gesammelte Schriften*, 3:392, translation from Kant, *Critique of Pure Reason*, 559 (A582/B610).

33. Russell, *Problems of Philosophy*, 93.

34. W. Heisenberg, *Physics and Philosophy*, 32.

35. Geier, *Kants Welt*, 144.

36. Ibid., 147.

37. Ibid., 171.

38. See Kuehn, *Kant*, 270.

39. Kant, *Gesammelte Schriften*, 10:391, translation from Kuehn, *Kant*, 270.

40. Hare, "Augustine, Kant, and the Moral Gap," 254.

41. Kant, *Gesammelte Schriften*, 6:37, translation from Kant, *Religion Within the Limits of Reason Alone*, 32.

42. Kant, *Gesammelte Schriften*, 6:40, translation from Kant, *Religion Within the Limits of Reason Alone*, 40.

43. Hare, "Augustine, Kant, and the Moral Gap," 252.

44. Augustine, *Confessions*, 2:244 (11.26 [33]), translation from Chadwick, *Confessions*, 240.

6. IN THE BLINK OF AN EYE

1. Rubenstein, *When Jesus Became God*, 75–81.

2. Ibid., 96.

3. Augustine, *Confessions*, 2:254 (11.29 [39]), translation from Chadwick, *Confessions*, 244.

4. See United States Conference of Catholic Bishops, "What We Believe."

5. Hegel, *Lectures on the History of Philosophy*, 404–5; Remes, *Neoplatonism*, 19.

6. Hegel, *Vorlesungen über die Geschichte der Philosophie*, 3:44, translation from Hegel, *Lectures on the History of Philosophy*, 415.

7. Augustine, *Confessions*, 2:254 (11.29 [39]), translation from Chadwick, *Confessions*, 243–44.

8. Augustine, *Confessions*, 2:254 (11.29 [39]), translation from Chadwick *Confessions*, 244.

9. Williamson, *Borges*, 207.

10. Plotinus, *Enneads*, 299.

11. Borges, *Obras*, 1:388, translation from Borges, "History of Eternity," 136.

12. Borges, "History of Eternity," 136.

13. Williamson, *Borges*, 217.

14. Ibid., 218.

15. Borges, *Obras*, 1:414, translation from Borges, *Collected Fictions*, 82.

16. Borges, *Obras*, 1:416, translation from Borges, *Collected Fictions*, 84.

17. Kant, *Gesammelte Schriften*, 5:76–77, translation from Kant, *Practical Philosophy*, 202.

18. Williamson, *Borges*, 51.

19. Ibid., 55.

20. Quoted in ibid., 58.

21. Ibid., 59.

22. Block de Behar, *Borges*, 95.

23. Ibid., 166.

24. Borges, *Obra*, 208, my translation.

25. Eco, *Search for the Perfect Language*, 26.

26. Kaplan, *Sefer Yetzirah*, 124 (2.5), translation from Eco, *Search for the Perfect Language*, 29.

27. Eco, *Search for the Perfect Language*, 29.

28. Williamson, *Borges*, 63–65.

29. Borges, *Obras*, 1:666, translation from Borges, *Collected Fictions*, 283.

30. Borges, *Obras*, 1:661, translation from Borges, *Collected Fictions*, 277.

31. Borges, *Obras*, 1:664, translation from Borges, *Collected Fictions*, 280.

32. Borges, *Obras*, 1:666, translation from Borges, *Collected Fictions*, 282.

33. Borges, *Obras*, 1:666, translation from Borges, *Collected Fictions*, 282.

34. Borges, *Obras*, 1:666, translation from Borges, *Collected Fictions*, 283.

35. Borges, *Obras*, 1:667, translation from Borges, *Collected Fictions*, 283–84.

36. Williamson, *Borges*, 295.

37. See ibid., 276.

38. See ibid., 279.

39. Ibid., 281.

40. Canto, *Borges a contraluz*, 96, translation from Williamson, *Borges*, 281.

41. Dante, *Paradiso*, 246–47 (27.106–7).

42. Ibid., 252–53 (28.16–21).

43. See Williamson, *Borges*, 282.

44. See ibid., 285.

45. Borges, *Obras*, 1:376, translation from Borges, "History of Eternity," 124.

46. See Greene, *Elegant Universe*, 136.

7. THE UNIVERSE (WHICH OTHERS CALL THE LIBRARY)

1. Lewis, *Discarded Image*, 118–19.

2. Grant, "Cosmology," 272. See also Aristotle, *Physics*, 312–15 (4.212a.8–31).

3. Lindberg, *Beginnings of Western Science*, 192.

4. Egginton, "On Dante, Hyperspheres, and the Curvature of the Medieval Cosmos"; Duhem, *Le système du monde*, 6:166; Grant, "Cosmology," 272–73.

5. Lewis, *Discarded Image*, 116.

6. Dante, *Paradiso*, 244–46 (27.68–72). The translations here and following are mostly adapted from Allen Mandelbaum with some ideas from James Finn Cotter.

7. Ibid., 246 (27.100–102).

8. Ibid., 246–48 (27.106–16).

9. Ibid., 254 (28.53–54).

10. Borges, *Aleph and Other Stories*, 169.

11. Williamson, *Borges*, 230–31.

12. Ibid., 238.

13. Borges, *Obras*, 1:446, translation from Borges, *Collected Fictions*, 91.

14. Borges, *Obras*, 1:449, translation from Borges, *Collected Fictions*, 94.

15. Borges, *Obras*, 1:446–47, translation from Borges, *Collected Fictions*, 91.

16. Borges, *Obras*, 1:447, translation from Borges, *Collected Fictions*, 91.

17. Borges, *Obras*, 1:447, translation from Borges, *Collected Fictions*, 91–92.

18. Borges, *Ficcionario*, 127, translation from Borges, "Total Library," 215.

19. Borges, *Ficcionario*, 127, translation from Borges, "Total Library," 215. Borges attributes this to Aldous Huxley. The earliest instance I could find was our friend Arthur Eddington.

20. Borges, *Obras*, 1:385, translation from Borges, "Doctrine of Cycles," 115.

21. Borges, *Obras*, 1:390, translation from Borges, "Doctrine of Cycles," 120.

22. Borges, *Obras*, 1:391, translation from Borges, "Doctrine of Cycles," 121.

23. Borges, *Obras*, 1:391, translation from Borges, "Doctrine of Cycles," 122.

24. Williamson, *Borges*, 231.

25. Borges and Sorrentino, *Siete conversaciones*, 73, translation from Williamson, *Borges*, 241.

26. Borges, *Ficcionario*, 129, translation from Borges, "Total Library," 216.

27. See Williamson, *Borges*, 259.

28. Ibid., 260.

29. Ibid.

30. Ibid.

31. See ibid., 223, 344.

32. Ibid., 261.

33. Ibid., 265.

34. See Rodríguez Monegal, *Jorge Luis Borges*, 443.

35. Borges, *Obras*, 1:465, translation from Borges, *Collected Fictions*, 112.

36. Borges, *Obras*, 1:467, translation from Borges, *Collected Fictions*, 114.

37. Borges, *Obras*, 1:466, translation from Borges, *Collected Fictions*, 113.

38. Borges, *Obras*, 1:467, translation from Borges, *Collected Fictions*, 114–15.

39. Bloch, *Unimaginable Mathematics*, 16.

40. Ibid., 18.

41. Ibid., 19–20.

42. Borges, *Obras*, 1:465–66, translation from Borges, *Collected Fictions*, 113.

43. Like the two-dimensional beings in Abbott's 1884 *Flatland*.

44. Borges, *Obras*, 1:465, translation from Borges, *Collected Fictions*, 112.

45. Dante, *Paradiso*, 248 (27.109–11), my translation.

46. Borges, *Obras*, 1:364, translation from Williamson, *Borges*, 214.

47. Borges, *Obras*, 1:468, translation from Borges, *Collected Fictions*, 115.

48. Borges, *Obras*, 1:469, translation from Borges, *Collected Fictions*, 116.

49. Borges, *Obras*, 1:469, translation from Borges, *Collected Fictions*, 117.

50. Borges, *Obras*, 1:470, translation from Borges, *Collected Fictions*, 117.

51. Borges, *Obras*, 1:470, translation from Borges, *Collected Fictions*, 118.

8. GRAVITAS

1. E. Heisenberg, *Inner Exile*, 27–28.
2. W. Heisenberg, *Encounters with Einstein*, 112.
3. W. Heisenberg, *Gesammelte Werke*, C3:91, translation from W. Heisenberg, *Physics and Beyond*, 63.
4. Isaacson, *Einstein*, 332.
5. Greene, *Elegant Universe*, 3.
6. Ibid., 129.
7. P. Frank, *Einstein: Sein Leben und seine Zeit*, 350, translation from P. Frank, *Einstein: His Life and Times*, 216.
8. Einstein, *Über die spezielle und die allgemeine Relativitätstheorie*, 17–18, translation from Einstein, *Relativity*, 29.
9. Newton, *Correspondence, 1688–1694*, 254.
10. Quoted from Isaacson, *Einstein*, 145.
11. Reid, *Hilbert—Courant*, 142. See also Isaacson, *Einstein*, 596n89.
12. Einstein, *Über die spezielle und die allgemeine Relativitätstheorie*, 49, translation from Einstein, *Relativity*, 76.
13. Rosenthal-Schneider, *Begegnungen mit Einstein, von Laue und Planck*, 60, translation from Rosenthal-Schneider, *Reality and Scientific Truth*, 74.
14. Rosenthal-Schneider, *Begegnungen mit Einstein, von Laue und Planck*, 60, translation from Isaacson, *Einstein*, 259.
15. See Isaacson, *Einstein*, 251, 599n5.
16. As Einstein put it, "In the general theory of relativity, space and time cannot be defined in such a way that differences of the spatial co-ordinates can be directly measured by the unit measuring-rod, or differences in the time co-ordinate by a standard clock." Einstein, "Die Grundlage der allgemeinen Relativitätstheorie," 85–86, translation from Einstein, "Foundation," 117.
17. Einstein, "Die Grundlage der allgemeinen Relativitätstheorie," 86, translation from Einstein, "Foundation," 117.
18. Greene, *Elegant Universe*, 49–51.
19. As per Garson O'Toole, this quip was first written by Ray Cummings in a 1919 story called *The Girl in the Golden Atom*, and subsequently borrowed by diverse figures from Sir Arthur Eddington to John Wheeler to Susan Sontag; see O'Toole, "Time Is What Keeps Everything from Happening at Once." Sontag, it should be said, quoted it while reminiscing about late nights as a philosophy student struggling with Kant.
20. Isaacson, *Einstein*, 223.
21. See Clark, *Einstein*, 200, 663n200.
22. Einstein, "Die Grundlage der allgemeinen Relativitätstheorie," 70, translation from Einstein, *Relativity*, 108.
23. Einstein, "Cosmological Considerations on the General Theory of Relativity," 180.

24. See Isaacson, *Einstein*, 252, 599n8.

25. Einstein, "Kosmologische Betrachtungen zur allgemeinen Relativitätstheorie," 139, translation from Einstein, "Cosmological Considerations on the General Theory of Relativity," 187–88.

26. Einstein, *Über die spezielle und die allgemeine Relativitätstheorie*, 73, translation from Einstein, *Relativity*, 112.

27. Greene, *Elegant Universe*, 82.

28. Dante, *Paradiso*, 246 (27.100–102), my translation.

29. W. Heisenberg, *Gesammelte Werke*, C3:91, translation from W. Heisenberg, *Physics and Beyond*, 62.

30. W. Heisenberg, *Gesammelte Werke*, C3:92, translation from W. Heisenberg, *Physics and Beyond*, 63.

31. W. Heisenberg, *Gesammelte Werke*, C3:95, translation from W. Heisenberg, *Physics and Beyond*, 66.

32. W. Heisenberg, *Gesammelte Werke*, C3:98, translation from W. Heisenberg, *Physics and Beyond*, 68.

33. W. Heisenberg, *Gesammelte Werke*, C3:92, translation from W. Heisenberg, *Physics and Beyond*, 63.

34. W. Heisenberg, *Gesammelte Werke*, C3:98, translation from W. Heisenberg, *Physics and Beyond*, 68.

35. W. Heisenberg, *Physics and Beyond*, 78.

36. W. Heisenberg, *Gesammelte Werke*, C3:92, translation from W. Heisenberg, *Physics and Beyond*, 63.

37. W. Heisenberg, *Gesammelte Werke*, C3:98, translation from W. Heisenberg, *Physics and Beyond*, 68.

38. Hawking and Mlodinow, *Grand Design*, 107.

39. Ibid.: "The universe doesn't have just a single history, but every possible history, each with its own probability; and our observations of its current state affect its past and determine the different histories of the universe, just as the observations of the particles in the double-slit experiment affect the particles' past."

40. Ibid., 159.

41. Dante, *Paradiso*, 252–53 (28.16–21).

42. Hawking and Mlodinow, *Grand Design*, 172.

43. In Hawking's view, "The universe appeared spontaneously, starting off in every possible way." Ibid., 174.

44. Gleiser, *Tear at the Edge of Creation*, 68.

45. Gleiser, *Island of Knowledge*, 79.

46. Borges, "John Wilkins' Analytical Language," 231.

47. W. Heisenberg, *Physics and Beyond*, 168.

48. W. Heisenberg, *Physics and Philosophy*, 32.

49. Isaacson, *Einstein*, 238.

50. Ibid., 97–98.

9. MADE TO MEASURE

1. Landsman, "Fine-Tuning Argument."
2. Ibid.
3. Ibid.
4. Rees, *Before the Beginning*, 259.
5. Kenny, *Five Ways*, 96.
6. Kant, *Critique of the Power of Judgment*, 245–46 (5:374).
7. Kremer, *Das Problem der Theodicee in der Philosophie und Literatur des 18. Jahrhunderts mit besonderer Rücksicht auf Kant und Schiller*, 95, translation from Cassirer, *Kant's Life and Thought*, 338.
8. Voltaire, *Candide*, 2 (chap. 1).
9. Weinberg, *Dreams of a Final Theory*, 149.
10. Mendelssohn, *Saemmtliche Werke*, 6:vi, translation from Kuehn, *Kant*, 251.
11. Kuehn, *Kant*, 318–19.
12. Ibid., 322.
13. Hamann, *Briefwechsel*, 7:148, translation from Kuehn, *Kant*, 323.
14. Kuehn, *Kant*, 323.
15. Hasse, *Merkwürdige Äusserungen Kant's von einem seiner Tischgenossen*, 6–7, translation from Kuehn, *Kant*, 325.
16. Kuehn, *Kant*, 325.
17. Wegenstein, *Conductor*.
18. Kant, *Gesammelte Schriften*, 5:363, translation from Kant, *Critique of the Power of Judgment*, 236.
19. Cassirer, *Kants Leben und Lehre*, 319.
20. Kant, *Critique of the Power of Judgment*, 97–99 (5:212–13).
21. Kuehn, *Kant*, 351.
22. Ibid., 353.
23. Kant, *Gesammelte Schriften*, 8:249, translation from Kuehn, *Kant*, 354.
24. Kuehn, *Kant*, 354–55.
25. Kant, *Gesammelte Schriften*, 2:434, translation from Cassirer, *Kant's Life and Thought*, 356.
26. Kant, *Gesammelte Schriften*, 5:250, translation from Kant, *Critique of Aesthetic Judgement*, 98.
27. Kant, *Gesammelte Schriften*, 5:161, translation from Kant, *Practical Philosophy*, 269.
28. Kant, *Gesammelte Schriften*, 5:360, translation from Kant, *Critique of Teleological Judgement*, 4.
29. See Rovelli's discussion of the relational interpretation of quantum mechanics in *Helgoland*, as I also exposit in chapter 12.
30. W. Heisenberg, *Gesammelte Werke*, C1:226, translation from W. Heisenberg, *Reality and Its Order*, 29.
31. Kant, *Gesammelte Schriften*, 5:388, translation from Kant, *Critique of Teleological Judgement*, 38.

10. FREE WILL

1. Boethius, *Consolation*, 398–400 (bk. 5, prose 3), translation from Slavitt, *Consolation*, 155.
2. Harris, *Free Will*, 4.
3. Ibid., 5.
4. Boethius, *Consolation*, 422 (bk. 5, prose 6), translation from Slavitt, *Consolation*, 168.
5. Borges, *Obras*, 1:391, translation from Borges, "Doctrine of Cycles," 122.
6. Kant, *Gesammelte Schriften*, 8:40, translation from Kant, "Answer to the Question," 21.
7. See Cassirer, *Kant's Life and Thought*, 376.
8. Ibid.
9. Ibid., 380.
10. Kant, *Gesammelte Schriften*, 8:338, translation from Cassirer, *Kant's Life and Thought*, 393.
11. Kant, *Gesammelte Schriften*, 7:6, translation from Cassirer, *Kant's Life and Thought*, 394.
12. Kuehn, *Kant*, 379.
13. Kant, *Gesammelte Schriften*, 7:6, translation from Cassirer, *Kant's Life and Thought*, 394.
14. See Cassirer, *Kant's Life and Thought*, 395.
15. Kant, *Gesammelte Schriften*, 7:10, translation from Kant, "Conflict of the Faculties," 242.
16. Kant, *Gesammelte Schriften*, 6:487, translation from Kant, *Practical Philosophy*, 599.
17. Kant, *Gesammelte Schriften*, 7:19, translation from Kant, "Conflict of the Faculties," 242.
18. Kant, *Gesammelte Schriften*, 6:213, translation from Kant, *Practical Philosophy*, 375.
19. In fact, recent research has shown that RP (readiness potential) is a factor for arbitrary decisions but as much for deliberative ones, suggesting that deliberation may escape our technological abilities to predict decisions. See Maoz et al., "Neural Precursors of Decisions That Matter."
20. Harris, *Free Will*, 4.
21. Strawson, "Your Move."
22. Ibid.
23. Kant, *Gesammelte Schriften*, 4:455, translation from Kant, *Groundwork of the Metaphysics of Morals*, 59.
24. Harris, *Free Will*, 3.
25. Ibid., 4.
26. Greene, *Until the End of Time*, 147.
27. Kant, *Gesammelte Schriften*, 4:455, translation from Kant, *Groundwork of the Metaphysics of Morals*, 60.
28. Greene, *Until the End of Time*, 149.

29. Ibid., 150.
30. As J. T. Ismael has noted, this way of thinking is not shared by most scientists, but it is more common among philosophers and cosmologists. As she puts it, because this kind of thinking is focused on the emergent "laws that describe the universe as a whole," as opposed to local laws describing behavior in open systems, they (philosophers and cosmologists) "invert the order of determination and reify the laws, so that now it looks like the laws are not simply descriptions of a pattern" but "iron rails." Ismael, *How Physics Makes Us Free*, 110–11.
31. Kant, *Gesammelte Schriften*, 4:457, translation from Kant, *Groundwork of the Metaphysics of Morals*, 61.
32. García Márquez, *Cien años de soledad*, 49, my translation.
33. Warda, "Ergänzungen zu E. Fromm's zweitem und drittem Beitrage zur Lebensgeschichte Kants," 78, translation from Kuehn, *Kant*, 386.
34. See Abegg, *Reisetagebuch von 1798*, 186–91, translation from Kuehn, *Kant*, 392.
35. Vaihinger, "Briefe aus dem Kantkreis," 290, translation from Kuehn, *Kant*, 410.
36. Warda, *Briefe an und von Johann George Scheffner*, 2:424, translation from Kuehn, *Kant*, 410.
37. Jachmann, *Immanuel Kant geschildert in Briefen an einen Freund*, 196, translation from Kuehn, *Kant*, 415.
38. Wasianski, *Immanuel Kant in seinen letzten Lebensjahren*, 48, translation from Kuehn, *Kant*, 416.
39. Kuehn, *Kant*, 417.
40. Kuehn, *Kant*, 422. Literally, the German reads, "It is good."
41. Borges, *Obras*, 1:490, translation from Borges, *Collected Fictions*, 137.
42. Wasianski, *Immanuel Kant in seinen letzten Lebensjahren*, 51, translation from Kuehn, *Kant*, 416.
43. Bruner, "Foreword," xxii.

11. FORKING PATHS

1. Carroll, *Something Deeply Hidden*, 113.
2. See Byrne, *Many Worlds of Hugh Everett III*, 171.
3. Carroll, *Something Deeply Hidden*, 135.
4. The physics community seems to have found out about Borges's story in 1972. See DeWitt and Graham, *Many-Worlds Interpretation of Quantum Mechanics*, iv–vi. See also Rojo, "Garden of the Forking Worlds."
5. Borges, *Obras*, 1:477, 479, translation from Borges, *Collected Fictions*, 125, 127.
6. Borges, *Obras*, 1:478, translation from Borges, *Collected Fictions*, 126.
7. Borges, *Obras*, 1:479, translation from Borges, *Collected Fictions*, 127.
8. Borges, *Collected Fictions*, 128.
9. Williamson, *Borges*, 345.

10. Ibid., 348.

11. Personal anecdote recounted to the author by Vicchio.

12. Williamson, *Borges*, 374.

13. Ibid., 375.

14. Ibid., 391.

15. Gómez López-Quiñones, *Borges y el nazismo*, 103, translation from Williamson, *Borges*, 256.

16. Williamson, *Borges*, 271.

17. See ibid., 409, 528n12.

18. See ibid., 410, 528n14.

19. See ibid., 410, 528n15.

20. Teitelboim, *Los dos Borges*, 216, translation from Williamson, *Borges*, 422.

21. Williamson, *Borges*, 425.

22. Frost, *Complete Poems*, 131.

23. Borges, *Obras*, 1:364, translation from Williamson, *Borges*, 214.

24. Mateo, *El otro Borges*, 200, translation from Williamson, *Borges*, 454.

25. See Williamson, *Borges*, 454, 532n2.

26. See ibid., 458, 533n15.

27. Slavuski, "The Old Man and the City," 11.

28. See Williamson, *Borges*, 454, 532n5.

29. Harris, *Free Will*, 4.

30. Williamson, *Borges*, 370.

31. Ibid., 388.

32. Alifano, *Borges*, 128, translation from Williamson, *Borges*, 395.

33. Williamson, *Borges*, 395.

34. Borges, *Obras*, 3:50, translation from Borges, *Collected Fictions*, 457.

35. Borges, *Obras*, 3:49, translation from Borges, *Collected Fictions*, 457.

36. Borges, *Obras*, 3:50, translation from Borges, *Collected Fictions*, 458.

37. Borges, *Obras*, 3:51, translation from Borges, *Collected Fictions*, 459.

38. Borges, *Obras*, 2:197, translation from Borges, *Collected Fictions*, 324.

39. I owe the term to the physicist Andrei Linde, who explained it to me over dinner while making matchsticks jump from his hands in an ostensible demonstration of quantum fluctuations.

12. PUTTING THE DEMON TO REST

1. Dawidoff, *Catcher Was a Spy*, 72.

2. Cassidy, *Uncertainty*, 492.

3. Ibid., 498.

4. See Cassidy, *Beyond Uncertainty*, 367, 453n31.

5. Cassidy, *Uncertainty*, 499.

6. Goudsmit, *Alsos*, 48.

7. The size of that difference is as tiny as the fact of it is huge: i x *h-bar*, or the square root of –1 (an imaginary number) multiplied by Planck's constant divided by 2π.

8. Feynman, *Character of Physical Law*, 129.

9. Borges, *Obras*, 1:258, translation from Borges, "Avatars of the Tortoise," 202.

10. See Rovelli, *Helgoland*, 75.

11. See ibid., 83.

12. Cassidy, *Uncertainty*, 255.

13. See ibid., 256, 592n29.

14. Heisenberg, "Die Kausalgesetz und Quantenmechanik," 181, translation from Camilleri, *Heisenberg and the Interpretation of Quantum Mechanics*, 135, italics added.

15. W. Heisenberg, *Gesammelte Werke*, C3:164, translation from W. Heisenberg, *Physics and Beyond*, 118.

16. These exchanges are as recalled by Heisenberg in his memoir; see W. Heisenberg, *Physics and Beyond*, 118–19.

17. Ibid., 119–20. Heisenberg's explanation is a little murky, so I've paraphrased it here.

18. Ibid., 122.

19. W. Heisenberg, *Gesammelte Werke*, C3:171, translation from W. Heisenberg, *Physics and Beyond*, 123.

20. While Heisenberg continued to believe that modern physics had moved the needle on what counted as a priori in terms of our ability to know, his interactions with Hermann and Weizsäcker clearly had an effect. He told Bohr as much in a letter shortly after the visit, and he would go on to write in an article the following year that Kant's forms of intuition and the law of causality underlay every experiment in modern physics, and indeed without them no inference concerning the properties of observed objects could ever be made. See W. Heisenberg, *Physics and Beyond*, 123; and Camilleri, *Heisenberg and the Interpretation of Quantum Mechanics*, 142–43.

21. Weizsäcker himself was critical that Cassirer had gone too far down the road of logical empiricism, hence sacrificing much of what Kant's thought had enabled; see Camilleri, *Heisenberg and the Interpretation of Quantum Mechanics*, 143. Indeed, as Stephan Körner writes in his introduction to Cassirer's timeless exposé of Kant's life and thought, many philosophers believed and continue to believe that the discoveries of general relativity and quantum mechanics were "incompatible with the Kantian a priori principles of causality and continuity"; Körner, "Introduction," ix–x.

22. W. Heisenberg, *Physics and Philosophy*, 90.

23. Ibid., 64.

24. Ibid., 101. And yet even while overlooking that Kant had, in fact, foreseen the very paradox that quantum mechanics codified, when considering the question of the shape of the cosmos, Heisenberg saw that same paradox in its cosmological version and called it by its name, antinomy. See ibid., 124: "Space cannot be finite, since we cannot imagine that there should be an end to space; to whichever point in space we come we can always

imagine that we can go beyond." Having recognized the antinomy of the edge of the universe, Heisenberg would need only to connect the dots to see that the wrench in the wheel of full correspondence between quantum mechanics and Kant's system was, in fact, already part of that system.

25. W. Heisenberg, *Gesammelte Werke*, C3:171, translation from W. Heisenberg, *Physics and Beyond*, 123.

26. Ibid.

27. C. Frank, *Operation Epsilon*, 78.

28. Frayn, *Copenhagen*, 36. Frayn's dialogue is based on Heisenberg's own reconstructions in his memoirs, so the phrasing of this famous question is clouded by multiple layers of guesswork.

29. W. Heisenberg, "Über die Arbeiten zur technischen Ausnutzung der Atomkernenergie in Deutschland," 327, translation from Cassidy, *Uncertainty*, 510.

30. W. Heisenberg, "Über die Arbeiten zur technischen Ausnutzung der Atomkernenergie in Deutschland," 327, translation from W. Heisenberg, "Research in Germany on the Technical Application of Atomic Energy," 213.

31. W. Heisenberg, "Über die Arbeiten zur technischen Ausnutzung der Atomkernenergie in Deutschland," 329, translation from Cassidy, *Uncertainty*, 510.

32. Morrison, "*Alsos*," 365.

33. E. Heisenberg, *Das politische Leben eines Unpolitischen*, 134, translation from E. Heisenberg, *Inner Exile*, 109.

34. E. Heisenberg, *Inner Exile*, 109.

35. Goudsmit, *Alsos*, 121.

36. Ibid., 115.

37. Cassidy, *Uncertainty*, 519; see also 638n62.

38. Ibid., 531.

39. W. Heisenberg, "Nature of Elementary Particles," 38.

40. W. Heisenberg, *Gesammelte Werke*, C3:330, translation from W. Heisenberg, *Physics and Beyond*, 244.

41. Cassidy, *Uncertainty*, 522.

POSTSCRIPT

1. See Rovelli, *Helgoland*, 182.

2. See ibid., 137.

BIBLIOGRAPHY

Abegg, Johann Friedrich. *Reisetagebuch von 1798.* Edited by Walter Abegg, Jolanda Abegg, and Zwi Batscha. Frankfurt: Insel, 1976.

Alifano, Roberto. *Borges, biografía verbal.* Barcelona: Plaza & Janes, 1988.

Anderson, Abraham. *Kant, Hume, and the Interruption of Dogmatic Slumber.* Oxford: Oxford University Press, 2020.

Andrés, Alfredo. *Palabras con Leopoldo Marechal.* Buenos Aires: Carlos Pérez, 1968.

Aristotle. *The Physics.* Translated and edited by Philip Henry Wicksteed and Francis Macdonald Cornford. Cambridge, Mass.: Harvard University Press, 1929–34.

Augustine. *Confessions.* Translated and edited by Carolyn Hammond. Cambridge, Mass.: Harvard University Press, 2014.

Bastos, María Luisa. *Borges ante la crítica argentina, 1923–1960.* Buenos Aires: Ediciones Hispamérica, 1974.

Bernstein, Jeremy. *Quantum Profiles.* Princeton, N.J.: Princeton University Press, 1991.

Bloch, William Goldbloom. *The Unimaginable Mathematics of Borges's Library of Babel.* Oxford: Oxford University Press, 2008.

Block de Behar, Lisa. *Borges, the Passion of an Endless Quotation.* Translated by William Egginton and Christopher RayAlexander. 2nd ed. Albany: State University of New York Press, 2014.

Boethius, Anicius Manlius Severinus. *The Consolation of Philosophy.* Translated by S. J. Tester. In *Theological Tractates: The Consolation of Philosophy,* 2nd ed., 130–435. Cambridge, Mass.: Harvard University Press, 1973.

Bohr, Niels. "Can Quantum-Mechanical Description of Physical Reality Be Considered Complete?" *Physical Review* 48, no. 8 (1935): 696–702.

———. *Foundations of Quantum Physics I (1926–1932).* Translated and edited by Jørgen Kalckar. Vol. 6 of *Collected Works,* edited by Erik Rüdinger. Amsterdam: North-Holland, 1985.

Borges, Jorge Luis. *The Aleph and Other Stories, 1933–1969.* Translated and edited by Norman Thomas Di Giovanni. New York: Bantam, 1970.

———. "Avatars of the Tortoise." Translated by James East Irby. In *Labyrinths: Selected Stories and Other Writings,* edited by Donald Alfred Yates and James East Irby, 196–202. New York: New Directions, 1962.

———. *Collected Fictions.* Translated and edited by Andrew Hurley. New York: Penguin, 1998.

———. "A Defense of the Kabbalah." Translated by Eliot Weinberger. In *Selected Non-fictions,* 83–86.

———. "The Doctrine of Cycles." Translated by Esther Allen. In *Selected Non-fictions,* 115–22.

———. *Ficcionario: Una antología de sus textos.* Edited by Emir Rodríguez Monegal. Mexico: Fondo de Cultura Económica, 1985.

———. "A History of Eternity." Translated by Esther Allen. In *Selected Non-fictions,* 123–39.

———. *El idioma de los argentinos.* Buenos Aires: Seix Barral, 1994.

———. *Inquisiciones.* Buenos Aires: Proa, 1925.

———. "John Wilkins' Analytical Language." Translated by Eliot Weinberger. In *Selected Non-fictions,* 229–32.

———. "The Nothingness of Personality." Translated by Esther Allen. In *Selected Non-fictions,* 3–9.

———. *Obra poética, 1923–1977.* 2nd ed. Buenos Aires: Emecé, 1981.

———. *Obras completas.* Edited by Carlos V. Frías. Buenos Aires: Emecé, 1996.

———. "The Perpetual Race of Achilles and the Tortoise." Translated by Suzanne Jill Levine. In *Selected Non-fictions,* 44–47.

———. *Selected Non-fictions.* Edited by Eliot Weinberger. New York: Penguin, 1999.

———. *El tamaño de mi esperanza.* 2nd ed. Buenos Aires: Seix Barral, 1993.

———. "The Total Library." Translated by Eliot Weinberger. In *Selected Non-fictions,* 214–16.

Borges, Jorge Luis, and Antonio Carrizo. *Borges el memorioso: Conversaciones.* Mexico: Fondo de Cultura Económica, 1982.

Borges, Jorge Luis, and Fernando Sorrentino. *Siete conversaciones.* Buenos Aires: Casa Pardo, 1973.

Born, Max. *My Life: Recollections of a Nobel Laureate.* Edited by Gustav Born. New York: Scribner's, 1975.

———. "Zur Quantenmechanik der Stoßvorgänge." *Zeitschrift für Physik* 37, no. 12 (1926): 863–67.

———, ed. *Born-Einstein Letters: Correspondence Between Albert Einstein and Max and Hedwig Born from 1916 to 1955.* Translated by Irene Born. London: Macmillan, 1971.

Born, Max, and Werner Heisenberg. "La mécanique des quanta." In Lorentz, *Électrons et photons*, 143–81.

Borowski, Ludwig Ernst. *Darstellung des Lebens und Charakters Immanuel Kants.* Königsberg: Friedrich Nicolovius, 1804.

Bruner, Jerome Seymour. "Foreword to the First Edition." In Luria, *Mind of a Mnemonist*, xxi–xxv.

Bryson, Bill. *One Summer: America, 1927.* New York: Anchor, 2014.

Byrne, Peter. *The Many Worlds of Hugh Everett III: Multiple Universes, Mutual Assured Destruction, and the Meltdown of a Nuclear Family.* Oxford: Oxford University Press, 2010.

Cale, George. "The Anthropic Principle." *Scientific American* 245, no. 6 (1981): 154–71.

Camilleri, Kristian. *Heisenberg and the Interpretation of Quantum Mechanics.* Cambridge, U.K.: Cambridge University Press, 2009.

Canto, Estela. *Borges a contraluz.* Madrid: Espasa-Calpe, 1989.

Carroll, Sean. *From Eternity to Here: The Search for the Ultimate Meaning of Time.* New York: Dutton, 2010.

———. *Something Deeply Hidden: Quantum Worlds and the Emergence of Space-time.* New York: Dutton, 2019.

Cassidy, David Charles. *Beyond Uncertainty: Heisenberg, Quantum Physics, and the Bomb.* New York: Bellevue Literary Press, 2009.

———. *Uncertainty: The Life and Science of Werner Heisenberg.* New York: Freeman, 1992.

Cassirer, Ernst. *Kants Leben und Lehre.* Berlin: Bruno Cassirer, 1921.

———. *Kant's Life and Thought.* Translated by James Haden. New Haven, Conn.: Yale University Press, 1981.

Chadwick, Henry, trans. and ed. *Confessions,* by Augustine. Oxford: Oxford University Press, 1991.

Clark, Ronald William. *Einstein: The Life and Times.* New York: World, 1971.

Dante Alighieri. *The Divine Comedy.* Translated by James Finn Cotter. Stony Brook, N.Y.: Forum Italicum, 2006.

———. *Paradiso.* Translated by Allen Mandelbaum. Edited by Anthony Oldcorn, Daniel Feldman, and Giuseppe Di Scipio. New York: Bantam, 1986.

Dawidoff, Nicholas. *The Catcher Was a Spy: The Mysterious Life of Moe Berg.* New York: Pantheon, 1994.

DeWitt, Bryce Seligman, and Neill Graham, eds. *The Many-Worlds Interpretation of Quantum Mechanics: A Fundamental Exposition.* Princeton, N.J.: Princeton University Press, 1973.

Dresden, Max. *H. A. Kramers: Between Tradition and Revolution.* New York: Springer, 1987.

Duhem, Pierre. *Le système du monde: Histoire de doctrines cosmologiques de Platon à Copernic.* Paris: Hermann, 1913–59.

Eco, Umberto. *The Search for the Perfect Language.* Translated by James Fentress. Oxford: Blackwell, 1995.

Eddington, Arthur Stanley. *The Nature of the Physical World*. New York: Macmillan, 1928.

Egginton, William. "On Dante, Hyperspheres, and the Curvature of the Medieval Cosmos." *Journal of the History of Ideas* 60, no. 2 (1999): 195–216.

Einstein, Albert. "Autobiographisches." In *Albert Einstein: Philosopher-Scientist*, edited by Paul Arthur Schilpp, 1–95. New York: MJF, 1949.

———. *The Berlin Years: Writings and Correspondence, June 1925–May 1927*. Edited by Diana Kormos Buchwald, József Illy, A. J. Knox, Dennis Lehmkuhl, Ze'ev Rosenkranz, and Jennifer Nollar James. Vol. 15 of *Collected Papers*. Princeton, N.J.: Princeton University Press, 1989.

———. "Cosmological Considerations on the General Theory of Relativity." In Sommerfeld, *Principle of Relativity*, 177–88.

———. "The Foundation of the General Theory of Relativity." In Sommerfeld, *Principle of Relativity*, 109–64.

———. "Die Grundlage der allgemeinen Relativitätstheorie." In Sommerfeld, *Das Relativitätsprinzip*, 81–124.

———. "Kosmologische Betrachtungen zur allgemeinen Relativitätstheorie." In Sommerfeld, *Das Relativitätsprinzip*, 130–39.

———. "On a Heuristic Point of View About the Creation and Conversion of Light." In *The Old Quantum Theory*, edited and translated by Dirk Ter Haar, 91–107. Oxford: Pergamon, 1967.

———. "Quantentheorie des einatomigen idealen Gases. Zweite Abhandlung." *Sitzungsberichte der Preussischen Akademie der Wissenschaften* 1 (1925): 3–14.

———. *Relativity: The Special and the General Theory*. Translated by Robert W. Lawson. London: Routledge, 1993.

———. "Remarks to the Essays Appearing in This Co-operative Volume." Translated by Paul Arthur Schilpp. In *Albert Einstein: Philosopher-Scientist*, edited by Paul Arthur Schilpp, 663–88. New York: MJF, 1949.

———. *The Swiss Years: Writings, 1900–1909*. Edited by John Stachel. Vol. 2 of *Collected Papers*. Princeton, N.J.: Princeton University Press, 1989.

———. *Über die spezielle und die allgemeine Relativitätstheorie*. Berlin: Springer, 2001.

Epstein, Klaus. *The Genesis of German Conservatism*. Princeton, N.J.: Princeton University Press, 1966.

Feynman, Richard. *The Character of Physical Law*. Cambridge, Mass.: MIT Press, 1967.

Feynman, Richard, Robert Leighton, and Matthew Sands. *The Feynman Lectures on Physics*. New York: Basic, 2010.

Forman, Paul. "Alfred Landé and the Anomalous Zeeman Effect, 1919–1921." *Historical Studies in the Physical Sciences* 2 (1970): 153–261.

Frank, Charles, ed. *Operation Epsilon: The Farm Hall Transcripts*. Bristol: Institute of Physics Publishing, 1993.

Frank, Philipp. *Einstein: His Life and Times.* Translated by George Rosen. Edited by Shuichi Kusaka. New York: Knopf, 1947.

———. *Einstein: Sein Leben und seine Zeit.* Braunschweig: Vieweg, 1979.

Frayn, Michael. *Copenhagen.* New York: Anchor Books, 1998.

Frost, Robert. *Complete Poems.* New York: Holt, Rinehart and Winston, 1949.

García Márquez, Gabriel. *Cien años de soledad.* Madrid: Alfaguara, 1982.

García Márquez, Gabriel, and Plinio Apuleyo Mendoza. *The Fragrance of Guava.* Translated by Ann Wright. London: Verso, 1983.

———. *El olor de la guayaba: Conversaciones.* Bogotá: Oveja Negra, 1982.

Geier, Manfred. *Kants Welt: Eine Biographie.* Hamburg: Rowohlt, 2004.

Gleiser, Marcelo. *The Island of Knowledge: The Limits of Science and the Search for Meaning.* New York: Basic Books, 2014.

———. *The Tear at the Edge of Creation: A Radical New Vision for Life in an Imperfect Universe.* New York: Free Press, 2010.

Gómez López-Quiñones, Antonio. *Borges y el nazismo: Sur (1937–1946).* Granada: Universidad de Granada, 2004.

Goudsmit, Samuel A. *Alsos.* Woodbury, N.Y.: AIP Press, 1996.

Grant, Edward. "Cosmology." In *Science in the Middle Ages,* edited by David C. Lindberg, 265–302. Chicago: University of Chicago Press, 1978.

Greene, Brian. *The Elegant Universe: Superstrings, Hidden Dimensions, and the Quest for the Ultimate Theory.* New York: Vintage, 1999.

———. *The Fabric of the Cosmos: Space, Time, and the Texture of Reality.* New York: Random House, 2004.

———. *Until the End of Time: Mind, Matter, and Our Search for Meaning in an Evolving Cosmos.* New York: Knopf, 2020.

Gribbin, John. *In Search of Schrödinger's Cat: Quantum Physics and Reality.* Toronto: Bantam, 1984.

———. *Schrödinger's Kittens and the Search for Reality.* London: Weidenfeld & Nicolson, 1995.

Hamann, Johann Georg. *Briefwechsel.* Edited by Walther Ziesemer and Arthur Henkel. Frankfurt am Main: Insel, 1955–79.

Hare, John. "Augustine, Kant, and the Moral Gap." In *The Augustinian Tradition,* edited by Gareth Matthews, 251–62. Berkeley: University of California Press, 1999.

Harris, Sam. *Free Will.* New York: Free Press, 2012.

Hasse, Johann Gottfried. *Merkwürdige Äusserungen Kant's von einem seiner Tischgenossen.* Königsberg: Gottlieb Lebrecht, 1804.

Hawking, Stephen, and Leonard Mlodinow. *The Grand Design.* New York: Bantam, 2010.

Hegel, Georg Wilhelm Friedrich. *Greek Philosophy to Plato.* Translated by Elizabeth Sanderson Haldane. Vol. 1 of *Lectures on the History of Philosophy.* Lincoln: University of Nebraska Press, 1995.

———. *Plato and the Platonists.* Translated by Elizabeth Sanderson Haldane and Frances Simson. Vol. 2 of *Lectures on the History of Philosophy*. Lincoln: University of Nebraska Press, 1995.

———. *Vorlesungen über die Geschichte der Philosophie*. Edited by Karl Ludwig Michelet. 2nd ed. Berlin: Duncker und Humblot, 1840–44.

Heisenberg, Elisabeth. *Inner Exile: Recollections of a Life with Werner Heisenberg*. Translated by S. Cappellari and C. Morris. Boston: Birkhäuser, 1980.

———. *Das politische Leben eines Unpolitischen: Erinnerungen an Werner Heisenberg*. Munich: Piper, 1980.

Heisenberg, Werner. "The Development of the Interpretation of the Quantum Theory." In *Niels Bohr and the Development of Physics: Essays Dedicated to Niels Bohr on the Occasion of His Seventieth Birthday*, edited by Wolfgang Pauli, 12–29. New York: McGraw-Hill, 1955.

———. *Encounters with Einstein: And Other Essays About People, Places, and Particles*. Princeton, N.J.: Princeton University Press, 1983.

———. *Gesammelte Werke / Collected Works*. Edited by Walter Blum, Hans-Peter Dürr, and Helmut Rechenberg. Berlin: Springer/Piper, 1984–89.

———. "Die Kausalgesetz und Quantenmechanik." *Erkenntnis* 2 (1931): 172–82.

———. "The Nature of Elementary Particles." *Physics Today* 29, no. 3 (1976): 32–39.

———. *Physics and Beyond: Encounters and Conversations*. Translated by Arnold Julius Pomerans. New York: Harper & Row, 1971.

———. *Physics and Philosophy: The Revolution in Modern Science*. New York: HarperCollins, 2007.

———. *Reality and Its Order*. Translated by Martin B. Rumscheidt, Nancy Lukens, and Irene Heisenberg. Edited by Konrad Kleinknecht. Cham: Springer, 2019.

———. "Research in Germany on the Technical Application of Atomic Energy." *Nature* 160, no. 4059 (1947): 211–15.

———. *Der Teil und das Ganze: Gespräche im Umkreis der Atomphysik*. Munich: Piper Taschenbuch, 2009.

———. "Über die Arbeiten zur technischen Ausnutzung der Atomkernenergie in Deutschland." *Naturwissenschaften* 33, no. 11 (1946): 325–29.

Henderson, Bob. "The Rebel Physicist on the Hunt for a Better Story Than Quantum Mechanics." *New York Times Magazine*, June 25, 2020. www.nytimes.com.

Hentschel, Ann M., and Jennifer Nollar James, trans. *The Berlin Years: Writings and Correspondence, April 1923–May 1925*, by Albert Einstein. Edited by Diana Kormos Buchwald, József Illy, Ze'ev Rosenkranz, Tilman Sauer, and Osik Moses. Vol. 14 of *Collected Papers*. Princeton, N.J.: Princeton University Press, 2015.

Hermann, Armin. *Frühgeschichte der Quantentheorie (1899–1913)*. Mosbach: Physik, 1969.

———. *Werner Heisenberg in Selbstzeugnissen und Bilddokumenten*. Hamburg: Rowohlt, 1976.

Hippel the Elder, Gottlieb von. *Biographie des Königl. Preuss. Geheimenkriegsraths zu Königsberg.* Gotha: Justus Perthes, 1801.

Homer. *The Odyssey.* Translated by A. T. Murray. 2 vols. Cambridge, Mass.: Harvard University Press, 1919.

Hume, David. *An Enquiry Concerning the Principles of Morals.* Edited by Tom Beauchamp. Oxford: Oxford University Press, 1998.

———. *A Treatise of Human Nature.* Edited by Lewis Amherst Selby-Bigge. Oxford: Clarendon, 1888.

Isaacson, Walter. *Einstein: His Life and Universe.* New York: Simon & Schuster, 2008.

Ismael, J. T. *How Physics Makes Us Free.* Oxford: Oxford University Press, 2016.

Jachmann, Reinhold Bernhard, ed. *Immanuel Kant geschildert in Briefen an einen Freund.* Königsberg: Friedrich Nicolovius, 1804.

Jauch, Josef Maria. *Foundations of Quantum Mechanics.* Reading, Mass.: Addison-Wesley, 1968.

Johnson, Reed. "The Mystery of S., the Man with an Impossible Memory." *New Yorker,* Aug. 12, 2017. www.newyorker.com.

Kaes, Anton, Martin Jay, and Edward Dimendberg, trans. and ed. *The Weimar Republic Sourcebook.* Berkeley: University of California Press, 1994.

Kant, Immanuel. "An Answer to the Question: What Is Enlightenment?" In *Practical Philosophy,* translated and edited by Mary J. Gregor, 15–22. Cambridge, U.K.: Cambridge University Press, 1999.

———. *Briefwechsel.* Edited by Rudolf Malter. Hamburg: Meiner, 1986.

———. "The Conflict of the Faculties." Translated by Mary J. Gregor and Robert Anchor. In *Religion and Rational Theology,* 237–327. Cambridge, U.K.: Cambridge University Press, 1996.

———. *Correspondence.* Translated and edited by Arnulf Zweig. Cambridge, U.K.: Cambridge University Press, 1999.

———. *Critique of Aesthetic Judgement.* Translated and edited by James Creed Meredith. Oxford: Clarendon, 1911.

———. *Critique of the Power of Judgment.* Translated by Paul Guyer and Eric Matthews. Edited by Paul Guyer. Cambridge, U.K.: Cambridge University Press, 2000.

———. *The Critique of Pure Reason.* Translated and edited by Paul Guyer and Allen William Wood. Cambridge, U.K.: Cambridge University Press, 1998.

———. *Critique of Teleological Judgement.* Translated and edited by James Creed Meredith. Oxford: Clarendon, 1928.

———. *Gesammelte Schriften.* Berlin: Reimer/de Gruyter, 1902–97.

———. *Groundwork of the Metaphysics of Morals.* Translated and edited by Mary J. Gregor. Cambridge, U.K.: Cambridge University Press, 1997.

———. *Practical Philosophy.* Translated and edited by Mary J. Gregor. Cambridge, U.K.: Cambridge University Press, 1999.

———. *Reflexionen Kants zur kritischen Philosophie: Aus Kants handschriftlichen Aufzeichnungen.* Edited by Benno Erdmann. Leipzig: Fues, 1884.

———. *Religion Within the Limits of Reason Alone.* Translated and edited by Theodore Meyer Greene and Hoyt Hopewell Hudson. 2nd ed. New York: Harper & Row, 1960.

———. *Theoretical Philosophy, 1755–1770.* Translated by David Walford. Edited by David Walford and Ralf Meerbote. Cambridge, U.K.: Cambridge University Press, 1992.

Kaplan, Aryeh, ed. *Sefer Yetzirah: The Book of Creation in Theory and Practice.* 2nd ed. York Beach, Maine: Weiser, 1997.

Kenny, Anthony. *The Five Ways: St. Thomas Aquinas' Proofs of God's Existence.* London: Routledge, 1969.

Kirchhoff, Gustav. "On the Relation Between the Emissive and the Absorptive Power of Bodies for Heat and Light." In *The Laws of Radiation and Absorption: Memoirs by Prévost, Stewart, Kirchhoff, and Kirchhoff and Bunsen,* translated and edited by De Witt Bristol Brace, 73–97. New York: American Book Company, 1901.

———. "Ueber das Verhältniss zwischen dem Emissionsvermögen und dem Absorptionsvermögen der Körper für Wärme und Licht." *Annalen der Physik und Chemie* 185, no. 2 (1860): 275–301.

Knight, Will. "Entangled Photons Secure Money Transfer." *New Scientist,* April 22, 2004. www.newscientist.com.

Körner, Stephan. "Introduction to the English Edition." In Cassirer, *Kant's Life and Thought,* vii–xxi.

Kremer, Josef. *Das Problem der Theodicee in der Philosophie und Literatur des 18. Jahrhunderts mit besonderer Rücksicht auf Kant und Schiller.* Berlin: Reuther & Reichard, 1909.

Kuehn, Manfred. *Kant: A Biography.* New York: Cambridge University Press, 2001.

Landsman, Klaas. "The Fine-Tuning Argument: Exploring the Improbability of Our Existence." In *The Challenge of Chance: A Multidisciplinary Approach from Science and the Humanities,* edited by Klaas Landsman and Ellen van Wolde, 111–29. New York: Springer, 2016.

Lewis, Clive Staples. *The Discarded Image: An Introduction to Medieval and Renaissance Literature.* Cambridge, U.K.: Cambridge University Press, 1964.

Lindberg, David C. *The Beginnings of Western Science.* Chicago: University of Chicago Press, 1992.

Lindley, David. *Uncertainty: Einstein, Heisenberg, Bohr, and the Struggle for the Soul of Science.* New York: Anchor, 2008.

Lorentz, Hendrik, ed. *Électrons et photons: Rapports et discussions du cinquième Conseil de Physique tenu à Bruxelles du 24 au 29 octobre 1927 sous les auspices de l'Institut International de Physique Solvay.* Paris: Gauthier-Villars, 1928.

Lorentz, Hendrik, Niels Bohr, Marcel Brillouin, Théophile de Donder, Max Born, Albert Einstein, Wolfgang Pauli, Paul Dirac, Hendrik Anthony Kramers, Werner Heisenberg, Louis de Broglie, Auguste Piccard, Paul Langevin, Ralph Fowler, Erwin Schrödinger, Paul Ehrenfest, Owen Richardson, Irving Langmuir, and Arthur Compton. "Discussion générale des idées nouvelles émises." In Lorentz, *Électrons et photons,* 248–89.

Luria, Alexander. *The Mind of a Mnemonist.* Translated by Lynn Solotaroff. 2nd ed. Cambridge, Mass.: Harvard University Press, 1987.

———. *Romanticheskie ésse: Malen'kaĩa knizhka o bol'shoĩ pamĩati; Poteríannyĩ i vozvrashchennyĩ mir* [Романтические эссе. Маленькая книжка о большой памяти; Потерянный и возвращенный мир]. Moscow: Pedagogica [Педагогика], 1996.

Maoz, Uri, Gideon Yaffe, Christof Koch, and Liad Mudrik. "Neural Precursors of Decisions That Matter—an ERP Study of Deliberate and Arbitrary Choice." *ELife,* Oct. 23, 2019. elifesciences.org.

Mateo, Fernando, ed. *El otro Borges: Entrevistas, 1960–1986.* Buenos Aires: Equis, 1997.

Mehra, Jagdish, and Helmut Rechenberg. *The Historical Development of Quantum Theory.* New York: Springer, 1982–2001.

Mendelssohn, Moses. *Saemmtliche Werke.* Edited by Daniel Jenisch. Buda: Paul Burian, 1819–21.

Mermin, N. David. "Can You Help Your Team Tonight by Watching on TV? More Experimental Metaphysics from Einstein, Podolsky, and Rosen." In *Philosophical Consequences of Quantum Theory: Reflections on Bell's Theorem,* edited by James Thomas Cushing and Ernan McMullin, 38–59. Notre Dame, Ind.: University of Notre Dame Press, 1989.

———. "What's Wrong with This Pillow?" *Physics Today* 42, no. 4 (April 1989): 9–11.

Minev, Zlatko Kristev, Shantanu Omprakash Mundhada, Shyam Shankar, Phil Reinhold, Ricardo Gutiérrez-Jáuregui, Robert J. Schoelkopf, Mazyar Mirrahimi, Howard John Carmichael, and Michel H. Devoret. "To Catch and Reverse a Quantum Jump Mid-flight." *Nature* 570, no. 7760 (2019): 200–204.

Morrison, Philip. "*Alsos:* The Story of German Science." *Bulletin of the Atomic Scientists* 3, no. 12 (1947).

Nature. "New Problems in Quantum Theory." 121, no. 3050 (1928): 579.

Newton, Isaac. *The Correspondence of Isaac Newton, Vol. 3, 1688–1694.* Edited by Herbert Westren Turnbull. Cambridge, U.K.: Cambridge University Press, 1961.

New York Times. "Stimson Says Law Required Action." Dec. 11, 1932, 3. nyti.ms /3JV9VRJ.

Osserman, Robert. *Poetry of the Universe.* Stanford, Calif.: Stanford University Press, 1996.

O'Toole, Garson. "Time Is What Keeps Everything from Happening at Once." Quote Investigator, July 6, 2019. quoteinvestigator.com.

Pauli, Wolfgang. *Wissenschaftlicher Briefwechsel mit Bohr, Einstein, Heisenberg u.a.* Edited by Karl von Meyenn, Armin Hermann, and Victor Frederick Weisskopf. New York: Springer, 1979–2005.

Peterson, Mark. "Dante and the 3-Sphere." *American Journal of Physics* 47, no. 12 (1979): 1031–35.

Planck, Max. "Zur Theorie des Gesetzes der Energieverteilung im Normal-spectrum." *Verhandlungen der Deutschen Physikalischen Gesellschaft* 2, no. 17 (1900): 235–45.

Plato. *Opera.* Edited by John Burnet. Oxford: Clarendon, 1900–1907.

———. *Parmenides.* Translated by Mary Louise Gill and Paul Ryan. In *Complete Works,* edited by John Madison Cooper and D. S. Hutchinson, 359–97. Indianapolis: Hackett, 1997.

———. *Timaeus.* Translated by Donald J. Zeyl. In *Complete Works,* edited by John Madison Cooper and D. S. Hutchinson, 1224–91. Indianapolis: Hackett, 1997.

Plotinus. *The Enneads.* Translated by Stephen MacKenna. Edited by John Dillon. Abridged ed. London: Penguin, 1991.

Prudhomme, Paul. *Fork in the Road: A Different Direction in Cooking.* New York: William Morrow, 1993.

Rees, Martin. *Before the Beginning: Our Universe and Others.* London: Simon & Schuster, 1997.

Reicke, Rudolf. *Kantiana: Beiträge zu Immanuel Kants Leben und Schriften.* Königsberg: Theile, 1860.

Reid, Constance. *Hilbert-Courant.* New York: Springer, 1986.

Remes, Pauliina. *Neoplatonism.* Berkeley: University of California Press, 2008.

Rink, Friedrich Theodor. *Ansichten aus Immanuel Kant's Leben.* Königsberg: Göbbels und Unzer, 1805.

Rodríguez Monegal, Emir. *Jorge Luis Borges: A Literary Biography.* New York: E. P. Dutton, 1978.

Rojo, Alberto G. "The Garden of the Forking Worlds: Borges and Quantum Mechanics." *Oakland Journal* 9 (2005): 69–78. hdl.handle.net/10323/7649.

Rosenfeld, Léon. "Niels Bohr in the Thirties: Consolidation and the Extension of the Conception of Complementarity." In *Niels Bohr: His Life and Work as Seen by His Friends and Colleagues,* edited by Stefan Rozental, 114–36. Amsterdam: North-Holland, 1967.

Rosenthal-Schneider, Ilse. *Begegnungen mit Einstein, von Laue und Planck: Realität und wissenschaftliche Wahrheit.* Braunschweig: Vieweg, 1988.

———. *Reality and Scientific Truth: Discussions with Einstein, von Laue, and Planck.* Edited by Thomas Braun. Detroit: Wayne State University Press, 1980.

Rovelli, Carlo. *Helgoland: Making Sense of the Quantum Revolution.* Translated by Erica Segre and Simon Carnell. New York: Riverhead, 2021.

Rubenstein, Richard E. *When Jesus Became God: The Epic Fight over Christ's Divinity in the Last Days of Rome.* New York: Harcourt Brace, 1999.

Russell, Bertrand. *The Problems of Philosophy.* 2nd ed. Oxford: Oxford University Press, 1998.

Schilpp, Paul Arthur. *Kant's Pre-critical Ethics.* 2nd ed. Evanston, Ill.: Northwestern University Press, 1960.

Schlosser, Johann Georg. *Kleine Schriften.* Basel: Serini, 1779–93.

Schrödinger, Erwin. "Die gegenwärtige Situation in der Quantenmechanik." *Naturwissenschaften* 23, no. 48 (1935): 807–12.

———. "Die gegenwärtige Situation in der Quantenmechanik." *Naturwissenschaften* 23, no. 49 (1935): 823–49.

———. "An Undulatory Theory of the Mechanics of Atoms and Molecules." *Physical Review,* 2nd ser., 28, no. 6 (1926): 1049–70.

Scott, William Taussig. *Erwin Schrödinger: An Introduction to His Writings.* Amherst: University of Massachusetts Press, 1967.

Slavitt, David R., trans. *The Consolation of Philosophy,* by Anicius Manlius Severinus Boethius. Cambridge, Mass.: Harvard University Press, 2008.

Slavuski, Victoria. "The Old Man and the City; Chronicle of a Change of Heart: Borges's Late Love Affair with the People." *Times Literary Supplement,* Aug. 20, 1999, 10–12.

Sommerfeld, Arnold, ed. *The Principle of Relativity: A Collection of Original Memoirs on the Special and General Theory of Relativity.* Translated by Wilfried Perrett and G. B. Jeffery. New York: Dover, 1952.

———. *Das Relativitätsprinzip: Eine Sammlung von Abhandlungen.* 5th ed. Wiesbaden: Springer, 1923.

Strawson, Galen. "Your Move: The Maze of Free Will." *Opinionator* (blog), *New York Times,* July 22, 2010. opinionator.blogs.nytimes.com.

Swedenborg, Emanuel. *De caelo et ejus mirabilibus et de inferno: Ex auditis et visis.* Edited by Samuel Howard Worcester. 2nd ed. New York: American Swedenborg Printing and Publishing, 1890.

———. *Heaven and Hell; Also, The World of Spirits or Intermediate State from Things Heard and Seen.* Translated by John Faulkner Potts. Rotch ed. Boston: Swedenborg Printing Bureau, 1907.

Teitelboim, Volodia. *Los dos Borges: Vida, sueños, enigmas.* Mexico City: Hermes, 1996.

Unamuno, Miguel de. *Obras completas.* Edited by Ricardo Senabre. Madrid: Turner, 1995–2009.

———. *Tragic Sense of Life.* Translated by Anthony Kerrigan. Princeton, N.J.: Princeton University Press, 1972.

United States Conference of Catholic Bishops. "What We Believe." www.usccb.org.

Vaihinger, Hans. "Briefe aus dem Kantkreis." *Altpreussische Monatsschrift* 17 (1880): 286–99.

Van der Waerden, Bartel Leendert, ed. *Sources of Quantum Mechanics.* Amsterdam: North-Holland, 1967.

Verfassung des Deutschen Reiches vom 11. August 1919. 2nd ed. Berlin: Carl Heymann, 1920.

Voltaire. *Candide; or, Optimism.* Translated by Burton Raffel. New Haven, Conn.: Yale University Press, 2005.

Warda, Arthur. "Ergänzungen zu E. Fromm's zweitem und drittem Beitrage zur Lebensgeschichte Kants. I." *Altpreussische Monatsschrift* 38 (1901): 75–95.

———, ed. *Briefe an und von Johann George Scheffner.* Munich: Duncker & Humblot, 1916–38.

Wasianski, Ehregott Andreas Christoph, ed. *Immanuel Kant in seinen letzten Lebensjahren: Ein Beytrag zur Kenntniss seines Characters und häuslichen Lebens aus dem täglichen Umgauge mit ihm.* Königsberg: Friedrich Nicolovius, 1804.

Wegenstein, Bernadette, dir. *The Conductor.* Waystone, 2021.

Weinberg, Steven. *Dreams of a Final Theory: The Search for the Fundamental Laws of Nature.* London: Hutchinson Radius, 1993.

Williamson, Edwin. *Borges: A Life.* New York: Penguin, 2004.

———. "Borges in Context: The Autobiographical Dimension." In *Cambridge Companion to Jorge Luis Borges,* edited by Edwin Williamson, 201–25. Cambridge, U.K.: Cambridge University Press, 2013.

Wittgenstein, Ludwig. *Tractatus Logico-Philosophicus.* Translated by Charles Kay Ogden. 2nd ed. London: Kegan Paul, Trench, Trubner, 1933.

FURTHER READING

Abiko, Seiya. "Einstein's Kyoto Address: 'How I Created the Theory of Relativity.'" *Historical Studies in the Physical and Biological Sciences* 31, no. 1 (2000): 1–35.

Bitbol, Michel. *Schrödinger's Philosophy of Quantum Mechanics.* Dordrecht: Kluwer, 1996.

Borges, Jorge Luis. *Discusión.* Buenos Aires: Gleizer, 1932.

———. "The Translators of *The Thousand and One Nights.*" Translated by Esther Allen. In *Selected Non-fictions,* ed. Eliot Weinberger, 92–109. New York: Penguin, 1999.

Borges, Jorge Luis, and Roberto Alifano. *Conversaciones.* Madrid: Debate, 1986.

Campbell, Joseph. *The Ecstasy of Being: Mythology and Dance.* Edited by Nancy Allison. Novato: New World, 2017.

———. *The Masks of God.* New York: Penguin, 1968.

Canales, Jimena. *The Physicist and the Philosopher: Einstein, Bergson, and the Debate That Changed Our Understanding of Time.* Princeton, N.J.: Princeton University Press, 2015.

———. *A Tenth of a Second: A History.* Chicago: University of Chicago Press, 2009.

Carson, Cathryn. *Heisenberg in the Atomic Age: Science and the Public Sphere.* Cambridge, U.K.: Cambridge University Press, 2010.

Derrida, Jacques. *Margins of Philosophy.* Translated by Alan Bass. Chicago: University of Chicago Press, 1982.

D'Hoine, Pieter, and Marije Martijn, eds. *All from One: A Guide to Proclus.* Oxford: Oxford University Press, 2017.

Dillon, John, and Lloyd P. Gerson, eds. *Neoplatonic Philosophy: Introductory Readings.* Indianapolis: Hackett, 2004.

Egginton, William. *The Philosopher's Desire: Psychoanalysis, Interpretation, and Truth.* Stanford, Calif.: Stanford University Press, 2007.

Gleick, James. *Genius: The Life and Science of Richard Feynman.* New York: Vintage, 1992.

———. *Time Travel: A History.* New York: Pantheon, 2016.

Gleiser, Marcelo. *The Prophet and the Astronomer: A Scientific Journey to the End of Time.* New York: Norton, 2001.

Greene, Brian. *The Hidden Reality: Parallel Universes and the Deep Laws of the Cosmos.* New York: Vintage, 2011.

Gumbrecht, Hans Ulrich, ed. *What Is Life? The Intellectual Pertinence of Erwin Schrödinger.* Stanford, Calif.: Stanford University Press, 2011.

Hägglund, Martin. *This Life: Secular Faith and Spiritual Freedom.* New York: Pantheon, 2019.

Heelan, Patrick A. *Quantum Mechanics and Objectivity: A Study of the Physical Philosophy of Werner Heisenberg.* The Hague: Martinus Nijhoff, 1965.

Heidegger, Martin. *Being and Time: A Translation of "Sein und Zeit."* Translated by Joan Stambaugh. Albany: State University of New York Press, 1996.

———. *Kant and the Problem of Metaphysics.* Translated by Richard Taft. 5th ed. Bloomington: Indiana University Press, 1997.

Holt, Jim. *Why Does the World Exist?* New York: Liveright, 2012.

Huggett, Nick, ed. *Space from Zeno to Einstein: Classic Readings with a Contemporary Commentary.* Cambridge, Mass.: MIT Press, 1999.

Jammer, Max. *The Conceptual Development of Quantum Mechanics.* 2nd ed. New York: American Institute of Physics, 1989.

Janiak, Andrew. "Newton's Philosophy." In *The Stanford Encyclopedia of Philosophy,* edited by Edward N. Zalta. plato.stanford.edu.

Jaspers, Karl. *Drei Gründer des Philosophierens: Plato, Augustin, Kant.* Munich: Piper, 1967.

Johnson, David E. *Kant's Dog: On Borges, Philosophy, and the Time of Translation.* Albany: State University of New York Press, 2013.

Lloyd, Seth. *Programming the Universe: A Quantum Computer Scientist Takes On the Cosmos.* New York: Knopf, 2006.

Marcus, Russell, and Mark McEvoy, eds. *An Historical Introduction to the Philosophy of Mathematics: A Reader.* London: Bloomsbury, 2016.

Moore, Walter. *Schrödinger: Life and Thought.* Cambridge, U.K.: Cambridge University Press, 1989.

Nussbaum, Martha C. *The Fragility of Goodness: Luck and Ethics in Greek Tragedy and Philosophy.* Cambridge, U.K.: Cambridge University Press, 1986.

Rees, Martin. *Just Six Numbers: The Deep Forces That Shape the Universe.* New York: Basic Books, 2000.

Rigden, John S. *Einstein 1905: The Standard of Greatness.* Cambridge, Mass.: Harvard University Press, 2005.

Schilpp, Paul Arthur. *Albert Einstein: Philosopher-Scientist.* New York: MJF, 1969.

Schopenhauer, Arthur. *The World as Will and Idea.* Translated by Richard Burdon Haldane and John Kemp. 3rd ed. London: Kegan Paul, Trench, Trübner, 1896.

Schrödinger, Erwin. *Nature and the Greeks; and, Science and Humanism.* Cambridge, U.K.: Cambridge University Press, 1996.

————. *What Is Life? The Physical Aspect of the Living Cell; with Mind and Matter; and Autobiographical Sketches.* Cambridge, U.K.: Cambridge University Press, 1992.

Smith, Norman Kemp, trans. *Critique of Pure Reason,* by Immanuel Kant. 2nd ed. New York: St. Martin's, 1965.

Strobach, Nico. *The Moment of Change: A Systematic History in the Philosophy of Space and Time.* Dordrecht: Kluwer Academic, 1998.

Wheeler, John Archibald, and Wojciech Hubert Zurek, eds. *Quantum Theory and Measurement.* Princeton, N.J.: Princeton University Press, 1983.

INDEX

A NOTE ON THE TEXT

This book was set in Sabon, a typeface designed by the well-known German typographer Jan Tschichold (1902–74). Sabon's design is based upon the original letterforms of sixteenth-century French type designer Claude Garamond and was created specifically to be used for three sources: foundry type for hand composition, Linotype, and Monotype. Tschichold named his typeface for the famous Frankfurt typefounder Jacques Sabon (c. 1520–80).

Typeset by Scribe, Inc., Philadelphia, Pennsylvania

Printed and bound by Berryville Graphics,
Berryville, Virginia

Designed by Jo Anne Metsch